What t<
For in

Best Wishes
Charles

What to Listen For in Opera

An Introductory Handbook

CHARLES R. BECK

McFarland & Company, Inc., Publishers
Jefferson, North Carolina

I am grateful to my opera-loving friends Professor Josephine Reiter, Dr. Peter Dittami and Pearl Oliva for inspiring me to write this book. I am also thankful to the translators named below for their able assistance.

A Note on the Translations: The libretto English translations in Parts I and II were made by a team of foreign language experts: translations of Italian text by Pearl Oliva and Maria Figueroa, translations of French text by Mary-Ann Stadtler-Chester, and translations of German text by Albert Richer. The author of this handbook is responsible for boldfacing words in the original language text and the English translation to sensitize the reader to words that resemble each other in meaning in both languages.

A Note on the Illustrations: All drawings are by Sachiko Beck, my wife and professor emeritus of graphic design at Framingham State University, Massachusetts.

LIBRARY OF CONGRESS CATALOGUING-IN-PUBLICATION DATA

Beck, Charles R., 1941–
    What to listen for in opera : an introductory handbook / Charles R. Beck.
        p.   cm.
    Includes bibliographical references and index.

    ISBN 978-0-7864-9609-9 (softcover : acid free paper) ∞
    ISBN 978-1-4766-1714-5 (ebook)

    1. Operas—Analysis, appreciation. 2. Operas—Stories, plots, etc. I. Title.

MT95.B45 2014
782.1'117—dc23   2014029575

BRITISH LIBRARY CATALOGUING DATA ARE AVAILABLE

On the cover: *Women at the Odeon*, Eugène Samuel Grasset, 1890 (© 2014 PicturesNow)

Printed in the United States of America

McFarland & Company, Inc., Publishers
Box 611, Jefferson, North Carolina 28640
www.mcfarlandpub.com

Table of Contents

Part III. Literary and Rhyming Exercises

Preface

This handbook is designed as an introduction for those unfamiliar with opera as well as a guide to greater understanding for established fans. As a convenient and ready reference for listening to opera, it's intended to help listeners develop an appreciation for the vocal skills required to sing demanding songs. Why is it important to develop an understanding of the range of the operatic voice? In part, because a skilled opera singer helps to sensitize us to the many facets of human experience ranging from comedy, or romance, to jealousy, and tragedy. No other instrument can convey the human spirit with as much sensitivity as a highly cultivated voice. This helps to explain why opera audiences feel such a strong involvement with the characters on an opera stage, and why the tension reaches a climax, in a sustained high note, or resolution in a soothing soft note, many in the audience erupt with loud applause and cheers.

The handbook focuses on introducing readers to opera highlights and well-known songs rather than detailing complete operas that normally last from two to three hours. Learning to listen to an aria will enable the listener to more fully experience full-length operas. In addition to helping operagoers expand upon their appreciation, hopefully, it will assist teachers in exposing their students to the world of opera.

Part I: A Selection of Operas presents 14 well-known works with biographical information on the composer and a brief introduction to the opera. There is a synopsis of the plot and an introduction to each of the major songs (solos, duets, ensembles). Focusing on song highlights may be likened to reading a famous set of quotations from a Shakespearean play. With the famous songs preparing the reader to move on to the entire opera.

Part II: Arias by Composer presents a more in-depth analysis of 62 of the most popular arias by the 14 composers introduced in Part I. Each example is on an aria sheet that helps the listener to become more sensitive to the

1

emotional context and vocal challenges required. Each aria is divided into passages with comments on the setting and how the singer should respond to specific words and phrases. The aria sheets are useful guides prior to listening to famous songs.

Part III: Literary and Rhyming Exercises provides two interactive activities that are designed to encourage some literary, analytical, and poetic thinking. Readers should find this part enjoyable and challenging because many famous operas were based on literature and the librettos were composed in rhyme. As a literary exercise, readers are asked to match literary passages from novels with songs they appear to have inspired. As a poetic exercise, the reader has the opportunity to complete a set of rhyming song translations, identify their titles, their characters, and sequential position in the opera.

PART I

A Selection of Operas

The following 14 operas were selected based on several considerations. First, they were chosen to expose readers to the diverse talents of 14 great composers in three popular operatic languages—Italian, French, and German. Next, each opera has a distinctive sound that exemplifies the musical style of the composer. For example, the quick-paced patter songs of Rossini are clearly distinguishable from the sweet lyricism of Puccini and the heroic and uplifting sound of Beethoven. Finally, some consideration was given to including operas with cheerful endings, thus proving that not every serious plot ends on a tragic note.

Since Italy is considered the birthplace of opera, it's appropriate that six Italian works are included. But how does one select a single opera from a prolific composer like Verdi who wrote a series of masterpieces, including *Aida*, *La Traviata*, and *Rigoletto*? *Aida* was chosen because its exotic background and grand pageantry would appeal to the broadest audience. Selecting a single Puccini opera was another difficult task. The choice of *La Bohème* was based on its reputation as his most popular and frequently performed opera. Other choices required less deliberation. Most critics agree that Rossini's *Il Barbiere di Siviglia* and Donizetti's *L'Elisir d'Amore* are two of opera's most beloved comedies, and no Italian composer exemplified the bel canto style any better than Bellini, and *Norma* is generally considered his greatest accomplishment. Finally, Leoncavallo's only masterpiece, *I Pagliacci*, has a circus setting that appeals to a wide audience and a dark plot based on an actual murder.

The choice of four French operas was much easier when compared to the many Italian contenders. Bizet's *Carmen*, Gounod's *Faust*, and Offenbach's *Les Contes d'Hoffmann* are three of the most popular operas on the interna-

Scenes from *Die Zauberflöte* and *I Pagliacci*.

tional stage. And although Massenet's *Manon* is not as popular today as it was in his time, it still qualifies on a short list of favorite French operas. Another incentive for selecting these four French operas was the fact that they were all inspired by popular novels.

In selecting four German operas, most authorities would probably include Mozart's *Die Zauberflöte* and Beethoven's *Fidelio*. After composing several masterpieces in Italian to satisfy the Vienna Imperial Court, Mozart was proud to refer to his favorite and final opera, *Die Zauberflöte*, as his "German opera." Beethoven's only opera is as uplifting as his beloved Symphony #9 (Choral Symphony). As for the requisite Wagner opera, critics generally agree that *Der Fliegende Holländer* was his first mature opera and its more accessible than Wagner's later works. Finally Weber's *Der Freischütz* is considered the first pure German opera. The haunting "Wolf's Glen" and the conflict between good and evil create a folk tale setting very typical of early German romantic opera. Although not performed as often as it deserves, the songs are very melodic and romantic.

Italian Operas

Aida
by Giuseppe Verdi

Loving a commander from a different fatherland
Joining in death after revealing his battle plan

First performed in Cairo, December 24, 1871
Based on a book by Camille du Locle and
a sketch by Egyptologist Mariette Bey

Libretto by Antonio Ghislanzoni and Verdi
Translation by Pearl Oliva

*G*iuseppe Verdi was born in Roncole in 1813 and died in Milan in 1901. He was at a very mature stage in his life when he composed *Aida*, and was already the world's most famous and successful opera composer. He had already composed three of his most famous operas—*La Traviata, Rigoletto,* and *Il Trovatore*. He was considered a national hero in Italy, and his operas were performed in every major opera house. Verdi had received a commission to compose an opera by the Khedive, the ruler of Egypt. *Aida* premiered at the Cairo Royal Opera House in 1871. Verdi didn't attend the premiere because he didn't enjoy boat rides and festive and "superficial occasions." He jokingly told a friend that, if he journeyed to Egypt, he might end up being "mummified."

    Aida is considered a grand opera in the grandest tradition. Grand opera emphasizes spectacle and splendor often with a historical setting. It features huge casts, lavish set designs, and often ballet scenes. *Aida* contains wonderful and colorful orchestration. To create an oriental setting, Verdi used harps, oboes and flutes; for the triumphal scenes, he uses brass instruments, including Egyptian style trumpets. Verdi was primarily interested in portraying a powerful, tragic, and intimate human drama. For example, in the first act, Verdi makes a quick transition from a war-like chorus to an intimate portrait of Aida weeping and praying to the gods. This is followed by an intimate portrait of Aida's adversary Amneris. They are both in love with Radamès. Each of the three main characters—Aida, Radamès and Amneris—must confront their conflicting loyalties and emotions. In the end, Aida and Radamès lose their lives as a result of this conflict between love for each other and devotion to opposing countries.

Synopsis of Verdi's Aida

Main Characters

Aida, Ethiopian slave	Soprano
Radamès, Commander	Tenor
Amneris, King's daughter	Contralto
Amonastro, Aida's father	Baritone

Act I

    Radamès learns from the High Priest that the Ethiopians are threatening the Nile Valley and that the goddess, Isis, has decreed that a new commander should be chosen to defend Egypt. Radamès wants to be chosen commander of the Egyptian army to win fame and the lovely slave girl, Aida, for his wife (Song: **"Celeste Aida"**). When the king learns that the Ethiopians are marching toward Thebes, he appoints Radamès as commander and the crowd cries out for war and victory (Song: **"Su! del Nilo"**). After the crowd has left, Aida regrets that she cheered Radamès to victory because the Ethiopians are her own people and the King of Ethiopia is her secret father, Amonastro (Song: **"Ritorna vincitor!"**).

Act II

Amneris, the king's daughter, is in love with Radamès and jealous of Aida. At her royal apartment, she longs for the return of Radamès. She summons Aida and tricks her into admitting that she, too, loves Radamès (Song: **"Fu la sorte dell'armi"**). At the gate of Thebes, a crowd welcomes the victorious Radamès as part of a grand procession (Song: **"Gloria all'Egitto"**). The King of Egypt offers his daughter, Amneris, in marriage as a reward for Radamès' victory. The Ethiopian captives are in chains along with their king, Amonastro. Without revealing his identity, Amonastro pleads that the captives be given mercy (Songs: **"Suo padre"** and **"Ma tu, Re"**). Although his captives are freed, Amonastro is retained as a hostage, and Aida weeps over her father's capture.

Act III

On the moonlit banks of the Nile, next to the Temple of Isis, Aida has come to mourn her lost country and say farewell to Radamès (Song: **"O patria mia"**). Her father has followed her and begs her to draw from her lover his plans for the next military campaign. Aida protests against such treachery, but finally gives in to her father's impassioned pleas (Song: **"Rivedrò le foreste"**). When Radamès appears, Aida learns his tactics and begs him to flee with her, but he is reluctant to leave his homeland (Song: **"Fuggiam gli arbori inospiti"**). Amneris suddenly appears and accuses them of treachery, and the guards arrest Radamès as Aida and her father escapes.

Act IV

At the palace Judgment Hall, Amneris expresses her anger and sorrow at Radamès' treachery (Song: **"L'aborrita rivale"**). When the guards bring him in, she offers to help him if he will renounce Aida. He refuses to do so and she listens in despair at the guilty verdict of the priests as it echoes from the Judgment Hall. Radamès is sealed in a vault beneath the temple to die. He is surprised to find Aida has hidden herself in the vault to die with him. He regrets that she has chosen to sacrifice her youth and beauty (Song: **"Morir! sì pura e bella!"**). Together, they accept death while Amneris still mourns over Radamès (Song: **"O terra, addio"**).

Major Song Sketches

Act I

"Celeste Aida" (**"Celestial Aida"**). The high priest has informed Radamès that a commander will be chosen to fight the invading Ethiopians. The aria has two themes—glory and love. Radamès desires to be chosen commander of the Egyptian army because military glory will help him to win Aida as his wife. His voice must ring with the sound of trumpets with heroic high notes. He must then express his love for the Ethiopian slave, Aida. Verdi wanted the aria to have a dreamlike ending with the beautiful high notes sung softly and fading away. (See "Celeste Aida" in Part II for vocal skills.)

Celeste Aida, **forma divina.**	**Celestial** Aida, **divine form,**
Mistico serto di **luce** e **fior,**	**mystic** garland of **light** and **flowers,**
del mio pensiero tu sei **regina,**	you are the **queen** of my thought,
tu di mia vita sei lo **splendore.**	you are the **splendor** of my life.
Il tuo bel cielo vorrei ridarti,	I would like to give you once more your
le dolci **brezze** del patrio suol,	beautiful blue skies, the sweet **breezes** of
un **regal** serto cul crin posarti,	your native soil, a **royal** crown to deck your
ergerti un **trono** vicino al **sol.**	brow, a royal **throne** for you, in the **sun!**
Oh! Celeste Aida, forma divina,	Oh, celestial Aida, divine form,
mistico **raggio** di luce e fior,	mystic **ray** of light and flowers,
del mio pensiero *ecc.*	you are the queen, *etc.*

"Su! del Nilo" (**"Onward! To the Nile"**). This chorus occurs after the King of Egypt announces the appointment of Radamès as commander of the Egyptian army. The jubilant crowd leads Radamès away with a lively military march, including trumpets, soloists and chorus. Amneris, the king's daughter, shouts farewell with the words "Ritorna vincitor!" The crowd repeats the words as it marches away. Radamès delivers the melody in a majestic manner, while Aida repeats the melody with anguish as a kind of emotional counterpoint (combined musical themes). She is distressed because she knows that Radamès' victory will mean defeat for her father and Ethiopian homeland.

Chorus

Su! del **Nilo** al **sacro** lido	Onward! May our breasts be a fortress
sien barriera i nostri petti;	shielding the **sacred** banks of the **Nile.**
non echeggi che un sol grido	Let no cry sound but one, war
guerra e **morte** allo **stranier!** ecc.	and **death** to the **foreigner!** etc.

Aida

Per chi piango? Per chi **prego?**	For whom do I weep? For whom do I **pray?**
Qual **potere** m'avvince a lui!	What **power** ties me to him?
Deggio amarlo ed è costui	I must love him, he who is
un nemico uno **stranier!**	the enemy, a **foreigner!**

"Ritorna vincitor!" (**"Return a victor!"**). As soon as the military parade marches off stage, Verdi gives us an intimate portrait of Aida as she struggles with conflicting emotions. If Radamès is successful, her homeland and father, the King of Ethiopia, will be defeated. She begins with an anguished echo of the chorus's "Ritorna vincitor!" She bows to the earth and expresses her anguish by praying to the gods to have pity on her suffering. Her unrest can be heard in the lower strings followed by the return of her sorrowful melody. She is faced with the dilemma of betraying either the man she loves or her own father. (See "Ritorna vincitor!" in Part II for vocal skills.)

Ritorna vincitor! E dal mio labbro	**Return** a victor! My lips have spoken
uscì l'**empia** parola! Vincitor	the **impious** word! Victorious
del **padre mio** di lui che impugna	over **my father**, who takes up **arms**
l'**armi** per me per ridarmi	for me, to give me again
una patria, una reggia e il **nome**	a homeland, a kingdom, and an **illustrious**,
illustre che qui celar m'è forza.	**name** which here I must hide.
Numi, **pietà** del **mio soffrir!**	Gods, have **pity** on **my suffering!**
Speme non v'ha pel mio dolor.	There is no hope for my grief,
Amor fatal, tremendo amor,	**fatal love, trembling** love,
spezzami il cor, fammi morir!	rend my heart, make me die!

Act II

"Fu la sorte dell'armi" (**"The fortunes of war"**). The king's daughter Amneris tries to trick Aida into admitting that she loves Radamès. Amneris pretends that Radamès was killed in battle. Aida's cry of anguish convinces Amneris that Aida loves Radamès. In this confrontational duet, the voices respond to each other rather than singing together. The orchestra depicts Amneris' cunning and jealousy with agitated phrasing and Aida's increasing despair. Amneris' jubilant phrases announce her victory over Aida with the sound of triumphal music in the background. Aida falls at her rival's feet and begs for Amneris to show mercy. Amneris takes no pity and considers Radamès' victory march to be her hour of triumph.

Amneris

Fu la sorte dell'armi a'tuoi **funesta**,	The **fortunes** of war have gone against
povera Aida! Il lutto	your people! **Poor** Aida!
che ti pesa sul cor teco **divido**.	Your heart's grief I **share** with you.
Io son l'amica tua...	I am your friend. You shall have all
Tutto da me tu avrai, vivrai felice!	from me. You shall live happily.

Aida

Pietà ti prenda del mio dolor.	Let **pity** for my sorrow move you.
È vero, io l'amo d'**immenso amor**.	It is true, I love him with **immense love**.
Tu sei felice, tu sei **possente**,	You are happy, you are **powerful**,
io vivo solo per questo amor!	I live only for this love!

AMNERIS
Trema, **vil schiava!**   **Tremble, vile slave!**
Spezza tuo core;   Let your heart break;
segnar tua **morte** può questo **amore**;   this **love** can mean your **death**.
del tuo **destino** arbitra io sono,   I am master of your **destiny**, and my
d'odio **vendetta** le **furie** ho in cor.   heart **rages** with hate and **vengeance!**

AIDA
Numi, pietà del mio martir,   O gods, take pity on my suffering!
Speme non v'ha pel mio dolor! *ecc.*   There is no hope for my sorrow! *etc.*

"Gloria all'Egitto" ("Glory to Egypt"). This chorus is part of the famous Triumphal March in honor of Radamès and his victory over the Ethiopians. It is one of the grandest scenes in all opera. It begins with a patriotic chorus, followed by a march and trumpet fanfare, a short ballet, and Radamès' heroic arrival in a horse drawn chariot. There is a beautiful lyrical and gentle melody for the women followed by a contrasting theme for the priests. There is a sinister sound to their voices followed by troops with long trumpets. In the more lavish productions, the pageantry includes sacred vessels, statues of the gods, ballet dancers and live animals, such as elephants, camels and other wildlife that promise to behave and not frighten the orchestra and audience. After its premiere in Cairo, the Egyptian government adopted this triumphal chorus as its national hymn.

Gloria all'Egitto, ad **Iside**   **Glory** to **Egypt** and to **Isis**,
che il **sacro suol protegge;**   which the **sacred soil protects!**
al Re che il **Delta** regge   To the King who rules the **Delta**
inni **festosi** alziam, *ecc.*   **joyful** hymns we sing! *etc.*

S'intrecci il **loto** al **lauro**   Interweave the **lotus** and the **laurel**
sul crin dei **vincitori;**   into a crown for the **victors!**
nembo **gentil** di **fiori**   Let a **gentle** cloud of **flowers**
stenda sull'**armi** un vel.   veil the steel of their **arms.**

"Suo padre ... Ma tu, Re" ("Her father ... But you, king"). Following the triumphal scene, we are introduced to Aida's secret father, Amonasro, King of Ethiopia. Amonasro and his defeated troops are brought before the King of Egypt and the High Priests. He whispers to his daughter not to reveal his identity. His opening lines are sung with vigorous phrases. Beginning with the words "Ma tu Re," he makes a beautiful appeal to the Egyptian King to show mercy for prisoners who fought with courage for love of their country. His solo turns into a striking ensemble when the six principal characters join in to express their opposing feelings with a massive chorus in the background. Two melodies are sung at the same time as the Egyptian people call for mercy while the priests express their opposition. The ensemble of soloists and immense chorus succeed in winning the Egyptian King's mercy for the prisoners.

Suo **padre**. Anch'io pugnai,
vinti noi fummo, **morte invan** cercai.

Quest'assisa ch'io vesto vi dica
che il mio Re, la **mia patria** ho **difeso**:
fu la sorte a nostr'armi **nemica**.
Tornò vano de' forti l'ardir.
Ma tu, Re, tu **signore** possente,
a costoro ti volgi **clemente**;
oggi noi siam percossi dal **fato**,
doman voi potria il fato colpir.

Her **father**. I, too, fought.
We were conquered. I sought **death in vain**.
This uniform is witness
that I **defended** my King and **my country**.
Fate was our **enemy**,
our courage was in vain.
But you, King, you a mighty **lord**.
Look with **mercy** on these captives.
Today we are laid low by **fate**,
tomorrow, such might be your fate.

Act III

"O patria mia" ("Oh my homeland"). In a scene of romantic beauty, Aida secretly awaits her lover along the moonlit Nile. If Radamès abandons her, she will throw herself in the Nile and never see her beloved homeland again. This is Aida's most famous aria. It begins with anguish and yearning and then turns into a loving and tender hymn to her homeland. After singing in a lyrical voice, she must rise twice to a high note. A solo oboe introduces the song by suggesting a distant homeland, and a solo flute sounds like a shepherd's song in the distance. An offstage chorus chants a hymn to the goddess Isis. (See "O patria mia" in Part II for vocal skills.)

O **patria mia**, mai più ti rivedrò!
O cieli azzuri, o dolce aure **native**,

dove **sereno** il mio mattin brillò...
O verdi colli, o **profumate** rive,
O patria mia, mai più ti rivedrò! ecc.
O **fresche valli**, o **queto** asil beato,
che un dì **promesso** dall'amor mi fu;
or che d'**amore** il sogno è dileguato,
O patria mia, mai più ti rivedrò...

Oh **my homeland**, I shall never see you again! Oh blue skies, oh soft **native** breezes,
where shone the **serene** morning of my life, oh green hills, oh **fragrant** streams, oh homeland, I shall never see you again! etc.
Oh **fresh valleys**, blessed, **quiet** haven, which one day **promised** me by love, now that the dream of **love** is gone, oh my homeland, I shall never see you again...

"Rivedrò le foreste imbalsamate" ("I shall see again our fragrant forests"). This duet between Aida and her father, Amonasro, has three sections. First, the father gently reaches out to his daughter by appealing to her love for her homeland. He wants her to find out Radamès' secret military plans, but she resists because she doesn't want to expose Radamès to treason. Second, he reminds Aida that the Egyptians have defeated her homeland. His anger descends upon her as he reminds her that she must not abandon her native people. Finally, in a more soothing tone, he reminds her that she will once again see her homeland's beautiful forests. She begs for peace as she confronts her opposing loyalties. The orchestral agitation captures the conflicting emotions.

AIDA
Rivedrò le **foreste** imbalsamate,
le **fresche valli**, i nostri **templi** d'or.

I shall see again our fragrant **forests**,
the **cool valleys** and our golden **temples**.

AMONASRO
Sposa felice a lui che amasti tanto,
tripudii **immensi** ivi potrai gioir.

Happy bride of the one you so loved,
you shall enjoy **immense** exultations.

Pur rammenti che a noi l'**Egizio** immite,
le case, i **templi** e l'are **profanò**,
trasse in ceppi le **vergini** rapite;
madri vecchi,
fanciulli ei trucidò.

Also recall that pitiless **Egypt**
profaned our homes, **temples**, and altars,
carrying off our **maidens** in slavery,
murdering our old **mothers**,
and our children.

"Fuggiam gli arbori inospiti" (**"Let us flee from the hostile arbors"**). In this duet, Aida tries to convince Radamès that their only hope is to flee to her homeland. She sounds desperate as she tries to seduce him with lovely images of her homeland. The melody rises and falls to depict their emotional struggle. Aida pleads while Radamès expresses his reluctance to leave Egypt. Even though she has been a humble servant to Amneris, Aida rises to the occasion and expresses her strong determination. After questioning his love for her, he finally agrees to her plan with a passionate outburst. She repeats his outburst and they join together in a triumphal theme of love. When Radamès reveals his secret battle plans, Amneris and her guards overhear him. He is captured for treason, but Aida and her father manage to escape.

AIDA
Fuggiam gli arbori inospiti
di queste **lande** ignude;
una **novella patria**
al nostro **amor** si schiude.

Let us flee from the hostile arbors
of these bare **lands**.
A **new homeland**
reveals itself to our **love**.

RADAMÈS
Sovra una **terra estrania**
teco fuggir dovrei!
Abbandonar la patria
l'are de' nostri dei!

I ought to flee with you
to a **foreign land**!
To **abandon** my homeland
and the altars of our gods!

Act IV

"L'aborrita rivale" (**"My hated rival"**). This aria reveals the conflicting emotions expressed by Amneris when the priests judge Radamès a traitor and sentence him to death. The orchestral prelude suggests a restless motif (a short musical theme) as Amneris wrestles with jealousy, hate, passion, terror, and remorse. After expressing her jealousy and wishing revenge on Radamès and Aida, she frightens herself at the thought of his death. She reflects on her love for him in a sudden and lyrical burst of emotion and appeals to heaven to save him. The string instruments provide the accompanying melody. Amneris gives out three cries of anger when she hears the priests' judgment. She directs her wrath at the priests and ends with a furious high note.

L'aborrita **rivale** a me sfuggia...	My hated **rival** has escaped.
Dai sacerdoti Radamès **attende**	Radamès **awaits**, from the hands
dei **traditor** la pena. Traditor	of the priests, the **traitor**'s punishment.
egli non è. Pur rivelò di guerra	But he is not a traitor,
l'alto **segreto**. Egli fuggir volea,	even if he revealed the **secret** war plan.
con lei fuggire! Traditori tutti!	He meant to flee—with her!
A morte! A **morte**!	Traitors all! Death to them—**death**!
Oh! che mai parlo? Io l'amo,	Oh, what am I saying! I love him,
io l'amo sempre. **Disperato, insano**	I still love him, with a **desperate, mad**
è quest'**amor** che la mia vita strugge.	**love**, which is destroying my life.

"Morir! sì pura e bella!" ("**To die! So pure, so lovely!**"). After being sentenced to death, Radamès is sealed in a vault beneath the temple. He discovers that Aida has entered the vault secretly, and he is horrified that she will die in the beauty of her youth. Harps are heard in the background. Amneris begs the priests to show mercy for Radamès, but she doesn't know that Aida is also in the vault. To avoid a painful closing, Verdi creates a soft, melodic, and celestial atmosphere, as if their souls are about to leave their bodies. Radamès sings with an unearthly beauty while Aida greets the angel of death as an opportunity for their immortal love to enter heaven. In the background, we hear a transcendent choir of muted violins, strings, woodwinds and a harp.

RADAMÈS

Morir! sì **pura** e **bella**!	To die! So **pure**, so **lovely**!
Morir per me d'**amore**...	To die, for **love** of me!
Degli anni tuoi nel **fiore**	In the **flowering** of your youth,
fuggir la vita!	to give up your life!

AIDA

Vedi? Di **morte l'angelo**	See? The **radiant angel of death**,
radiante a noi s'**appressa**;	**approaches** us;
ne adduce a **eterni** gaudii	to bear us to **eternal** joys
sovra i suoi **vanni** d'or.	upon his golden **wings**.

"O terra, addio" ("**Oh earth, farewell**"). Aida and Radamès sing a luminous duet as they prepare to leave their earthly life. Verdi creates a hymn for two souls about to be released without a sign of suffering. Their voices are heard against the sound of the priests and echoes of the sacred dance. The words "o terra, addio" are repeated several times by two voices that sound as if they have begun their final journey. It is a sustained piece of delicate lyricism. The two souls are bound forever as the grieving Amneris prays for peace.

O terra, **addio**; addio, **valle** di pianti...	Oh earth, **farewell**—farewell, **vale** of tears,
sogno di gaudio che in dolor svanì.	dream of joy which vanished into sorrow.
A noi si schiude il ciel e l'alme erranti	Heaven opens to us, our wandering souls
volano al raggio dell'**eterno** dì, ecc.	fly fast towards the light of **eternal** day, etc.
O terra addio, ecc.	**Oh earth, farewell**, etc.
Ah! si schiude il ciel, ecc.	Ah! Heaven opens for us, etc.
O terra, addio, ecc...	Oh Earth, farewell, etc...

Il Barbiere di Siviglia
(The Barber of Seville)
by Gioacchino Rossini

Determined not to marry a hobbling old man
Rescued by a disguised count with a barber's plan

First performed in Rome, February 20, 1816
Based on a play by Pierre-Augustin de Beaumarchais

Libretto by Cesare Sterbini
Translated by Maria Figueroa

*G*ioacchino Rossini was born in Pesaro in 1792 and died in Passy in 1868.
Il Barbiere di Siviglia (The Barber of Seville) was his most famous opera

buffa (comic opera). He completed the 600 page manuscript in just 13 days. The story goes that he completed the opera without taking time to shave. He remarked to a friend, "If I had gone to visit my barber for a shave, I wouldn't have had time to finish the opera in 13 days." It was a disaster when it premiered in Rome in 1816. A series of events disrupted the opera and the audience began hissing and whistling. For example, a guitar string snapped during a serenade, a character became entangled in his robe, and a cat strolled across the stage. After Rossini revised the manuscript, it became a great success and Verdi referred to it as "The most beautiful opera buffa in existence." Rossini composed about 40 operas and became very successful and famous. He earned enough money to retire when he was only 37.

Rossini acquired the story from a popular stage comedy of the same name. The characters in *Il Barbiere di Siviglia* also appear in Mozart's *Le Nozze di Figaro* but under different circumstances. Both operas are based on different plays written by the same author, Pierre de Beaumarchais. Rossini's bel canto operas require very ornamental passages that demand exceptional vocal agility. The words flow rapidly with the passages. Rossini used staccato (pauses between notes) repetitions of the same notes in ascending (upward) and descending (downward) movements. He would repeat a phrase with increasing volume and instrumentation with every repetition of a passage. Rossini considered the voice to be the loveliest of all instruments, and his vocal requirements were very exacting and demanding. He often used fast talking ensembles (groups of characters) to create chaotic situations and humorous conversations.

Synopsis of Rossini's Il Barbiere di Siviglia

Main Characters

Rosina, Dr. Bartolo's ward	Soprano
Count Almaviva, Rosina's lover	Tenor
Figaro, a barber	Baritone
Dr. Bartolo, Rosina's guardian	Bass
Don Basilio, a music teacher	Bass

Act I

Count Almaviva and his hired band of musicians come at dawn to serenade Rosina beneath her balcony (Song: **"Ecco ridente in cielo"**). Her guardian, Dr. Bartolo, tries to prevent her from leaving the house because he hopes to marry her. When Rosina does not appear, the Count decides to wait until he sees her. The barber Figaro arrives and describes his busy life on his way to work (Song: **"Largo al factotum della città!"**). Figaro promises to help the Count win Rosina. The barber suggests that the Count disguise himself as a drunken soldier to enter Dr. Bartolo's house. Figaro thinks it is such a great idea that he should be rewarded with gold (Song: **"All'idea di quel metallo"**).

Act II

Alone in Dr. Bartolo's drawing room, Rosina dreams of the voice that touched her heart (Song: **"Una voce poco fa"**). She leaves when the Doctor arrives with her music teacher, Don Basilio. The Doctor is worried that the Count is trying to win Rosina. He agrees to Basilio's plan to ruin the Count's reputation with Rosina (Song: **"La calunnia è un venticello"**). Figaro, who has overheard the plan, warns Rosina and promises to give her affectionate letter to the Count (Song: **"Dunque io son ... tu non m'inganni?"**). The Doctor is unable to trap Rosina because she is too clever. When she outsmarts him, the Doctor gets angry and threatens her with his authority as guardian (Song: **"A un dottor della mia sorte"**). The Count arrives as a drunken soldier and slips a reply letter to Rosina. Meanwhile, the noise inside the house has attracted a crowd of townspeople on the street. The police arrive to restore order and arrest the drunken soldier. The Count removes his disguise and is instantly released. The Doctor is shocked by the events and the act closes with a noisy and large ensemble (sextet) commenting on the events of the day (Song: **"Freddo ed immobile"**).

Act III

Alone in his room, the Doctor is proud of himself for having gotten rid of the soldier. When the Count returns, he is dressed as a music teacher. He pretends to be one of Basilio's students, who he says is ill. The Doctor brings Rosina in for her lesson and she pretends not to recognize the Count (Song: **"Contro un cor che accende amore"**). Figaro is shaving the Doctor when Basilio arrives in good health. The Count convinces Basilio that he is really ill and should leave. As Basilio leaves, a farewell song is sung by a quintet (*Song:* **"Buona sera, mio signore"**). When night falls, the Count and Figaro climb through a window to help Rosina escape. At first she refuses until the Count reveals his identity. The trio sings about the joy of the moment as they prepare to escape (Song: **"Ah, qual colpo inaspettato!"**). When a marriage official arrives to marry the Doctor and Rosina, they convince the official to marry the Count and Rosina. When the Doctor arrives, it is too late to stop the wedding. The Doctor bestows his blessing and a sextet sings about the joyful occasion (Song: **"Di sì felice innesto"**).

Overture and Major Song Sketches

"Overture." The famous overture consists of joyful tunes that help to provide musical portraits of the main characters. It captures the tension, rapid chatter, the humor, and the joyful success of the lovers. After the opening chords suggest a moment of tension, an oboe relaxes the tension and the strings follow with a graceful melody. A new element of tension returns to suggest anger and urgency. The storm passes and the violins provide a more peaceful mood. The strings and woodwinds begin to chatter with increasing excitement and conflict. The orchestra reaches a crescendo (dramatic increase in volume) before breaking out with a dance-like melody. The pace grows in intensity leading to a joyful crescendo and triumphant conclusion.

Act I

"Ecco ridente in cielo" ("Low, in the smiling sky"). At the beginning of Act I, Count Almaviva comes at dawn with a group of musicians to serenade Rosina beneath her window. The Count strums a guitar while the accompanying woodwinds introduce the melody. The Count begins to sing the melody, encouraging Rosina to come to him. He never sees her because the balcony remains closed. The gentle tune becomes more ardent as he imagines seeing her. He erupts into little expressions of pleasure, in elaborate and ornamental (added vocal color) phrases, echoed by the orchestra. He is possessed by love and full of delight. His joys carry him to an ecstatic high C note without even seeing her. The song is richly ornamented and requires difficult technical skills to sing.

Ecco ridente in cielo	Low, in the smiling sky,
spunta la **bella aurora,**	the **beautiful dawn** is breaking,
e tu non sorgi ancora	and you are not awake,
e puoi dormir così?	and are you still asleep?
Sorgi, **mia dolce** speme,	Arise, **my sweet** love,
vieni bell'**idol mio,**	oh, come, **my idolized** one,
rendi men crudo, **o Dio,**	soften the pain, **oh God,**
lo stral che mi ferì.	of the dart which pierces me.

"Largo al factotum della città!" ("Make way for the handyman of the city!"). Figaro, the barber, pauses on his way to work to celebrate his success and importance as a handyman in the daily life of his town. He sees himself as a messenger between lovers, and looks forward to the financial reward for his services. He is in very high spirits and congratulates himself for his talents. This very popular song is a portrait of Figaro's character. The orchestra provides a vigorous and merry introduction. Even though it has a very fast tempo (speed), Figaro must sing with elegance, charm, amusement, and proper diction. He impersonates many characters that call on him for his services, and even calls his own name in their different voices. He pretends to be overcome by their demands. This rollicking song requires great vocal agility. This is one of the most famous baritone arias in opera. (See "Largo al factotum della città!" in Part II for vocal skills.)

La ran la le ra, la ran la la.	La ran la le ra, la ran la la.
Largo al **factotum** della **città**!	Make way for the **handyman** of the **city**.
La ran la la, ecc.	La ran la la, etc.
Presto a bottega	**Quickly** to his workshop
che l'alba è già.	for dawn is here.
Sono il factotum della città.	I am the handyman of the city.
Ah, che **bella** vita!	Ah! ah! what a **lovely** life!
Faticar poco, divertirsi assai,	Little work, and much amusement,
e in tasca sempre aver	always with some money in my pocket,
qualche doblone,	thanks to **my reputation**.
gran frutto della **mia riputazione**.	

"**All'idea di quel metallo**" ("**At the idea of that metal**"). The Count has just promised to pay Figaro for helping him win Rosina. In this jolly duet, Figaro begins with a lively tune that expresses his determination to help the Count, also known as Lindoro. The following exchange suggests that they are delighted with their agreement. In a waltz-like melody, Figaro gives the Count directions to his shop. Each one expresses satisfaction in counterpoint (two musical lines sung together) to the other. As they discuss their plan, the orchestra produces a chattering sound. The Count is delighted at the chance to win Rosina, and Figaro looks forward to the money he will earn. It ends with Figaro's D major waltz. The song is an interweaving of rapid patter and accompanied recitatives.

FIGARO

Son **pronto**. Ah, non sapete	I'm **ready**. You cannot imagine
i simpatici effetti **prodigiosi**	what a **prodigious** devotion
che ad appagare il mio signor Lindoro	the sweet thought of gold
produce in me la dolce idea dell'oro.	makes me feel towards Lindoro.
All'**idea** di quel metallo	At the **idea** of that marvelous,
portentoso, **onnipossente**,	**omnipotent** metal,
un **vulcan** la mia mente	my mind like a **volcano**
già **comincia** a diventar, sì.	**commences** to erupt, yes.

COUNT

Su, vediamo di quel **metallo**	Come, let's see what effect
qualche effetto sorprendente,	this **metal** will have on you,
del vulcan della tua mente	some real demonstration
qualche mostro singolar, sì.	of this volcano within you, yes.

Act II

"**Una voce poco fa**" ("**A voice just now**"). In this famous and difficult coloratura (a rapid and ornamental) aria, Rosina is alone in her guardian's drawing room. In the first part, she is reflecting on the voice that serenaded and touched her heart. She begins by singing softly to create an intimate mood as if she is thinking aloud. She speaks of her suitor's love, the trouble with her guardian, and her desire to marry the Count (Lindoro). The second part reveals her strong determination to reach her goal. The song sparkles with vitality and virtuoso skills. It provides a spirited and artful portrait of Rosina. The coloratura passages express her charm, wit and humor. She discards her sentimental mood and becomes more animated as she expresses her freedom. It ends with a passage that requires exceptional agility and technical skill. (See "Una voce poco fa" in Part II for vocal skills.)

Una **voce** poco fa	A **voice** just now
qui nel cor mi risuonò.	has touched my very heart.
Il **mio cor** ferito è già	**My heart** has already been pierced
e Lindoro fu che il piagò.	and it was Lindoro who hurled the dart.
Sì, Lindoro mio sarà,	**Yes**, Lindoro shall be mine,
lo giurai, la vincerò.	I've sworn it, I'll succeed.
Il **tutor** ricuserà,	My **guardian** won't consent,
io l'ingegno aguzzerò,	but I will sharpen my wits,
alla fin s'accheterà,	and at last, he will relent,
e **contenta** io resterò.	and I shall be **content**.

"**La calunnia è un venticello**" ("**Slander is a little breeze**"). Don Basilio provides a sermon-like melody on how to start a rumor and discredit a person's character. It is a song in praise of vicious gossip to discredit the Count. It has an explosive effect even though the vocal part is comparatively simple. It is a masterpiece of characterization. The music grows and intensifies as Don Basilio speaks and reaches a crescendo. The calumny (slander) grows from a whisper to an outburst—a typical Rossini crescendo. After his outburst, a new melody allows him to emphasize the danger of damaging one's reputation. The number of instruments playing gradually increases to signal a robust and dramatic Rossini crescendo. (See "La calunnia è un venticello" in Part II for vocal skills.)

No? Uditemi e tacete.	No? Then listen to me and be silent.
La **calunnia** è un venticello	**Slander** is a little breeze,
un'auretta assai **gentile**	a **gentle** breeze
che **insensibile**, **sottile**,	which **insensibly**, **subtly**,
leggermente, dolcemente,	lightly and sweetly,
incomincia a sussurrar.	**commences** to whisper.
Dalla bocca fuori uscendo	From the mouth it emerges
lo schiamazzo va **crescendo**,	the noise grows in **crescendo**,

prende **forza** a poco a poco,   gathers **force** little by little,
vola già di **loco in loco**,   runs its course from **place to place**,
sembra il tuono, la **tempesta**...   seems like the thunder of the **storm**...

"Dunque io son ... tu non m'inganni?" ("Then it is I ... you are not deceiving me?"). When Figaro learns that Rosina's guardian plans to discredit the Count's reputation, he warns her in this duet. Rosina expresses her delight when she learns that she is the object of her music teacher's affection. Figaro discovers during Rosina's coloratura passages that she is already aware of the game. He exclaims that it is difficult to figure out women. It is a duet of pure happiness with semi-ornamented passages. Figaro responds by echoing her melody and coloratura passages. The excitement bubbles up in a typical Rossini crescendo. Staccato repetitions of the same notes add a lively and humorous element.

ROSINA
Dunque io son ... tu non m'inganni?   Then it is I ... you are not deceiving me?
Dunque io son **la fortunata**!   Then I am **the fortunate** girl!
(Già me l'ero **immaginata**,   (But I had already **imagined** it,
lo sapevo pria di te.)   I knew it all along.)

FIGARO
Di Lindoro il vago oggetto   You are, **beautiful Rosina**,
siete voi, **bella Rosina**.   the object of Lindoro's love.
(Oh, che volpe sopraffina!   (Oh, what a clever little fox!
Ma l'avrà da far con me.)   But she'll have to deal with me.)

"A un dottor della mia sorte" ("For a doctor of my standing"). Dr. Bartolo is upset by Rosina's behavior toward him and lack of respect. He orders her to be locked up in her room. He warns her not to impose on a man of his distinguished character. It's an amusing expression of his insolent and pompous nature. He advises Rosina to think of better excuses when addressing a man of his dignity and intelligence. Rossini uses a very fast tempo in sonata form (three sections consisting of an exposition, a development, and a recapitulation) to depict the Doctor's status. It's an elaborate ornamented passage for a bass singer. Rosina provides a surprising interlude as she expresses her sad fate.

A un **dottor** della mia sorte   For a **doctor** of my standing
queste **scuse**, **signorina**,   these **excuses**, **young lady**,
vi consiglio, mia carina,   I advise you, my dear child,
un po' meglio a impostar.   to invent something better.

Eh! non servono le **smorfie**,   Now your **simpering** will not help you
faccia pur la gatta morta.   nor your **face** of injured innocence.
Cospetton! per quella **porta**,   I here assure you, through that **door**
nemmen l'**aria entrar** potrà,   the very **air** itself won't **enter**.

"Freddo ed immobile" ("Cold and motionless"). This is one of the most enthusiastic and unrestrained ensembles in opera. It has a calm beginning as each character comments on the strange events. As the pace quickens, the sextet of characters moves in different directions. As the confusion and frenzy approach a climax, Rosina's cheerful high notes express a need for silence and order. It is full of comic energy as several people talk at once. It becomes a chorus in which everyone agrees that the situation has become insane. A variety of musical ideas are used to portray different moods. They are combined in unison to create a complex dramatic situation and then repeated on a higher key. It's an amusing and clever climax to Act II.

COUNT

Freddo ed **immobile**	**Cold** and **motionless**
come **una statua,**	like **a statue,**
fiato non restagli	she has hardly
da **respirar!**	breath to **breathe!**

BARTOLO

Freddo ed immobile	Cold and motionless
come una statua,	like a statue,
fiato non restami	I have hardly
da respirar!	breath to breathe!

FIGARO

Guarda Don Bartolo,	**Look** at Don Bartolo,
sembra una statua!	he stands like a statue!
Ah, ah, dal ridere	Oh, I am ready to burst
sto per crepar!	with uncontrolled laughter!

Act III

"Contro un cor che accende amore" ("Against a heart ignited with love"). The Count has entered Dr. Bartolo's house disguised as a music professor. Rosina's part calls for an elaborate coloratura. In this "Lesson Scene," the Count pretends to give her a music lesson. Rosina sings a rondo (a song consisting of one slow and one fast section) while the Count accompanies her at the harpsichord. This gives the soprano the freedom to show off her virtuosity. Dr. Bartolo is also in the room seated in a chair listening to the lesson. When he falls asleep, they express their mutual affection.

ROSINA

Contro un cor che accende **amore**	**Against** a heart ignited with **love,**
di verace invitto ardore,	burning with inextinguishable fire,
s'arma invan poter **tiranno**	a ruthless **tyrant, cruelly** armed,
di rigor, di **crudeltà.**	wages war, but all in vain.
D'ogni **assalto vincitore,**	From every **assault** a **victor,**
sempre amore **trionferà.**	love will always **triumph.**

COUNT

Non temer, ti **rassicura**,	Fear not, be **reassured**,
sorte amica a noi sarà.	fate will be our friend.

"Buona sera, mio signore" ("Good night to you, my gentleman"). Figaro has arrived to shave Dr. Bartolo and distract him from the young lovers. The plan is going well until Don Basilio appears. He is offered money not to interfere with the plan. As Figaro shaves the doctor, Rosina sings a lively melody and is alerted to Figaro's plot. Dr. Bartolo overhears the plot and the angry doctor disrupts the plan. The Count, Rosina and Figaro convince Brasilia to go home and rest after persuading him that he is very ill. They all wish him good night.

COUNT, ROSINA, FIGARO

Buona sera, **mio signore**,	Good night to you, **my gentleman**,
presto andate via di qua.	**quickly** go away from here.

BASILIO

Buona sera, ben di core...	Well, good night, with all my heart,
Poi diman si parlerà.	then tomorrow we shall talk.

COUNT

Buona sera, via di qua,	Well, good night, away from here.
buona sera, mio signore,	Well, good night, my gentleman,
pace, sonno e sanità,	**peace**, sleep and good health.
presto andate via di qua.	Quickly go away from here.

"Ah, qual colpo inaspettato!" ("Oh, what an unexpected shock!"). In this trio, the Count and Rosina are planning their escape, while Figaro pats himself on the back for serving as their matchmaker. As the lovers continue to sing a passionate melody, Figaro becomes impatient and encourages them to make a quick escape. They express their anxiety to leave in the "Zitti, zitti" ("Quiet, quiet") trio. To add humor to the scene, he leads them to the balcony only to find that the ladder has been removed. The song moves at a very fast pace and especially designed for the Italian language. The three singers take turns singing the main melody before uniting to sing the melody.

ROSINA

(Ah, qual colpo **inaspettato!**	(Oh, what an **unexpected** shock!
Egli stesso? Oh Ciel! Che sento!	It is he himself! Heavens, what do I hear?
Di **sorpresa** e di contento	With **surprise** and with joy
son vicina a **delirar!**)	I am almost **delirious!**)

COUNT

(Qual **trionfo** inaspettato!	(What an unexpected **triumph!**
Me felice! Oh, **bel momento!**	I'm so happy! What a **beautiful moment!**
Ah, d'**amore** e di **contento**	With **love** and **contentment**
son vicino a delirar!)	I am almost delirious!)

FIGARO

(**Nodo!**) Andiamo. (**Nodo!**)	(Tie the **knot!**) Let's get going. (Tie the
Presto, andiamo. (**Paghi!**)	knot!) **Quickly**, Let's go. (**Pay!**)
Vi sbrigate.	Hurry up.
Lasciate quei sospir.	This is no time for sentiment.
Presto, andiam per carità.	Let's go quickly, for pity's sake.

"Di sì felice innesto" ("So happy a reunion"). This sextet and chorus brings the curtain down with a delightful and happy ending. The Count presents a gift to Dr. Bartolo of Rosina's dowry. The doctor accepts his defeat and gives his blessing to the lovers. Figaro, Rosina and the Count celebrate their good fortune. The opera ends with the main characters and chorus expressing their joy over the happy outcome. Rosina's voice sparkles above the joyous ensemble.

FIGARO

Di sì felice innesto,	So happy a reunion,
serbiam **memoria eterna**.	let's have **eternal memories**.
Io smorzo la **lanterna**,	I put out my **lantern**,
qui più non ho che far.	I am no longer needed.

CHARACTERS, CHORUS

Amor e **fede eterna**	May **love** and **faith eternal**
si vegga in voi regnar.	reign in both your hearts.
Rosina, Count	
Amor e fede eterna	May love and faith eternal
si vegga in noi **regnar**.	**reign** in both our hearts.

La Bohème
by Giacomo Puccini

Introducing herself as a seamstress to a bohemian poet
Meeting under candlelight and dying in his garret
First performed in Turin, February 1, 1896
Based on a novel, *Scènes de la vie de Bohème*, by Henri Murger
Libretto by Giuseppe Giacosa and Luigi Illica
Translation by Pearl Oliva

*G*iacomo Puccini was born in Lucca in 1858 and died in Brussels in 1924. *La Bohème* was his first great masterpiece and it made him wealthy and famous. It was followed by two more masterpieces—*Tosca* and *Madama Butterfly*. Even though the critics dismissed *La Bohème* as lightweight at its premiere in Turin, Italy, in 1896, it quickly became very popular with the public. Puccini never portrayed human passion as sensitively and poetically as he did in *La Bohème*. It is still Puccini's most popular opera, and its sad ending draws tears from the audience. It is based on a novel entitled *Scenes de la vie de Bohème* by Henri Murger. The book and the opera are a faithful picture of life in the poor artists' and students' quarter of Paris in the mid 19th century. Several of Puccini's other most popular operas include *Tosca, Madama Butterfly, and Turandot*.

After attending a performance of Verdi's *Aida*, Puccini became convinced that he wanted to compose music for the human voice. He studied composition for three years at the Milan Conservatory. Puccini's years as a poor student made him sympathetic to the Bohenian characters (poor artists and writers who tend to share living quarters) in *La Bohème*. Puccini and his librettists worked on the score for three strenuous years. He demanded that the words should reflect a tightly woven plot and precise articulation of the text. Puccini repeatedly told the librettists to simplify the words to match his music. He realized that the libretto could only carry the opera so far. The music would have to be the sealing element because opera, in the final analysis, is a musical drama.

Synopsis of Puccini's La Bohème

Main Characters

Rodolfo, a poet	Tenor
Mimì, an embroiderer	Soprano
Musetta, a singer	Soprano
Marcello, a painter	Baritone
Colline, a philosopher	Bass

Act I

Rodolfo is writing poetry in a cold attic apartment in Paris. His three Bohemian friends, who share the apartment, have just left to visit a café on

Christmas Eve. There is a knock at the door. His neighbor Mimì needs a match to light her candle. As she is about to leave, she drops her key and the candle blows out. In the darkness, Rodolfo tries to warm her cold hands and tell her of his dreams (Song: **"Che gelida manina!"**). Mimì responds by telling him about her lonely life as an embroiderer and her love for springtime and making flowers (Song: **"Mi chiamano Mimì"**). In the moonlit room, they express their affection for each other in a duet (Song: **"O soave fanciulia!"**). They leave the room arm-in-arm singing to join Rodolfo's friends.

Act II

Mimì, Rodolfo and his friends are seated at an outdoor café. Vendors are shouting their goods and a chorus of children is following the toy vendor (Song: **"Ecco Parpignol!"**). The painter Marcello is seated with his friends when his former sweetheart Musetta arrives with a wealthy and elderly admirer. She tries to regain Marcello's attention by singing about all the attention she attracts wherever she goes (Song: **"Quando me'n vo soletta"**). When her elderly friend leaves to repair her shoe, Musetta, Marcello and his friends leave before he returns to pay their bill.

Act III

At dawn on a snowy morning, Mimì comes to a tavern looking for Marcello's help. After an argument with Musetta, Marcello emerges and Mimì confesses to him that she is disturbed over Rodolfo's jealous accusations. She hides when Rodolfo appears. He tells Marcello that it is really Mimì's poor health that he cannot face. She comes forth to bid Rodolfo farewell with no regrets (Song: **"D'onde lieta uscì"**). They review the joys they will no longer share. Musetta runs from the tavern after Marcello catches her flirting with another man. In the quartet that follows, Marcello and Musetta carry on a quarrel while Rodolfo and Mimì decide to reunite until spring arrives (Song: **"Dunque è proprio finita"**).

Act IV

Rodolfo and Marcello have returned to their attic and they long to see their sweethearts. In a duet, they share their sentimental memories of Mimì and Musetta (Song: **"O Mimì, tu più non torni!"**). Musetta arrives and announces that Mimì is very weak and needs medicine. To raise money, the philosopher Colline prepares to pawn his overcoat. He sings about how faithfully it has served him (Song: **"Vecchia zimarra"**). Just before she is about to die, Mimì reminds Rodolfo of their happy days together (Song: **"Sono andati?"**).

Major Song Sketches

Act I

"Che gelida manina!" (**"What a cold little hand!"**). In the darkness of his attic, the poet Rodolfo pretends to be searching for Mimì's key. After touching her cold hand, he tells her of his dreams in a soft voice. He expresses compassion, cheerfulness and warmth. He admits that he has little material means, but his passion makes him richer than a millionaire. In the next part, his voice becomes more passionate as he reaches toward a high note of C to express his growing attraction for Mimì. It is an expression of pure beauty and radiance. It is one of the most famous tenor arias in opera. (See "Che gelida manina!" in Part II for vocal skills.)

Che gelida manina!	What a cold little hand!
Se la lasci riscaldar.	Let me warm it for you.
Cercar che giova?	What's the use of searching?
Al buio non si trova.	It can't be found in the dark.
In **povertà** mia lieta	I delight in **poverty**,
scialo da **gran signore**	I pretend to be a **great gentleman**
rime ed inni d'**amore**.	of **rhymes** and songs of **love**.
Per sogni e per chimere	When it comes to hopes and dreams
e per **castelli in aria**	and **castles-in-air**,
l'anima ho **milionaria**.	I have the soul of a **millionaire**.

"Mi chiamano Mimì" (**"They call me Mimì"**). After Rodolfo completes his introductory aria, Mimì describes her simple life in a touching melody. The opening notes serve to identify Mimì's motif (a short unit of music that identifies her character in several parts of the opera). We learn that she accepts her present life by dreaming of a more pleasant future. We learn that Mimì and Rodolfo both have a poetic nature that helps to draw them together. (See "Mi chiamano Mimì" in Part II for vocal skills.)

Mi chiamano Mimì,	They call me Mimì,
ma il **mio nome** è Lucia.	but **my name** is Lucia.
La **storia** mia è **breve**.	My **story** is **brief**.
A tela o a seta	On canvas or on silk,
ricamo in **casa** e fuori.	I embroider at **home** or outside.
Son **tranquilla** e lieta,	I'm **tranquil** and happy,
ed è mio svago far gigli e **rose**.	and my pastime is making lilies and **roses**.
Ma quando vien lo sgelo	But when the thaw comes
il **primo sole** è **mio**,	the **first sunrays** are **mine**.
il primo bacio dell'**aprile** è mio!	The first kiss of April is mine!
Il primo sole è mio.	The first sunrays are mine!

"O soave fanciulia!" (**"Oh! Lovely girl!"**). Rodolfo and Mimì sing a famous duet that captures the love they feel for each other. Rodolfo ignores the voices of his friends from the street below as he gazes at Mimì's moonlit face. He uses his charm to describe her sweet face in the moonlight and in his dreams. Her short phrases express her need for security and a mutual attachment. Their voices blend together and the duet has a dreamy ending as they leave the room arm-in-arm. Their voices fade into the cold evening air on Christmas Eve. Part of the duet is a reprise of Rodolfo's opening aria.

RODOLFO

O soave fanciulia, o dolce viso,	Oh! Lovely girl! Oh, sweet face
di mite circonfuso alba **lunar**,	bathed in the soft **moonlight**.
in te ravviso il sogno	I recognize my dream in you
ch'io vorrei sempre sognar!	which I would always want to dream!
Fremon nell'anima	I already taste an
dolcezze estreme, ecc.	**extreme sweetness!**
Nel bacio freme **amor!**	**Love** trembles in our kiss!

MIMÌ

(Oh! come dolci scendono	(Oh! How sweetly his enticements
le sue lusinghe al core...	enter my heart...
Tu sol **comandi, amor!**)	You alone **command love!**)

Act II

"Ecco Parpignol!" (**"Here is Parpignol!"**). Mimì, Rodolfo and his friends are seated in front of a café. It is Christmas Eve and a cheerful crowd has gathered in the square. A chorus of children greets the toy seller, Parpignol. The words "Ecco Parpignol!" are heard twice in a remote key, and a chorus of kids follows this. They follow the toy maker and sing a festive song. Other vendors stroll by selling their wares.

Parpignol! Parpignol! Parpignol!...	Parpignol! Parpignol! Parpignol!
Ecco Parpignol! Parpignol!	Here is Parpignol! Parpignol!
Col **carretto** tutto **fior!**	With a **cart** covered in **flowers!**
Ecco Parpignol!	Here is Parpignol!
Voglio la **tromba**, il cavallin!	I want the **trumpet**, the toy horse!
Il **tambur, tamburel**...	The **drum, tambourine**...
Voglio il **cannon**, voglio il frustin,	I want the **cannon**; I want the riding whip,
dei **soldati** i drappel.	the group of **soldiers.**

"Quando me'n vo soletta" (**"When I walk alone"**). Marcello's former lover, Musetta, arrives with an elderly and wealthy escort. When she sees Marcello, she tries to regain his affection but he tries to ignore her. She sings this famous waltz designed to arouse his jealousy. She marvels at how people stop to look and admire her beauty. The conversations of the main characters are skillfully integrated into the waltz. As Musetta expresses her flirtatious character, Mimì sings a counter theme expressing her different character. (See "Quando me'n vo soletta" in Part II for vocal skills.)

Quando me'n vo **soletta**	When I walk **alone**
per la via,	on the street,
la gente sosta e mira,	people stop to look
e la **bellezza mia**	and **my beauty**
tutta ricerca in me,	they search for in me,
ricerca in me da capo a piè.	looked for from head to toe.
Ed assaporo allor la bramosia	And then I savor the subtle
sottil che dagli occhi traspira	longing that shows in their eyes,
e dai palesi vezzi intender sa	and from my visible charms, they can
alle occulte beltà.	appreciate the hidden beauties.

Act III

"**D'onde lieta uscì**" ("**From the place I left**"). Mimì has just overheard Rodolfo expressing his concern to Marcello about her failing health. She learns that he still loves her but he cannot face her terminal illness. She comes forth to sing him a touching farewell without judging him or expressing any regrets. Mimì's lyrical farewell has a tender beginning and becomes more melodic as it grows in strength. It begins with a soft violin solo based on her act one aria. After her theme is played very softly, the music becomes desperately sad and suggests her lonely room. Mimì must sing beautifully with a broken heart knowing that her death is near and that she will have to face it alone. Her strength and steady voice gives Rodolfo more strength. They decide to stay together until spring, and they leave with his arm around her.

D'onde lieta uscì al tuo grido	From the place I left happily
d'**amore** torna sola Mimì.	at your call of **love**.
Al **solitario** nido	Mimì returns **alone**
ritorna un'altra volta	to a lonely nest. She **returns**
a intesser **finti fior**.	again to make **false flowers**.
Addio senza **rancor**.	**Good-by**, without **resentment**.
Ascolta, ascolta.	Listen, listen.
Le poche robe aduna che lasciai	Gather up the few things
sparse. Nel mio cassetto	I left behind. In my drawer
stan chiusi quel **cerchietto**	there are the little golden **circlets**
d'or e il **libro** di preghiere.	and my prayer **book**. Wrap everything
Involgi tutto quanto in un grembiale	in an apron and I'll send
e manderò il **portiere**...	the **porter** for them...

"**Dunque è proprio finite**" ("**So it's really finished!**"). This famous quartet immediately follows Mimì's farewell. A sweet and tragic melody unites Mimì and Rodolfo, while Marcello and Musetta conduct a jealous argument.

The contrasting emotions of a quarreling couple and a reuniting couple make this one of the most outstanding quartets in Italian opera. Marcello is angry at Musetta's flirting, and she declares she is not answerable to him. At the same time, Mimì and Rodolfo are singing of their future happiness. Puccini uses this quartet to capture the personalities and paint a vivid portrait of the characters. He depicts their tensions and links them to a very expressive melody.

RODOLFO
Dunque è proprio **finita**.
Te ne vai, la mia piccina?
Addio, sogni d'**amor**!

So it's really **finished**!
You're leaving, my little one?
Good-bye, to dreams of **love**!

MIMÌ
Addio dolce svegliare alla **mattina**.

Good-bye to the sweet awakening
In the **morning**!

MARCELLO
Vana, frivola civetta!
Ve ne andate? Vi ringrazio,
or son **ricco** divenuto.

Vain, frivolous flirt!
Are you leaving? I thank you:
now I've become a **rich** man.

MUSETTA
Fo all'**amor** chi mi **piace**.
Non ti garba?
Fo all'amor con chi mi piace.
Musetta se ne va.

I'll make **love** with whom I **please**.
You don't like it?
I'll make love with whom I please.
Musetta is going away.

Act IV

"O Mimì, tu più non torni!" (**"Oh Mimi, you're not coming back anymore!"**). Rodolfo and Marcello are back in their apartment attic and they miss Mimì and Musetta. Their loving memories are expressed in this lovely and sentimental duet. It has a haunting sound as they engage in nostalgic memories. Their thoughts stray from their work to their sweethearts because Mimì and Musetta were recently seen in carriages. Their voices overlap even though their lyrics (words) pertain to two different women. The orchestra completes the melody after they complete their lines and reflect on their memories.

RODOLFO
O Mimì, tu più non torni.

Oh Mimì, you're not coming back anymore!

O giorni **belli**,
piccole mani, odorosi capelli...
collo di **neve**! Ah! Mimì,
mia breve gioventù.

Oh **beautiful** days,
small hands, sweet-smelling hair...
snowy **neck**! Ah! Mimì,
my brief youth.

MARCELLO
Se pingere mi **piace**
o cielo o **terre**

If I like I **paint**
either heaven or **earth**,

o inverni o **primavere**,	or winters or **springs**,
egli mi traccia due pupille nere	the brush draws two dark eyes
e una bocca procace,	and a provocative mouth,
e n'esce di Musetta il viso ancor...	and Musetta's face emerges from it...

"Vecchia zimarra" (**"Listen, my venerable coat"**). Colline, the philosopher, has just learned that Mimì needs medicine. He has decided to sell his coat to raise money for Mimì's weak condition. Before he parts with his coat, he sings a short and touching aria out of praise and respect for his coat. Colline tries to cover his sadness with a joke about how he will stay on a lower level while his coat ascends to a higher level. His farewell to his faithful coat is followed by a sweet orchestral interlude based on the love motif that united Rodolfo and Mimì in the first act.

Vecchia zimarra, senti,	Listen, my venerable coat,
io resto al pian, tu **ascendere**	I'm staying behind, while you have to
il **sacro monte** or devi.	**ascend** to the **holy mount**.
Le mie **grazie ricevi**.	**Receive** my **thanks**.
Mai non curvasti il logoro	You never bent your tired **back**
dorso ai **ricchi** ed ai **potenti**.	to the **rich** or **powerful**.
Passar nelle tue tasche	Your pockets held
come in antri **tranquilli**	**philosophers** and **poets**
filosofi e **poeti**.	as if in **tranquil** recesses.
Ora che i giorni lieti	Now that those happy days have fled
fuggir, ti dico addio,	I bid you farewell,
fedele amico mio. Addio.	my **faithful friend**. Farewell.

"Sono andati?" (**"Have they gone?"**). In this duet, Mimì and Rodolfo sing about the happy times they have spent together. The orchestra introduces this final duet by playing brief melodies presented earlier, including the duet from the first act. She faints at the end as she recalls Rodolfo's words when they first met. Puccini tells us that the dying Mimì is dreaming of the past. The hushed tones suggest a reflective atmosphere as Rodolfo kneels next to Mimì's bedside.

MIMÌ

Sono andati? Fingevo di dormire	Have they gone? I was pretending to sleep
perché volli con te **sola** restare.	because I wanted to be **alone** with you.
Ho tante cose che ti voglio dire,	I have so many things that I want to tell you,
o **una** sola ma **grande** come il mare,	I have **one** as **large** as the sea,
come il mare **profonda** ed **infinita**...	as the sea **profound** and **infinite**...
Sei il mio **amor** ... e tutta la **mia vita**.	You are my **love** ... and **my** entire **life**.

RODOLFO

Ah Mimì, **mia bella** Mimì!	Ah Mimì, **my beautiful** Mimì!

MIMÌ
Son bella ancora?   Am I beautiful still?

RODOLFO
Bella come un'aurora.   Beautiful as the dawn.

L'Elisir d'Amore
(The Elixir of Love)
by Gaetano Donizetti

Sighing and wishing to attract a lovely landowner
Thinking an elixir instead of his inheritance won her over

First performed in Milan, May 12, 1832
Based on a play, *Le Philtre*, by Eugène Scribe

Libretto by Giuseppe Felice Romani
Translation by Maria Figuero

*G*aetano Donizetti was born in Bergamo in 1797 and died in Bergamo in 1848. He was a versatile operatic dramatist, ranging from comedy to tragedy. He had a remarkable gift for melody and humorous character inventions, such as the quack Doctor Dulcamara in *L'Elisir d'Amore (The Elixir of Love)*. Italy was known for its development of vocal techniques, and Donizetti had a rare skill for voice composition. He composed music at a remarkable speed and left over 70 operas in his name. It is reported that he composed *L'Elisir d'Amore* in just two weeks. Donizetti and Bellini both lived during the first half of the 19th century. Both were drawn to the Romantic Movement and excelled in the bel canto repertory. They also collaborated with the same librettist, Felice Romani, on their most famous operas—Donizetti's *L'Elisir d'Amore* and Bellini's *Norma*. Unfortunately, they both lived short lives—Bellini died at 33 and Donizetti at 50. Even though Donizetti was most famous for his comedies, his life ended in tragedy—his wife and children died before he died in a state of insanity.

L'Elisir d'Amore was Donizetti's most successful opera. It remains one of the most charming and popular Italian comic operas known as "opera buffa." The characters are very appealing and lovable, such as the lovesick Nemorino and the coquettish Adina. The story is based on a book, *Le Philtre*, by a French dramatist of the 19th century. In Italy, opera was popular with all classes and not simply the wealthy. *L'Elisir d'Amore* contains simple and light-hearted melodies with a folk song appeal. Its make believe world of eternal sunshine, love, and a happy ending achieved immediate popularity and mirrored the romantic spirit of the times.

Synopsis of Donizetti's L'Elisir d'Amore

Main Characters

Nemorino, a young peasant	Tenor
Adina, a prosperous landowner	Soprano
Belcore, village sergeant	Baritone
Dr. Dulcamara, quack doctor	Bass
Gianetta, a peasant girl	Soprano

Act I

The farm workers are resting from their labor in the courtyard of Adina's farm. The lovesick Nemorino gazes at Adina and sighs because he can't arouse her affection (Song: **"Quanto è bella, quanto è cara!"**). She is reading a story of how Tristan drank a love potion to help him win Isolde's eternal love. She shares her amusement with the farm workers (Song: **"Della crudele Isotta"**). Sergeant Belcore arrives with a detachment of soldiers. He tries to win Adina's affection with a bouquet of flowers (Song: **"Come Paride vezzoso"**). She resists his advances and turns her attention to Nemorino. She tells him to stay near his sick uncle and forget about trying to win such a frivolous woman such as herself (Song: **"Chiedi all'aura lusinghiera"**). The villagers gather in the market place to welcome the quack Doctor Dulcamara. From the steps of his colorful carriage, he tells the crowd that he has special cures to treat every ailment (Song: **"Udite, udite, o rustici"**). Nemorino asks the doctor if he has a love potion (elixir) after hearing the story of Tristan and Isolde. Dulcamara sells him a flask of red wine but convinces Nemorino that it contains a love potion (Song: **"Voglio dire, lo stupendo elisir"**). After a couple of drinks, the tipsy Nemorino confronts Adina in a jolly mood. He pretends that she doesn't matter to him because the love potion is not supposed to work until the following day. When Nemorino finds out that Adina has agreed to marry Belcore that very day, he implores her to wait another day (Song: **"Adina credimi, te ne scongiuro"**). She ignores his plea and invites the crowd to her wedding.

Act II

A wedding feast has been prepared at the village inn. Dr. Dulcamara offers to entertain the guests with a lively barcarolle from Venice and invites Adina to join him. He sings the part of a rich senator while she sings the pretty girl gondolier (Song: **"Io son ricco e tu sei bella"**). Nemorino begs the doctor for a second bottle of love potion. In order to pay for it, he enlists in the army and receives an advance payment. He returns to Adina's farm confident the second bottle will work a miracle (Song: **"Dell'elisir mirabile"**). Nemorino doesn't know that his uncle has just died and left him a fortune. The village girls have heard about his inheritance, and they are trying to attract his attention. Nemorino thinks all of this attention is due to the love potion. When Adina learns from Dulcamara that Nemorino has sold his freedom to win her love, her heart softens for him (Song: **"Quanto amore! Ed io, spietata!"**). She conveys her feeling for him with a tear in her eye because her magic potion lies in her glance. Nemorino hopes that the tear he noticed in her eye means that her heart belongs to him (Song: **"Una furtiva lagrima"**). Adina tells him that she has bought off his recruitment contract. He tells her he would rather die as a soldier than live without being loved. She then confesses her love for him and they embrace (Song: **"Prendi, per me sei libero"**). Belcore takes his loss like a good soldier. Dulcamara announces that his magic potion has brought Nemorino both love and wealth. The villagers surround the quack doctor requesting samples of his elixir for themselves.

Major Song Sketches

Act I

"**Quanto è bella, quanto è cara!**" ("**How lovely she is, how dear she is!**"). This tender and sweet aria characterizes Nemorino's mellow and hesitant personality. He can only sigh at Adina from a distance. This is his entrance song with a very lyrical sound in the bel canto (elegant and smooth with a beauty of tone) style. As the song draws to a close, several phrases end on a high note. Just before and at the close of Nemorino's aria, Gianetta, a peasant girl, and the farm workers express their joy at resting in the shade during the noonday heat. Nemorino sings to himself while Adina reads a book under a tree.

Quanto è **bella**, quanto è cara!	How **beautiful** she is, how dear she is!
Più la vedó e più mi piace,	The more I see her, the more I like her,
ma in quel cor non son **capace**	but in her heart I am **incapable**
lieve **affetto** ad **inspirar**.	of **inspiring** the least **affection**.
Essa legge, **studia**, impara,	She reads, **studies**, learns,
non vi ha cosa ad essa ignota;	there's nothing she doesn't know;
io non sempre un **idiota**,	I'm a complete **idiot**,
io non so che sospirar.	I only know how to sigh.

"**Della crudele Isotta**" ("**For cruel-hearted Isolde**"). While the farm workers relax, Adina reads a book about how Tristan's magic love potion (elixir) attracted the hard-hearted Isolde. She finds the story amusing and reads it aloud in a waltz-like narrative. The violins suggest the magical power of the love potion. In her cavatina (short entrance song), she reads mockingly and laughs aloud at the absurd story. As she sings, there is a choral refrain and contrasting dance rhythm. The farm workers join in the closing section with growing excitement.

Della **crudele** Isotta	For **cruel-hearted** Isolde
il bel **Tristano** ardea,	the handsome **Tristan** longed,
nè fil di speme avea	he had not the slightest hope
di possederla un dì,	of winning her one day.
quando si trasse al piede	He went to a wise **enchanter**
di saggio **incantatore**	who gave him a phial
che in un vasel gli diede	of a special **love** potion
certo elisir d'**amor**,	which caused the **beautiful**
per cui la **bella** Isotta	**Isolde** to no longer avoid him.
da lui più non fuggi.	

"**Come Paride vezzoso**" ("**In the same way as the charming Paris**"). Sergeant Belcore is introduced by a swaggering march that portrays his boastful personality. His cavatina (romantic piece) is in two stanzas. In the first stanza, he presents a bouquet of flowers to Adina and compares himself to the handsome Paris when he gave a golden apple to Aphrodite. The second stanza is more embellished because he boasts that no fair maid can resist his uniform. His cavatina develops into a sizable ensemble as others join in.

Come **Paride** vezzoso	In the same way as the charming **Paris**
porse il pomo alla più **bella,**	presented the apple to the most **beautiful,**
mia diletta villanella,	**my darling village** girl,
io ti porgo questi **fior.**	I give these **flowers** to you.
Ma di lui più **glorioso,**	But more **glorious** than he,
più di lui felice io sono,	happier than he am I,
poichè in premio del mio dono,	for as a reward for my gift,
ne riporto il tuo bel cor.	I receive your dear heart.

   "Chiedi all'aura lusinghiera" (**"Ask the flattering breeze"**). In this duet, Adina compares her nature to a fickle breeze while Nemorino responds that he is as constant as a river. They sing identical melodies even though they characterize themselves as having opposite natures. The duet has two distinctive parts. The first part has a soft melody, and the second part has a spirited rhythm with a more ornamented (colorfully decorated) passage. Adina finds his sighs and pleas too modest for her more capricious nature.

ADINA

Chiedi all'aura lusinghiera	Ask the flattering breeze
perchè vola senza posa	why it flies without settling
or sul giglio, or sulla **rosa,**	now on the lily, now on the **rose,**
or sul prato, or sul ruscel:	now on the meadow, now on the brook:
ti dirà che è in lei **natura**	it will tell it is its **nature**
l'esser **mobile** e **infedel.**	always to be **moving** and **unfaithful.**

NEMORINO

Chiedi al rio perchè gemente	Ask the river why, moaning
dalla balza ov'ebbe vita	from the rock from which it sprang,
corre al mar che a sè l'**invita,**	it runs down to the sea which **invites** it on,
e nel mar sen va a morir:	and goes to its death in the ocean:
ti dirà che lo strascina	it will tell you it is dragged there
un **poter** che non sa dir.	by a **power** it cannot explain.

   "Udite, udite, o rustici" (**"Listen, listen, country folk"**). Doctor Dulcamara's entrance aria is accompanied by the delightful sound of a trumpet. This outstanding comic aria is performed by a base buffo voice. He is given a showman's entrance in a colorful carriage or in a gondola suspended from a large balloon. The quack doctor is introduced with appropriate rhythms as he tries to sell his elixirs (magic cures). The villagers sway to the trumpeter's waltz tune. Dulcamara presents his elixirs with very quickly spoken words. This fast talking comic style is known as a "patter song." This song includes a long and rapid amount of patter to a series of melodies.

Udite, udite, o rustici;	Listen, listen, country folk;
atteni, non fiatate.	pay **attention**, hold your breath.
Io già suppongo e **immagino**	I presume and **imagine**
che al par di me sappiate	that you know as well as I do
ch'io sono quel **gran medico**,	that I'm that **great doctor**,
dottore enciclopedico,	**encyclopedic doctor**,
chiamato Dulcamara,	called Dulcamara,
la cui **virtù** preclara,	whose **virtuous** power
e i portenti **infiniti**	and **infinite** marvels
son noti all'**universo**	are known throughout the **universe**
e ... e ... e in altri siti.	and ... and ... and in other places.

"Voglio dire, lo stupendo elisir" ("I mean the wonderful elixir"). Nemorino decides to buy a magic elixir from Dulcamara to help him win Adina's affection. The scene builds up from a recitative with keyboard to recitative with orchestra. This lively duet consists of a series of crescendos (passages that reach an increasing volume) with a comic style accompaniment. The opening exchanges are short and brisk. It becomes a full-fledged comic duet with their voices together. It is an excellent example of an Italian patter (fast talking) ensemble. Dulcamara sells Nemorino a magic love potion while comparing him to a simpleton. The elixir is nothing more than a bottle of red wine.

NEMORINO

Voglio dire, lo **stupendo**	I mean the **wonderful**
elisir che desta **amore**.	elixir that awakens **love**.

DULCAMARA

Ah! sì, sì, capisco, intendo.	Oh! Yes, yes, I understand what you mean.
Io ne son **distillatore**.	I am the **distiller**.

NEMORINO

Obbligato, ah! sì obbligato!	Much **obliged**! Oh, yes, much obliged!
Son felice, son **contento** (beato).	I am happy, I am **content**.
L'elisire di tal bontà,	A **blessing** on the person
benedetto chi ti fa!	for making an elixir of such goodness!

DULCAMARA

Nel paese che ho girato	Traveling about the countryside
più d'un gonzo ho ritrovato,	I've met more than one simpleton,
ma un **eguale** in verità	but, truly, one to **equal** this
non si trova, non si dà.	would be hard to find.

"Adina credimi, te ne scongiuro" ("Believe me, Adina, I beseech you"). Nemorino has learned that Adina is pledged to marry Belcore. He implores her to wait until tomorrow. He sings a very lovely lament with great tenderness. It is a heartfelt plea with a tragic touch. Adina then takes up the melody. It becomes a trio when Belcore refers to Nemorino as a buffoon and warns him to keep out of his way. Nemorino still thinks his love potion will work if Adina will postpone her wedding. She is looking for revenge because he treated her with indifference after drinking the elixir.

NEMORINO

Adina credimi, te ne scongiuro,	Believe me, Adina, I beseech you,
non puoi sposarlo, te ne assicuro,	you can't marry him. I swear to you,
aspetta ancora un giorno **solo**,	delay just **one** day,
un **breve** giorno, io so perchè.	one **short** day. I know the reason why.

BELCORE

Il ciel ringrazia, o babbuino,	Thank your lucky stars, dunce,
che matto, o preso tu sei dal **vino**!..	that you're either mad or drunk from **wine**!..
Infin ch'io tengo a fren le mani,	While I still hold my hand in check,
va via, **buffone**, ti ascondi a me.	off with you, **buffoon**, stay out of my way.

ADINA

Lo compatite, egli è un ragazzo:	Excuse him, he's just a boy:
un malaccorto, un mezzo pazzo;	imprudent, half-mad;
si è **fitto** in capo ch'io debba amarlo,	he has it **fixed** in his head that I love him
perch'ei **delira** d'amor per me.	because he's **delirious** with love for me.

Act II

"Io son ricco e tu sei bella" (**"I am rich and you are beautiful"**). Dulcamara invites Adina to sing a duet with him to entertain the guests. They blend their voices in a lilting Venetian barcarole involving a wealthy senator and a pretty lady gondolier. Dulcamara plays the clown and Adina the coquette. He produces the written music from his pocket and together they sing a captivating duet. He pretends he is a senator suggesting love to his attractive gondolier.

DULCAMARA

Io son **ricco** e tu sei **bella**,	I am **rich** and you are **beautiful**,
io ducati, e vezzi hai tu.	I have money and you have charm.
Perchè a me sarai rubella,	Why be so difficult with me,
nina mia, che vuoi di più?	my darling, what more could you want?

ADINA

Quale **onore**! Un **senatore**	What an **honor**! A **senator**
me d'**amore** supplicar!	begging for my **love**!
Ma, **modesta gondoliera**,	But I am a **modest gondolier** girl, and
un par mio mi vuo' sposar.	want to marry a man of my own station.

"Dell'elisir mirabile" ("I've drunk a great amount"). The village girls
have learned that Nemorino just inherited his uncle's wealth. He thinks his
sudden popularity is due to the love potion because he hasn't heard that his
uncle just passed away. His popularity has aroused Adina's jealousy. Dulcamara
attributes Nemorino's female gathering to the elixir. The scene turns into a
sparkling ensemble with a variety of different responses.

NEMORINO
Dell'elisir **mirabile**   I've drunk a great amount
bevuto ho in abbondanza,   of the **admirable** elixir,
e mi **promette** il **medico**   and the good **doctor promised** me
cortese ogni beltà.   all the pretty girls.

GIANNETTA AND VILLAGE GIRLS
Caro quell Nemorino!   That darling Nemorino!
Davver è un uom **amabile**,   He's really an **amiable** man,
ha l'aria da **signor.**   he looks like a **gentleman.**

ADINA
Credea trovarlo a piangere,   I thought I would find him in tears,
e in giuoco, in **festa** il trovo;   and I see him **festive** and rejoicing.
ah! non saria **possibil**   Oh, it couldn't be **possible**
se a me pensasse ancor.   that he might still think of me.

DULCAMARA
Io cado dalle nuvole,   I'm amazed,
il **caso** è **strano** e **nuovo**;   this is a **strange, new case;**
sarei d'un filtro **magico**   am I really the **possessor**
davvero **possessor?**   of a **magic** formula?

"Quanto amore! Ed io, spietata!" ("Such love! And I was pitiless!").
In this duet, Dulcamara offers to concoct an elixir for Adina to help her attract
Nemorino because he has been acting indifferent. She tells him that she has a
more potent elixir—a smile and tender gesture. Adina sings a melody above
Dulcamara's patter (fast spoken words) and bassoon sounding voice. As the
song progresses, the pace increases, and the duet has an allegro (fast) ending.
The song has a comic irony because she uses her charm to counter his charm
and quack treatment.

ADINA
Quanto **amore!** Ed io, **spietata!**   Such **love!** And I was **pitiless!**
Tormentai si **nobil** cor!   I **tortured** such a **noble** heart!

DULCAMARA
Prendi su la mia ricetta,   Come now, take my prescription,
che l'**effetto** ti farà.   that it will have an **effect** on you.

ADINA
Io **rispetto** l'elisire,   I **respect** the elixir,

ma per me ve n'ha un maggiore.	but for me there is a better one.
La ricetta è il mio visimo,	The formula is my pretty face,
in quest'occhi è l'elisir.	the elixir is in my eyes.
Una **tenera** occhiatina, ecc.	A **tender** glance, etc.

DULCAMARA

Sì, briccona.	Yes, rogue.
Ah! lo vedo, bricconcella, ecc.	Oh, I see, you little rogue, etc.
Ah! vorrei cambiar coi tuoi	Oh, I would like to exchange
i miei **vasi** d'**elisir**.	my **jars** of **elixir** with yours.

"Una furtiva lagrima" (**"A furtive tear"**). Nemorino's melancholy *romanza* is one of the most famous tenor arias in all opera. It has a hauntingly beautiful and memorable melody. The song has a tenderness, innocence, and pathos that appeal directly to the heart. The song is introduced by a combination of bassoon obbligato, harp, and pizzicato (plucked) strings. Nemorino expresses his inward joy at seeing a tear in Adina's eye as proof she cares for him. It reflects his growing maturity and convinces us that his feelings are completely sincere. (See "Una furtiva lagrima" in Part II for vocal skills.)

Una **furtiva** lagrima	A **furtive** tear
negl'occhi suoi spuntò:	welled up in her eyes:
quelle **festose** giovani	those **festive** girls
invidiar sembrò:	she seemed to be **envious**:
che più cercando io vo?	why should I look any further?
M'ama, sì, m'ama,	She loves me, yes, she loves me.
lo vedo, lo vedo.	I can see it, I can see it.
Un **solo istante i palpiti**	To feel for just **one instant**
del suo **bel** cor sentir!	the **pounding** of her **lovely** heart!

"Prendi, per me sei libero" (**"Take it, I have liberated you"**). In this duet, Adina tells Nemorino that she has bought back his enlistment papers because she realizes how much he loves her. He will not have to leave her by joining the military. She confesses her love for him. Adina's cavatina has a melodic simplicity and dignity. She expresses her sensitivity to his sincere love, and proves that she is not a mere coquette. The song provides a joyful ending as they embrace and exchange vows of love.

ADINA

Prendi, per me sei **libero**:	Take it, I have **liberated** you:
resta nel suol **natio**;	stay in your **homeland**.
non v'ha **destin** sì rio,	There is no **destiny** so hard
che non si cangi un dì. **Resta.**	that will not change one day. **Remain.**

NEMORINO

Ebben, tenete.	Well, take it back.
Poichè non sono amato,	Since I am not loved,
voglio morir **soldato**;	I want to die a **soldier**;

non v'ha per me più **pace**,	there's no more **peace** for me
se m'ingannò il **dottor**.	if the **doctor** deceived me.

ADINA
Ah! fu con te verace,	Oh, he was honest with you,
se presti **fede** al cor.	if you have **faith** in your heart.
Sappilo **alfin**, sappilo,	Know it, **finally**, know it,
tu mi sei caro.	you're dear to me.
Si, t'amo, t'amo, t'amo.	Yes, I love you, I love you.

NEMORINO
Oh! gioia **inesprimibile**!	Oh! **inexpressible** joy!
Non m'ingannò il dottor.	The doctor didn't deceive me.

Norma
by Vincenzo Bellini

Realized too late that he betrayed his devoted lover
Returned to the dishonored priestess to die together

First performed in Milan, December 26, 1831
Based on a story by Alexander Soumet and Louis Belmontet

Libretto by Giuseppe Felice Romani
Translation by Pearl Oliva

$\mathcal{V}$incenzo Bellini was born in Catania in 1801 and died in Puteaux in 1835. He was one of the most important and popular opera composers of the 19th century. He had a special gift for melody and his operas are permeated with beautiful and passionate songs in the bel canto (melodic and smooth) style. His operas are noted for their strong pathos, sublime dignity, and individual expression. Verdi wrote of Bellini that "...there are long, long melodies in his work such as no one has ever written." He collaborated with librettist Felice Romani on a series of successful operas, including his most famous opera—*Norma* (1831). Romani's texts were elegant and revealed strong emotions that matched Bellini's serious temperament. They both identified closely with the Romantic Movement of the 19th century. Bellini spent the last few years of his brief life in Paris where the artistic community warmly received him.

Bellini's *Norma* is based on a French stage play called *Norma ou l'infanticide*. Bellini and Romani decided to eliminate the infanticide, even though Norma considers killing her children. *Norma* is considered one of the greatest and most demanding female roles in opera. She must express the profound emotions of a high priestess and mother, abandoned lover, and vengeful rival. Her inner conflicts lead to her tragedy because she is unable to reconcile her religious vows with her human needs and desires. Norma must express her undying love for Pollione, in spite of his infidelity, and her love for her children. The plot has a limited amount of physical action because it focuses on the psychological and emotional tension created by a triangular love affair.

Synopsis of Bellini's Norma

Main Characters

Norma, Druid High Priestess	Soprano
Pollione, Roman Proconsul	Tenor
Adalgisa, temple virgin	Mezzo-soprano
Oroveso, Archdruid	Bass

Act I

In a sacred forest of ancient Gaul (land to the northwest of Italy), the Druids have gathered at an altar. They want revenge against the occupying Romans. Oroveso, the Archdruid, tells them to assemble on the hilltop for a sacred ritual led by Norma, the High Priestess (Song: **"Ite sul colle, oh Druidi"**). After the Druids depart, Pollione, the Roman Proconsul (governor), tells his friend that he has decided to leave Norma for a young priestess named Adalgisa (Song: **"Mecco all'altar di Venere"**). Norma greets the Druids and tells them to be patient until the gods speak to her of rebellion. She then prays for peace by addressing the moon goddess (Song: **"Casta Diva"**). Her thoughts turn to Pollione, the father of her children. She loves him very much and hopes that he will return to her (Song: **"Ah! Bello a me ritorna"**). Adalgisa, a young priestess, prays for the strength to resist her Roman lover. Pollione interrupts her worship, and she tries to send him away. In a pair of connected duets, he begins by telling her that he can never leave her, and then he asks her to flee with him to Rome (Songs: **"Va, crudele, al Dio spietato"** and **"Vieni in Roma, ah! vieni, oh cara"**). Norma is in a cave dwelling where she has hidden her children. In the first of a pair of duets, Adalgisa tells Norma that she has been meeting a lover in the temple. In the second duet without knowing the name of the lover, Norma forgives Adalgisa and frees her from her vow of chastity (Songs: **"Oh, rimembranza!"** and **"Ah sì, fa' core abbracciami"**). Norma's kindness turns to anger when Pollione appears and she learns that he is Adalgisa's lover. A trio of emotions follows with Norma's anger directed at Pollione (Song: **"Oh, Di qual sei tu vittima"**).

Act II

After learning that Pollione wishes to leave her, Norma considers killing their children. Instead, she decides to sacrifice her own life. She asks Adalgisa to take care of the children and marry Pollione. Adalgisa replies that she will try to persuade Pollione to return to Norma and their children. They sing three connected duets that end with the two priestesses pledging eternal friendship (Songs: **"Deh! con te, con te li prendi"** and **"Mira, oh Norma, ai tuoi ginocchi"** and **"Sì, fino all'ore estreme"**). Norma is horrified to learn that Adalgisa was unable to persuade Pollione to return. Norma receives a report that a Roman intruder has violated the temple by trying to abduct Adalgisa. The warriors drag Pollione before Norma. In a tense duet, she offers him a pardon if he will renounce Adalgisa, but he refuses to stop seeing her (Song: **"In mia man alfin tu sei"**). He pleads with her not to harm their children or Adalgisa. Norma calls on the Druids to light the funeral pyre because a priestess has broken her vows. She announces that she is the guilty priestess and will sacrifice her own life (Song: **"Qual cor tradisti"**). Pollione suddenly realizes that she is his true love and that he shares her guilt. She asks her father Oroveso to care for her children and not blame them for her behavior (Song: **"Deh! Non volerli vittime"**). He watches in horror as his daughter and Pollione together sacrifice their lives.

Major Song Sketches

Act I

"Ite sul colle, oh Druidi" ("To the hills, oh Druids"). Oroveso, the Archdruid, is addressing a gathering of Druids and warriors. The scene opens in a simple manner with bass instruments repeating the tone in a major key. After this simple tone color is established, a series of melodious phrases create an atmosphere of nobility. Oroveso enters and tells them he shares their desire to be free, but tells them to be patient. The High Priestess will perform a sacred ritual on the hilltop. As they depart, they express a somber commitment and a controlled desire to be free.

Ite sul colle, oh Druidi,	To the hills, oh Druids,
ite a spiar ne' cieli,	to watch the heavens;
quando il suo **disco** argenteo	when her silvery **disc** unveils
la **nuova luna** sveli, ed il **primier**	the **new moon**, and the **first**
sorriso del **virginal** suo viso	smile of her **pure** face **announces**
tre volte **annunzi** il **mistico**	three times the **mystical**,
bronzo sacerdotal...	priestly **bronze** gong...

"Meco all'altar di Venere" ("At the altar of Venus"). In this cavatina (a short entrance aria), Pollione is telling his aide about the conflict he faces. He has grown tired of his relationship with Norma and wishes to be with a younger priestess. The phrases to his song are carefully accentuated to clarify his position. His ardent desire is revealed in the lively and expressive conclusion.

Meco all'**altar** di **Venere**	At the **altar** of **Venus**,
era Adalgisa **in Roma**,	with me was Adalgisa **in Rome**,
cinta di bende candide,	dressed in white with
sparsa di **fior** la chioma;	**flowers** in her hair.
udia d'Imene i cantici,	I heard the hymns of Hymen
vedea fumar gl'**incensi**,	and saw the holy **incense** smoking;
eran **rapiti** i **sensi**	my **senses** were **enraptured**
di voluttade e **amor**...	with delight and **love**...

"Casta Diva" ("Chaste goddess"). This beautiful coloratura aria is the most famous song in the opera. A flute solo or obbligato introduces it. This instrumental introduction establishes a serene and lovely setting. Norma is praying to the moon goddess to bring peace to her people and free them from the Romans. The tension increases, as each section of melody is repeated higher and higher with increasing volume. Each contour of the melody has the sound of a pure ritual and magic spell. It is a luminous cantilena (a flowing and sustained melodic line). (See "Casta Diva" in Part II for vocal skills.)

Casta Diva, che inargenti	**Chaste goddess**, who bathes these
queste **sacre antiche** piante,	**sacred, ancient** trees in silver,
a noi volgi il bel sembiante	turn thy lovely face toward us,
senza nube e senza vel...	unclouded and unveiled...
Tempra, oh Diva, tempra tu de' cori	**Temper**, oh goddess, temper these **ardent**
ardenti, tempra ancora lo **zelo audace**,	hearts, temper the bold **zeal** of the
spargi in terra quella **pace**	**audacious**. Spread that **peace** upon the earth
che **regnar** tu fai nel ciel...	which thou causes to **reign** in heaven...

"**Ah! bello a me ritorna**" ("**Ah! handsome one return to me**"). This song is introduced with an energetic recitative. This leads directly into a florid cabaletta (ornamented ending). Norma speaks of her love for Pollione and her desire for his return to her side. Norma admits that if Pollione returns, she will defend his life. This decorated passage with its colorful intervals expresses Norma's grand and commanding stature.

Ah! bello a me **ritorna**	Ah! handsome one **return** to me
del **fido amor primiero**,	the **faithfulness** of our **first love**,
e contro il mondo intiero	and against the entire world
difesa a te sarò.	I will be your **defense**.
Ah! bello a me ritorna	Ah! handsome one return
del raggio tuo **sereno**;	to me your **serene** gaze;
e vita nel tuo seno,	and life at your breast, and
e **patria** e cielo avrò.	**fatherland** and heaven I will have.

"**Va, crudele, al Dio spietato** and **Vieni in Roma, ah! vieni, o cara**" ("**Go cruel one, and offer my blood** and **Come to Rome, ah! come oh dear one**"). These are two closely connected duets sung by Pollione and Adalgisa. He has just interrupted her religious duties to express his infatuation. After begging him to leave her in peace, the first duet begins. He refers to her as a cruel woman for choosing the altar instead of him. Both duets have a similar rhythm and harmony. They are repeated twice with the first melody given to the tenor and then the mezzo-soprano. In spite of this conventional format, the duets are expressed with charm and conviction.

POLLIONE	
(1) Va, **crudele**, al Dio spietato	Go, **cruel** one, and **offer** my blood
offri in dono il sangue mio;	as a gift to your heartless god;
tutto, ah! tutto ei sia versato,	let all my blood be spilt,
ma **lasciarti** non poss'io...	but I cannot **leave** you,
Non poss'io, no, no nol posso!	I can't no, no, I cannot.
ADALGISA	
(1) E tu pure, ah! tu non sai	And you also, ah, you do not know
quanto **costi** a me dolente!	the suffering it has **cost** me!
All'**altare** che oltraggiai	To the **altar** which I have violated, I
lieta andava ed **innocente**...	used to go in happiness and **innocence**...

POLLIONE
(2) Vieni in **Roma**, ah! vieni, o cara,
dove è **amor**, è gioia, è vita;
inebbriam nostr'alme a gara
del **contento** a cui ne **invita**.

Voce in cor parlar non senti,
che **promette eterno** ben?

ADALGISA
(2) Ciel! così parlar l'ascolto
sempre, ovunque, al **tempio** istesso...
con quegli occhi, con quel volto
fin sull'ara il veggo impresso.
Ei **trionfa** del mio pianto,
del mio duol **vittoria** ottien.

Come to **Rome**, ah! come oh dear love,
where there is **love**, and joy, and life;
let us become **intoxicated** with each other
vieing for the **contentment** which it
  invites.

Don't you hear the **voice** in your heart
which **promises eternal** happiness?

Heavens! I always hear him speak like
this everywhere, even the **temple** itself...
with those eyes, with that visage,
I see even on the altar.
He **triumphs** over my tears,
and achieves **victory** over my grief.

"Oh, rimembranza!" and **"Ah sì, fa' core, abbracciami"** (**"Oh, what memories!"** and **"Ah! Yes, take heart and embrace me"**). These two duets between Norma and Adalgisa are closely connected. In the first duet, Adalgisa has come to tell Norma that she has been secretly meeting a lover at the temple. Norma reflects on her own encounter "Oh, what memories!" The main melody is attached to Adalgisa's long phrases. Her emotional state is conveyed in a persuasive and classical manner. The following duet is introduced by Norma with the words "Yes—take heart, embrace me." She forgives Adalgisa and frees her from the sacred bonds. The melody grows in strength with each successive stanza. The duet is decorated with coloratura passages (rapid trills). The duet ends with a passionate cadenza (a virtuoso passage) that expresses their warm and joyful friendship.

NORMA
(1) (Oh, **rimembranza**! Io fui

così rapita, al sol mirarlo in volto.)

ADALGISA
(1) Sola, **furtiva** al **tempio**
io l'aspettai sovente;
ed ogni dì più **fervida**
crebbe la **fiamma ardente**.

NORMA
(1) (Io stessa arsi così.
Oh **rimembranza**: io fui così **sedotta**!)

NORMA
(2) Ah sì, fa core, **abbracciami**.
Perdono e ti compiango.

(Oh, what **memories**! I was so enraptured
by just observing his face.)

Alone, **furtively**, I often waited
for him in the **temple**,
and each day more **fervently**
grew the **ardent flame**.

(I too felt the same.
Oh, **memory**: I was so **seduced**!)

Ah! yes, take heart and **embrace me**.
I **pardon** you and pity you.

Dai voti tuoi ti **libero**,
i tuoi legami io frango.

ADALGISA
(2) **Ripeti**, o ciel, ripetimi
sì lusinghieri accenti:
Per te, per te, s'acquetano
i lunghi miei **tormenti**.

I **free** you from your vows,
and break your bonds.

Repeat, oh heaven, repeat to me
such flattering words: for you,
for you, my long
torments are eased.

"**Oh, di qual sei tu vittima**" ("**Oh, you are the victim**"). Norma has just learned that Pollione is Adalgisa's secret lover. After a dramatic recitative, Norma sings a short introductory song (cavatina) that sets off a trio of conflicting emotions. It contains smooth and flowing phrases. Norma's anger is directed at Pollione's deception. Pollione pleads for understanding, and Adalgisa expresses her misfortune and broken heart. The opposing emotions are skillfully intertwined to create a persuasive trio.

NORMA
Oh, di qual sei tu **vittima**
crudo e funesto inganno!
Pria che costui conoscere
t'era il morir men danno.

Oh! you are the **victim** of a **cruel**
and disastrous deception!
Instead of knowing him, death
would have been less harmful to you.

POLLIONE
Norma, de' tuoi **rimproveri**
segno non farmi adesso.
Deh! a questa afflitta **vergine**
sia respirar concesso...

Norma, do not cite to me
your **reprimands** now!
Ah! that this suffering pure
virgin be permitted to breathe.

ADALGISA
Oh, qual **mistero orribile**!
trema il mio cor di chiedere,
trema d'udire il vero.

Oh, what a **horrible mystery**!
My heart **trembles** to ask,
it trembles to hear the truth.

Act II

"**Deh! con te, con te li prendi**" and "**Mira, o Norma, ai tuoi ginocchi**" and "**Sì, fino all'ore estreme**" ("**Ah, take them with you, with you**" and "**Look, oh Norma, at your knees**" and "**Yes, until our final hours**"). This duet is broken into three sections. It demonstrates Bellini's skill at sustaining a series of intertwined melodic passages. Section one is Norma's plea that Adalgisa take her children to Rome with Pollione. In section two, Adalgisa asks Norma to take pity on her children and remain with them. This exchange gives the priestesses an appealing opportunity to rely on vocal nuance to express their concerns. The final section represents reconciliation and a pledge of lasting friendship. The tension in the duet increases as each section of melody is repeated on a higher level. A remarkable melody ties the sections together, and the pace quickens in the final section. The three connected sections demonstrate Bellini's skill at sustaining an integrated melody.

NORMA
(1) Deh! con te, con te li prendi...
li **sostieni**, li **difendi**...
Non ti chiedo **onori** e fasci;
a' tuoi figli ei fian serbati...

Ah, take them with you, with you...
sustain them, **defend** them...
I do not ask of you **honors** and respect;
that will be reserved for your sons...

ADALGISA
(1) Norma, ah Norma! ancor amata,
madre ancora sarai per me.
Tienti i figli. Ah! non fia mai
ch'io mi tolga a queste arene.

Norma, ah Norma! Again dearly loved,
you will still be a beloved **mother** to
me. Keep your children. Ah! let me never
be taken away from this land.

ADALGISA
(2) Mira, O Norma, a' tuoi ginocchi
questi cari tuoi pargoletti.
Ah! pietade di lor ti **tocchi**,
se non hai di te **pieta**.

Look, oh Norma, at your knees,
where are these dear children of yours.
Ah! be **touched** by your pity for them
even if you have no **pity** for yourself.

NORMA
(2) Ah! perchè la mia **costanza**
vuoi scemar con molli **affetti**?
Più lusinghe, ah più speranza
presso a morte un cor non ha.

Ah, why do you try to weaken my
constancy with soft **affections**?
No more illusions, ah no more hope
for a heart near death.

NORMA AND ADALGISA
(3) Sì, fino all'ore estreme
compagna tua m'avrai;
per ricovraci, per ricovrarci insieme
ampia è la terra assai, è la terra assai.
Teco del **fato** all'onte
ferma opporrò la fronte...

Yes, until our final hours, I will
remain your **companion**;
to protect us, to protect us together
the earth is large enough.
Together we will resolutely face
the hostilities of **fate**...

"In mia man alfin tu sei" (**"You are in my hands at last"**). Pollione has been captured while trying to abduct Adalgisa from the temple. Just as she was unable to murder her children, she is unable to sentence Pollione to death. After dismissing the angry crowd, Norma offers Pollione his life if he will abandon Adalgisa. They plead and argue in this emotional duet. The theme is repeated several times. The melody is tense with strong opposing emotions of anger and love. It is a moving duet with a passionate statement. After they reach a grand conclusion, the chorus reappears.

NORMA
In mia man alfin tu sei;
niun potria spezzar tuoi nodi:
Io lo posso!

You are in my hands at last;
no one can break your bonds.
I can do so!

POLLIONE

Tu nol dêi...	You must not...
E come?	And why would you?

NORMA

M'odi:	Hear me:
pel tuo **Dio**, pe' figli tuoi	for your **God**, for your children,
giurar dêi che d'ora in poi	you must swear from henceforth
Adalgisa fuggirai...	you will leave Adalgisa...
all'**altar** non la torrai...	You will not remove her from the **altar**...
E la vita io ti **perdono**,	I will then **pardon** your life,
e mai più ti rivedrò.	and never again will I see you.

"Qual cor tradisti" (**"The heart you betrayed"**). In Norma's final outstanding aria, she condemns herself as the priestess who broke her holy vows. Her words are depicted in a series of soft sounding chords as she prepares to sacrifice her life. Pollione is shocked by her confession, and his love for her is reawakened by her moving passage.

Qual cor **tradisti**, qual cor perdesti	The heart you **betrayed**, that a heart you
quest'ora **orrenda** ti **manifesti**.	lost, this **horrible** hour **manifests** itself to
Da me fuggire tentasti **invano**;	you. You tried to flee from me in **vain**;
crudel Romano, tu sei con me.	**cruel Roman**, you are with me.
Un Nume, un **fato** di te più forte	A god, a **fate** mightier than you
ci vuole **uniti** in vita e in morte.	wants us **united** in life and in death.

"Deh! Non volerli vittime" (**"Oh! Do not let them become victims"**). Norma sings this short cavatina in a mournful and minor key asking her father to take care of her children. In a more dignified minor key, she sings this anguished arioso (short passage). The beautiful melody reaches a great height of emotional intensity as she pleads with her father to show mercy. The final E major section rises to a stirring climax. The opera ends as Norma and Pollione mount the funeral pyre.

Deh! non volerli **vittime**	Oh! do not let them become **victims**
del mio **fatale errore**...	of my **fatal error**...
Deh! non troncar sul **fiore**	Oh, do not cut off their **flowering**
quell'**innocente** età.	at that **innocent** age.
Pensa che son tuo sangue...	Consider that they are your blood...
abbi di lor pietade,	have pity on them.
Oh padre, abbi di lor,	**Oh father**, have **pity** on them,
di lor **pietà**!	have pity on them!

I Pagliacci
by Ruggiero Leoncavallo

Continuing her affair in spite of his dire warning
Turning a clown performance into a fatal stabbing

First performed in Milan, May 21, 1892
Based on a court trial in Naples

Libretto by Ruggiero Leoncavallo
Translation by Maria Figuero

*R*uggiero Leoncavallo was born in Naples in 1857 and died in Bagni di Montecatini in 1919. *I Pagliacci* is a short two act opera that premiered in Milan in 1892. It was an immediate success and it made the composer rich and famous. Leoncavallo based it on an actual courtroom case in Naples. As a young boy, he was present in his father's court when an actor was on trial for murdering his wife after a performance. Whereas Verdi, Puccini, and Rossini found librettists to write the words to their operas, Leoncavallo wrote both the music and the words to *I Pagliacci*. Unfortunately, he was very disappointed when he was unable to compose a second successful opera.

Leoncavallo helped to define a new style of Italian opera called "verismo."

Verismo deals with common people and their strong and often violent emotions. The famous prologue captures the verismo nature of the opera when one of the actors, Tonio, announces that the drama is about real human beings with ordinary feelings. The audience learns that they are about to see a play within a play. Leoncavallo was very impressed with Wagner's use of motifs or short themes to identify characters and situations. The prologue to *I Pagliacci* includes motifs that are repeated as the drama unfolds, such as the love theme, the jealousy theme, and the players' theme.

Synopsis of Leoncavallo's I Pagliacci

Main Characters

Canio, leader of the players	Tenor
Nedda, Canio's wife	Soprano
Tonio, a clown	Baritone
Beppe, a harlequin	Tenor
Silvio, a villager	Baritone

Prologue

Tonio, a member of a troupe of traveling actors, appears in front of the curtain. He announces to the audience that the drama they are about to see is based on reality and not make believe (Song: **"Il Prologò: Si può?"**).

Act I

The leader of the troupe of actors, Canio, announces to the villagers that there will be an evening performance. In a display of jealous anger, he also announces that he will take revenge if he finds another man flirting with his wife (Song: **"Un tal gioco"**). When the church bells begin to ring, the villagers sing a bell chorus on their way to church (Song: **"Din, don. Suona vespero"**). After everyone has left, Canio's wife Nedda worries about her husband's jealousy, and then sings a bird song as she observes the birds flying overhead (Song: **"Qual Fiamma avea nel guardo ... Hui! Stridono lassù"**). When the misshapen Tonio confesses his love for her, she drives him away with a whip. The villager Silvio arrives and asks Nedda to run away with him. In a duet, they express their love for each other (Song: **"Non mi tentar!"**). Tonio observes the lovers and tells Canio about his wife's secret lover. When Canio arrives, Silvio escapes and Nedda refuses to reveal her lover's name. Left alone, Canio confesses how he must play his role as a clown even with a broken heart (Song: **"Vesti la giubba"**).

Act II

There is a festive chorus as the villagers gather for the evening performance. In a comic setting, a simple servant, Taddeo (played by Tonio), tries to attract his mistress, Columbina (played by Nedda), while his master, Pagliaccio (played by Canio), is away. Columbina's lover, Harlequin (played by Beppe), arrives and serenades her (Song: **"O Colombina, il tenero"**). He escapes when Pagliaccio returns home. Tonio takes the play seriously and questions Nedda and demands the name of her lover. He is so jealous that he can no longer separate the make believe play from his own rage (Song: **"No, Pagliaccio non son"**). The villagers are horrified to realize that this is no longer a comic play but a tragic slice of reality. Tonio forgets his part in the play and stabs Nedda to death. When Nedda calls for Silvio in the audience, he rushes on stage and Canio stabs him also.

Prelude, Intermezzo and Songs

Prelude

The prelude has a lively beginning associated with the players. This is followed by a sharp change of mood, as a solo French horn provides a sorrowful theme. This theme will be heard in Canio's broken-hearted aria at the close of Act I. The mood changes briefly to the love duet of Nedda and Silvio played by the violins. The low strings portray Canio's suspicion and jealousy. Finally, there is a return to the energetic opening and a sudden break to make way for the famous prologue.

Act I

"Il Prologo: Si può? Si può?" (**"The Prologue: May I? May I?"**). The clown Tonio steps in front of the curtain and introduces himself to the audience with an apology. He explains that the author of the play chose a prologue to explain the serious and real life emotions that are about to be presented. Instead of a make believe play, it's based on the passions of real men and women. The orchestral accompaniment becomes more somber as Tonio sets the stage for the deeply conflicting emotions that are about to unfold. The orchestra plays the themes of love and hatred, grief and laughter. As he nears the end of the prologue, he switches to a passionate melody to encourage the audience to have sympathy for the actors. He ends with a dramatic cry, on a high note, for the show to begin! (See "Il Prologo: Si può? Si può?" in Part II for vocal skills.)

Si può? Si può?
Signore! Signori! Scusatemi
se da sol mi **presento**. Io sono il **Prologo**.
L'**autore** ha cercato invece pingervi
uno squarcio di vita.
Egli ha per **massima** sol che l'**artista**
è un uom, e che per gli uomini
scrivere ei deve. Ed al vero **ispiravasi**.

Dunque, vedrete amar sì come s'amano
gli esseri **umani**, vedrete dell'odio
i tristi **frutti**. Del dolor gli spasimi,
urli di rabbia, udrete, e risa **ciniche!**

May I? May I?
Ladies! Gentlemen! Excuse me
if I **present** alone. I am the **Prologue**.
Our **author** has endeavored, rather,
to paint for you a slice of life.
His only **maxim** being that the **artist**
is a man, and he must write for men.
And seek his **inspiration** from the truth.

Now, then, you will see how **human**
beings love when they love, and you will
see the sad **fruit** of hate. And you will
hear shouts both of rage and pain, and
cynical laughter.

"Un tal gioco" (**"Not to play such a game"**). Canio appears dressed in his Pagliaccio (clown) costume beating a large drum before a group of villagers. This song serves as a preview of the sinister plot the villagers will witness during the evening performance. It also provides a dire warning that Canio has a carefully planned trap to gain vengeance. The villagers don't realize that Canio is very jealous of his wife because he suspects her of infidelity. They tease him because they think his threats are part of his act. The song helps to define Canio's suspicious and jealous nature. Canio is introduced by a sparkling theme in the violins. The music builds to a climax based on Canio's jealous theme. His wife, Nedda, shutters when she hears canio's warning.

Un tal gioco, credetemi,
è meglio non giocarlo con me, miei cari;
e a Tonio, e un poco a tutti or parlo
il **teatro** e la vita non son la stessa
cosa...
Ma se Nedda sul serio **sorprendessi**,
altramente finirebbe **la storia**,
com'è ver che vi parlo.
Un tal gioco, credetemi,
è meglio non giocarlo.

My dears, believe me, it's better
not to play such a game with me;
I say to Tonio, and in part to all of you
I say, the **stage** and life are not the
same thing...
But if I seriously **surprised** Nedda,
as sure as I am speaking to you,
the story would end.
It's better not to play
such a prank, believe me.

"Din, don. Suona vespero" (**"Bell Song"**). A procession crosses the back of the stage to remind the villagers that church is about to begin. The cheerful and charming bell chorus follows as the villagers file out. The sound of chimes is paired with the chorus imitating the ding, dong of the bells. The chorus has an attractive harmonic progression and fades quietly. This leaves an empty stage for Nedda's ballad that follows.

Din, don. Suona **vespero**,
ragazze e garzon,
a **coppie** al tempio affrettiamoci

Ding, dong! Vespers is ringing,
girls and lads, let us join
in **pairs** and now we

c'affrettiam! Din, don!	hasten. Ding, dong!
Diggià i culmini,	Already the sun kisses
din, don, vuol baciar.	the western heights, ding, dong!
Le **mamme** ci adocchiano,	Look out, companions,
attenti, compar.	our **mothers** are watching us.
Din, don. Tutto **irradiasi**	Ding, dong! The world **radiates**
di **luce** e d'**amor**.	with **light** and **love**.

"Qual fiamma avea nel guardo! ... Hui! Stridono lassù" ("What a fire he had in his glance! ... Hui! How wildly they shriek up there"). Nedda is alone and she worries about the jealous glance she saw in Canio's eyes. The orchestra plays some gentle chords as she raises her face toward the warm sun. The orchestra produces a shimmering sound to suggest a flight of birds. The flutes produce a chirping sound over the strings to introduce Nedda's yearning for freedom like the birds overhead. The violins trill upward to suggest birds in flight. After imitating the birds' screeching sound, she sings a happy, carefree, and lighthearted song with a swaying melody with pretty instrumentation. Her ballatella (small ballad) has a simple melody. (See "Qual fiamma avea nel guardo ... Hui! Stridono lassù, liberamente" in Part II for vocal skills.)

Qual **fiamma** avea nel **guardo**.	What a **fire** he had in his **glance!**
Gli occhi abbassai per tema ch'ei	I lowered my eyes for fear
leggesse il mio pensier **segreto**.	that he read my **secret** thought.
Oh! S'ei mi **sorprendesse**,	Oh! if he should **surprise** me,
brutale come egli è. Ma basti, orvia.	**brutal** as he is! But enough! Away now.
Oh! Che volo d'augelli, e quante **strida**!	Oh, what a flight of birds, and what
Che chiedon? Dove van? Chissà.	**shrieking!** What do they want?
	Where are they going? Who knows!
Hui! Stridono lassù. Liberamente	Hui! How wildly they shriek up there.
lanciati a vol come frecce, gli augel.	Freely **launched** like arrows on their flight.
Che incalzi il vento e latri la **tempesta**,	Let the wind blow, and let the **tempest**
con l'ali aperte san tutto sfidar;	roar, with their wings spread they can
la pioggia, i **lampi**, nulla mai li **arresta**,	dare all; the rain, the **lightning**,
e vanno, sugli **abissi** e i mar.	nothing ever **stops** them, and they fly
	over **abysses** and seas.

"Non mi tentar!" ("Oh, do not tempt me!"). The orchestra announces the arrival of the villager Silvio with a love theme. He urges Nedda to elope with him, but she resists his proposal while insisting that she loves only him. The duet has a dream-like quality with a profound sense that the lovers want to withdraw from reality. They begin with the words "Let us forget everything." The tender love duet has a long and poetic melody. Their passion rises in intensity but the tension in the orchestra suggests their love will be ill fated. The duet provides a lyrical interlude from the mounting tension. As their passion pours forth, they lose sight of caution. Canio's arrival is signaled by his sinister jealousy theme. Silvio manages to escape and Nedda refuses to reveal her lover's name.

NEDDA
Non mi **tentar**! Vuoi tu perder la mia vita? Taci, Silvio, non più. E **deliro**, è follia! Io mi **confido** a te cui diedi il cor. Non **abusar** di me, del mio febbrile amor! Non mi tentar!

Oh, do not **tempt** me! Would you ruin my life? Quiet, Silvio, no more. This is **madness**! I put my **trust** in you, to whom I gave my heart. Do not **abuse** my ardent passion! Do not tempt me!

SILVIO
Se tu scordasti l'ore fugaci io non lo posso, e voglio ancor que' spasmi **ardenti**, que' caldi baci che tanta **febbre** m'han meso in cor!

If you forgot those fleeting hours, I cannot do so: I still desire those ardent pangs and those **ardent** kisses that kindled such a **fever** in my heart!

NEDDA
Nulla scordai, sconvolta e turbata m'ha questo **amor** che nel **guardo** ti sfavilla.

I forgot nothing: I have been stirred and shaken by this **love** which sparkles in your **glance**.

"**Vesti la giubba**" ("**Put on the costume**"). Canio dresses in his clown's suit and sings one of the most famous tenor arias. He is alone and grief-stricken because of his wife's infidelity. The opening begins with strong staccato chords designed to introduce his anguish. His disturbed state of mind is reflected in his bitter laugh. Even though he has a broken heart, the play must go on. His opening word is "Recitar!" ("Perform the play!"). A soliloquy follows his outburst of grim laughter and ends with sobbing. He knows that he must entertain his audience even though he is suffering in his real life. He will have to play out his real pain on the stage. (See "Vesti la giubba" in Part II for vocal skills.)

Recitar! Mentre preso dal **delirio** non so più quel che dico e quel che faccio! Eppur ... è d'uopo...**sforzati**!

Perform! While I'm racked by **delirium**, I no longer know what I say or what I do! And yet ... I must ... ah, **force** myself to do it!

Bah, se' tu forse un uom!
Tu se' **Pagliaccio**!

Bah! If you were a man!
You are the **clown**!

Vesti la giubba e la **faccia** infarina. La gente **paga** e rider vuole qua. E se **Arlecchin** t'invola Colombina, ridi Pagliaccio, e ognun **applaudirà**! Tramuta in lazzi lo spasmo ed il pianto...

Put on the costume, and powder your **face**. The people **pay** and want to laugh. And if **Harlequin** steals your Columbine, laugh, Pagliaccio, and all will **applaud** you! Change all your tears and anguish into clowning...

Intermezzo

With the curtain closed between acts, the orchestra plays two themes. The orchestra begins by expressing the anguish felt by Canio over his wife's infidelity. The violins cry out Canio's words "Laugh, clown, laugh!" When the violins recede and calm is restored, the passionate sound of Tonio's prologue returns. It is heavy with sorrow and has a passionate ending with basses sounding Canio's despair. The composer, Leoncavallo, thought this intermezzo would help to calm the audience after Canio's dramatic aria at the close of act one.

Act II

"O Colombina, il fido" (**"Oh Columbine, your faithful"**). After a festive chorus of villagers arrives for the performance, the Harlequin (played by Beppe) serenades Columbine (played by Nedda) with a brief make-believe statement of his love for her. A solo flute and oboe accompanies beppe as he plucks the strings of his mandolin with his off-stage serenade. He sings a gentle and sweet love song. He makes a fast escape when Pagliaccio (played by Canio) returns unexpectedly. Suddenly we hear a guitar tuning up off stage as the Harlequin prepares to sing a charming serenade to his love.

Ah! Colombina, il **tenero**	**Oh Columbine**, your **faithful**
fido Arlecchin	and **tender Harlequin**
è a te vicin!	is near!
Di te chiamando,	Calling your name and
e sospirando, aspetta il **poverin!**	sighing, the **poor** fellow awaits you!
Ah! Colombina schiudimi	Oh, Columbine,
il finestrin, che a te vicin	open your window for me; your **poor,**
di te chiamando	Harlequin is near you
e sospirando è il **povero** Arlecchin!	calling your name and sighing!
A te vicin è Arlecchin!	Harlequin is near to you!

"No, Pagliaccio non son" (**"No, I am not Pagliaccio"**). Canio takes off his cap to show the play-acting is over. He tells the audience that they are no longer watching Pagliaccio. He passionately declares he will defend his honor against a woman he married and saved from starvation. His broad melody tells how he built his hopes on Nedda. His passionate outburst builds to a terrible curse on a high B flat. The audience shouts its appreciation for the fine acting not realizing that Canio is expressing his true feelings. When he demands the name of her lover, she cries "No!" and tries to escape. After stabbing his wife and her lover, he announces "The comedy is ended." The curtain falls and the orchestra blares out Canio's sad theme "laugh, Pagliaccio" from his famous aria. The song is a great tirade of jealousy and overpowering emotion. The turbulent sounding strings set the mood.

No, Pagliaccio non son; se il viso è	No, I am not Pagliaccio! If my face
pallido è di vergogna e smania di	is white, it is for shame and for the lust

vendetta! L'uom **riprende** i suoi dritti,
e il cor che sanguina vuol sangue a
lavar l'onta, o maledetta! No,
Pagliaccio non son!
Sperai, tanto il **delirio**
Accecato m'aveva,
Se non **amor**, pietà, **mercè**!

for **vengeance**! The man **reclaims** his
rights, the heart that bleeds wants blood to
wash away the shame, o cursed woman!
No I am not a clown!
So much blinded by my **delirium**
that I had hoped, if not for **love**,
at least for **merciful** compassion!

French Operas

Carmen
by Georges Bizet

Attracted to a sensuous gypsy who loved her liberty
Confronted his jealousy and accepted her destiny

First performed in Paris, March 3, 1875
Based on a novel by Prosper Mérimée

Libretto by Henri Meilhac and Ludovic Halévy
Translation by Mary-Ann Stadtler-Chester

*G*eorges Bizet was born in Paris in 1838 and died in Bougival in 1875. He was considered a child prodigy with remarkable musical skills. He described *Carmen* as "a work that is all clarity and vivacity, full of color and melody." The rehearsals were difficult and its premiere in Paris was met with apathy and critical reviews. Bizet was disappointed by the response and died a few months later at age 37. *Carmen* became a triumphant success a few years later and, today, it is considered one of the most perfect operas ever written. While French critics failed to appreciate *Carmen*, Tchaikovsky predicted it would soon enjoy worldwide popularity. Richard Strauss marveled over its rich orchestration and economy. He remarked, "...every note and rest is in its proper place."

Carmen is often referred to as the first "verismo" opera—an Italian word meaning strong and violent emotions. Later, this style became very popular in Italy. The strong emotions and sensuous behavior probably offended many Parisians and their bourgeois moral code. Furthermore, they were accustomed to operas with happy endings. The libretto to *Carmen*, by Henri Meilhac and Ludovic Halévy, is considered one of the most outstanding in the history of opera.

Synopsis of Bizet's Carmen

Main Characters

Carmen, a gypsy	Mezzo-soprano
Don José, a corporal	Tenor
Micaëla, a country girl	Soprano
Escamillo, a toreador	Baritone
Frasquita, a gypsy	Soprano
Mercedes, a gypsy	Mezzo-soprano

Act I

In a town square in 19th century Seville, a group of military officers and local people are gathered outside a cigarette factory near a guardhouse. The cigarette girls stroll leisurely out of the factory during their morning break. Carmen, an attractive gypsy, appears last and is surrounded by her admirers to whom she expresses the fickleness of love (Song: **"L'amour est un oiseau rebelle"**). Irritated by the indifference of Don José, she throws a flower at him and returns to the factory. Micaëla, Don José's shy sweetheart, appears and delivers a message of affection from his mother (Song: **"Ma mère, je la vois!"**). After she leaves, the girls pour out of the factory announcing that Carmen has wounded a worker. She is arrested and placed under Don José's guard until imprisonment. She seduces him to untie her bonds by promising him a rendezvous (Song: **"Près des remparts de Séville"**). As she is being led off to prison, Don José loosens her bonds and she breaks free. He is held responsible for her escape and placed under arrest.

Act II

At a tavern near Seville, Carmen and her friends describe the joys and sounds of gypsy life (Song: **"Les tringles des sitres tintaient"**). The toreador, Escamillo, arrives with a party of friends and admirers and he recounts the excitement and danger of the bullring (Song: **"Votre toast, je peux vous le rendre"**). Two smugglers ask Carmen and her gypsy friends to help them slip some goods past the customs guards (Song: **"Nous avons en tête une affaire"**). Don José arrives freed from the guardhouse where he served time for allowing Carmen to escape. Carmen dances for him but gets angry when he tells her he must return to his military barracks (Song: **"Je vais danser en votre honneur"**). He assures her of his passion by showing her the flower she once threw to him (Song: **"La fleur que tu m'avais jetée"**). Carmen insists that if he loves her, he should follow her to the mountains and join a group of smugglers.

Act III

The smugglers and gypsies are transporting their goods through a mountain pass. Don José has joined the smugglers to be close to Carmen, but she is more interested in the toreador, Escamillo. Carmen, along with her two gypsy friends, decides to read their fortunes in cards. When Carmen deals the pack several times, she only finds death (Song: **"En vain pour éviter les réponses amères"**). As the gypsies carry their bales away, the terrified Micaëla appears in search of Don José. In the foreboding darkness, she tries to convince herself that she has nothing to fear (Song: **"Je dis, que rien ne m'épouvante"**). After she is discovered behind the rocks, she tells Don José that his mother is dying. Before he leaves to see his mother, he warns Carmen, who is tiring of him that they will meet again.

Act IV

A festive crowd has gathered outside the bull arena awaiting the entrance of the toreadors and picadors. As the procession passes, the spectators comment on the appearance of the participants and the weapons they carry (Song: **"Les voici! Voici la quadreille!"**). After the spectators and participants enter the arena, Carmen bravely meets Don José who is lurking nearby. He pleads with her to return to him, but her heart is no longer his (Song: **"Carmen, il est temps encore"**). As Escamillo's triumph echoes from the arena, Carmen refuses to give in and Don José stabs her to death in the square.

Prelude and Major Song Sketches

"**Prelude.**" The famous prelude depicts three major themes: Carmen's wild character, the majesty of the bullfighter, and Carmen's ominous fate. The opening melody provides an exciting and wild portrait of Carmen. The noble theme of the toreador provides a sharp contrast to Carmen's character. It begins in a soft tone and is repeated in a louder tone. The third theme is a tragic motif (a brief musical unit) associated with Carmen throughout the opera. The strings and lower instruments convey her somber fate. The orchestration deepens and becomes more foreboding. The tension builds to the breaking point and then suddenly ends on a dramatic and dissonant chord. After a silence, the curtain rises on a town square.

Act I

"**L'amour est un oiseau rebelle**" ("**Love is a rebellious bird**" or "**Habanera**"). This is Carmen's most famous song. It sounds part gypsy and part Moorish and it has a Hispanic American dance rhythm. It introduces Carmen's personality and attitude toward love as a game of hide-and-seek and give-and-take back. It conveys a sense of mystery and a warning not to take her too seriously. The voice should convey a sinuous flexibility and warm seduction. The listener should realize that getting caught in Carmen's web could turn out to be fatal. As Carmen sings, Don José pretends to be indifferent to her seductive song, but he has already fallen under her spell. The orchestra and chorus help to accent the melody and are integrated with Carmen's voice. (See "L'amour est un oiseau rebelle" in Part II for in-depth analysis.)

L'**amour** est un oiseau **rebelle**	**Love** is a **rebellious** bird
que nul ne peut apprivoiser,	that no one can tame,
et c'est bien en **vain** qu'on l'appelle,	and it's in **vain** that one call's him
s'il lui convient de **refuser**.	if it suits him to **refuse**.
Rien n'y fait, **menace** ou prière,	Nothing moves him, neither **threat** nor
l'un parle bien, l'autre se tait;	plea, one man speaks freely, the other
et c'est l'autre que je **préfère**	keeps mum; and it's the other one I **prefer**
il n'a rien dit, mais il me plaît.	he's said nothing, but I like him.

"**Ma mère, je la vois!**" ("**I see my mother**"). This is a sweet and innocent duet in sharp contrast to the sensuous "Habanera." It reflects Don José's sentimental feelings for his home, his mother, and his childhood sweetheart, Micaëla, who has come to deliver a message. After delivering the message, Micaëla's part becomes more melodic and heartfelt. José replies with cheerful memories of his home life. They then join voices by responding to each other's sentiments. The song is typical of French opera in the late 1800's—fluent melody, tender but not overly passionate expression. It provides a sharp contrast to the more sensuous and tragic tone of the opera.

DON JOSÉ	
Ma mère, je la vois!	I see **my mother!**
Oui, je revois **mon village!**	Yes, I see **my village** again!
O **souvenirs** d'autrefois,	O **souvenirs** of bygone days,
doux souvenirs du pays!	sweet souvenirs of home!
MICAËLA	
Sa **mère**, il la revoit!	He sees his **mother** again!
Il revoit sa **village!**	He sees his **village** again!
O souvenirs d'autrefois!	O souvenirs of bygone days!
Souvenirs du pays!	Souvenirs of home!
Vous remplissez son coeur	**You** fill his heart with
de **force** et de **courage!**	**strength** and **courage!**

"**Près des remparts de Séville**" ("**By the ramparts of Seville**" or "**Sequidilla**"). This alluring aria is meant to seduce Don José into letting her escape. The song characterizes Carmen's longing for freedom and passion. Forbidden to speak, Carmen pretends to be thinking aloud and singing to herself, at least in the beginning. It starts with a very subdued volume, sparkling in timbre and very legato. The change of mood is designed to catch José's attention and arouse jealousy. After announcing that she has a lover, she reveals that she has sent him packing and needs a replacement. The song should be sung with force and sensuousness but with a lovely voice. It shows the wiles of a clever woman skilled in the art of handling men. She is completing the spell that she only described in the "Habanera." When José unties her wrists, she finishes the song with a triumphant voice. She repeats the melody with a bold and intense ending with a shout of joy. (See "Près des remparts de Séville" in Part II for in-depth analysis.)

Près des **remparts de Séville**,	By the **ramparts of Seville**,
chez mon ami Lillas Pastia,	at my friend Lillas Pastia's place,
j'irai **danser** la **séguedille**,	I'm going to **dance** the **seguidilla**
et boire du **manzanilla**.	and drink **manzanilla**.
J'irai chez mon ami Lillas Pastia!	I'm going to my friend Lillas Pastia's!
Oui, mais toute seule on s'ennuie,	**Yes**, but one is bored alone,
et les vrais **plaisirs** sont à **deux**.	and real **pleasures** are for **two**.
Donc, pour me tenir **compagnie**,	So, to keep me **company**,
j'emmènerai **mon amoureux!**	I shall take along **my lover!**

Act II

"**Les tringles des sitres tintaient**" ("**The sistrums' rods were ringing**" or "**The gypsy song**"). The orchestral prelude to Act II sets the mood for this song and dance act. Carmen and her gypsy friends sing and dance in a growing frenzy for their tavern audience on the outskirts of town. The song expresses the heart and soul of Carmen's lifestyle. As the tempo (speed) quickens, Carmen and her friends join in the whirling dance. The music becomes more mesmerizing as it gets faster and faster until it drops from exhaustion. It has a hypnotic effect on the listener and on José, like a few too many margaritas.

Les tringles des sitres tintaient avec un éclat **métallique**, et sur cette **étrange musique** les zingarellas se levaient. **Tambours** de basque allaient leur train, et les **guitares forcenées** grinçaient sous des mains obsinées, même **chanson**, même **refrain**. Tralalalala...	**The sistrums**' rods were ringing with a **metallic** clatter, and at this **strange music** the zingarellas leapt to their feet. **Tambourines** were keeping time and the **frenzied guitars** creaked out under persistent hands, the same **song**, the same **refrain**. Tralalalala...

"**Votre toast, je peux vous le rendre**" ("**I can return your toast**" or "**Toreador's song**"). Escamillo arrives at the gypsy tavern and is welcomed like a victorious general. He describes his feelings of mastery during a bullfight. The singer should behave like a polished gentleman by thanking his hosts and returning their toast. He should avoid sounding loud, violent and swaggering. He then paints a vivid, cheerful, and animated picture of an arena bursting with anticipation and reaching a climax. In the center of the storm, the toreador must appear cool, composed and sure of himself. After describing his exploits in the ring, his voice changes to a major key with the words "toreador en garde!" Already he sees his reward in Carmen—a beauty with dark eyes. When Carmen and her gypsy friends take turns singing "L'amour," Escamillo answers each one. In the second stanza of the aria, Escamillo stresses the crowd's mood in short phrases that suggest the movements of the bull. It is his elegance, courage, and skill that attract his audience. The audience serves as a chorus to echo Escamillo's confident and expressive cadenza or virtuoso passage. (See "Votre toast, je peux vous le rendre" in Part II for in-depth analysis.)

Votre **toast**, je peux vous le rendre, **señors**, car avec les **soldats**, oui, les **toréros** peuvent s'**entendre**, pour **plaisirs** ils ont les **combats**! **Le cirque** est plein, c'est jour de **fête**, le cirque est plein du haut en bas.	I can return your **toast**, **gentlemen**, for **bullfighters** can get along with **soldiers**—yes—their **pleasures** lie in **combat**! **The arena** is packed, it's a **festive** day, the arena is full from top to bottom.
Et songe bien, oui, songe en **combattant**, qu'un oeil noir te **regarde** et que l'**amour t'attend**! Toréador, l'amour t'attend!	And remember, yes, remember as you **fight** that a dark eye **watches** you, and that **love awaits** you! Toreador, love awaits you!

"Nous avons en tête une affaire" ("We have a scheme in mind"). This quintet is a clever song with sparkling humor. The two smugglers have a plan for moving some contraband (illegal goods) and they want Carmen and her friends to help. The women will flirt with the guards so they can slip past customs. The humor is evident in this rough rhyming translation from French to English: "When it's a question of achieving, whether by thieving or deceiving, you will do well, I've always found, having a few women around."

Carmen decides to stay behind with José and the other four depart singing the melody in mocking laughter. The parts of the theme are distributed among the five voices. The voices follow each other very quickly and then join together. This lighthearted song helps to relieve the tension between Carmen and José.

SMUGGLERS
Nous avons en tête une affaire.

We have a scheme in mind.

GYPSIES
Est-elle bonne, dites-nous?

Tell us, is it good?

SMUGGLERS
Elle est **admirable, ma chère**;
mais nous avons besoin de vous.
Car nous l'avouons **humblement**,
et fort **respectueusement**;
quand il s'agit de **tromperie**,
de **duperie**, de volerie,
il est toujous bon, sur ma foi,
d'avoir les **femmes** avec soi.

It's **admirable, my dear**;
but we require your services.
For we **humbly**
and most **respectfully** admit
when it's a question of **trickery**
of **deception**, of thieving,
it's always good, I swear,
to have **women** around.

"Je vais danser en votre honneur" ("I am going to dance in your honor"). Carmen has decided to lavish her love upon José by dancing for him alone. As she dances, she hums a wordless melody. He is mesmerized as she moves slowly to the accompaniment of castanets and her own voice. They are both absorbed in the seductive spirit of the dance until a distant bugle breaks the spell. As the bugle call increases in loudness, Carmen's dance grows in intensity. Even when she dances with more vigor, he rises to return to his barracks. She explodes with anger and complains that he loves a bugle more than her.

Je vais **danser** en votre **honneur**,
et vous verrez, **seigneur**,
comment je sais moi-même
accompagner ma danse!
Mettez-vous là, Don José, je **commence!**
"Taratata, **mon Dieu!** C'est la **retraite!**
Taratata, je vais être en retard!"

I am going to **dance** in your **honor**,
and you will see, my **lord**,
how I am able to
accompany my dance myself!
Sit down there, Don José, I'll **begin!**
"Taratata, **my God!** It's the **retreat!**
Taratata, I'm going to be late!"

Il court, il perd la tête,	He takes leave of his senses, he rushes
et voilà son **amour**!	off, and that's his **love**!

"La fleur que tu m'avais jetée" (**"The flower that you threw me"** or **"The flower song"**). The flower song is an eloquent and lyrical expression of José's psychological state. After being driven to the point of outrage by Carmen's taunting, he curbs his temper and returns to his good nature and intense passion. He draws forth Carmen's flower and sings a song of devotion, torment, remorse and passionate love. His voice is intense in feeling as it suggests the sweet lure of the flower's perfume. He felt resentment toward her in the solitude of jail. Then José expresses an explosion of desire and of incurable passion. His plea must touch Carmen's heart. The end of the song and fast tempo expresses worship and submission. It ends on a pianissimo (very soft note) to the accompaniment of woodwinds. He has surrendered his body and soul to Carmen and their tragic fate has been sealed. (See "La fleur que tu m'avais jetée" for in-depth analysis.)

La fleur que tu m'avais jetée,	**The flower** that you threw me
dans **ma prison** m'était restée.	stayed with me in **my prison**.
Flétrie et sèche, cette fleur	Withered and dried up, that flower
gardait toujours sa douce **odeur**;	always kept its sweet **smell**;
et pendant des **heures** entières,	and for **hours** on end,
sur mes yeux, fermant mes paupières,	with my eyes closed,
de cette odeur je m'enivrais	I became drunk with its smell
et dans **la nuit** je te voyais!	and in **the night** I used to see you!

Act III

"Prelude." The prelude is an exquisite and lovely orchestral introduction that paints a peaceful and moonlit setting. It is very different from the vibrant scenes and lively preludes in the preceding acts. A soaring flute solo carries the melody, and it removes the listener from the bustling city life to the solitude of the country.

"En vain pour éviter les réponses amères" (**"In vain to avoid bitter replies"** or **"The card song"**). This song begins as a duet between Carmen's two gypsy friends as they play cards. As they shuffle and cut the cards, they see good fortune and love. The orchestra changes from a cheerful melody to a more tragic overtone as Carmen reads her cards. Carmen's dark voice becomes very somber as she reads her tragic fate in cards. The short recitative preceding the song suggests that Carmen realizes that Jose would rather kill her than leave her. The cards simply confirm her suspicion. The first three lines are an earnest statement of her conviction that death awaits her. The next several lines are a vision of good fortune sung with a much brighter voice. The final lines are colored by tragedy and her voice conveys a sense of helplessness.

GYPSIES

Mêlons! **Coupons!**

Shuffle! **Cut!**

Et maintenant, parlez, **mes belles,**
de l'avenir, donnez-nous des nouvelles;
dites-nous qui nous trahira,
dites-nous qui nous aimera!

And now speak, **my lovelies,**
of the future, enlighten us;
tell us who will betray us,
tell us who will love us!

CARMEN

En vain pour éviter les **réponses** amères,
en vain tu mêleras;
cela ne sert à rien, **les cartes**
sont **sincères** et ne mentiront pas!

In vain to avoid bitter **replies,**
in vain will you shuffle;
it's no use, **the cards**
are **sincere** and will not lie!

"Je dis, que rien ne m'épouvante" (**"Nothing frightens me"** or **"Micaëla's air"**). This is a song of vocal beauty and personal dignity. Micaëla has just arrived at the smugglers' cove in search of José. She has come to tell him that his mother is dying. Micaëla is aware that she is in a dangerous and forbidding environment. Her voice must shine brightly, as a sign of courage, in this intimidating and dark setting. The opening recitative expresses some initial fear followed by confidence. Her absolute faith in the Lord overcomes her fear. Her total confidence restores her poise and fortitude. She is determined to fulfill her mission by locating José and confronting Carmen with firmness and courage. The melody is carried by the cellos and suggests her unshakable faith in the Lord. It provides a welcome ray of light in a dark and dangerous setting.

Je dis, que rien ne m'épouvante,
je dis, hélas! que je **réponds** de moi;
mais j'ai beau faire la **vaillante,**
au fond du coeur, je meurs d'**effroi!**
Seule en ce lieu **sauvage,**
toute seule j'ai peur,
mais j'ai tort d'avoir peur;
vous me donnerez du **courage,**
vous me **protégerez, Seigneur.**

I say that nothing terrifies me, I say, alas,
that I am **responsible** for myself;
I have tried in vain to be **brave,**
but at heart I'm dying of **fright!**
Alone in this **savage** place,
all alone, I'm afraid,
but I am wrong to be afraid;
you will give me **courage,**
you will **protect** me, Lord.

Act IV

"Prelude." The brief prelude to Act IV suggests the excitement outside the bullring as the spectators gather to watch the procession of toreadors and picadors. The prelude leads directly into the procession chorus. It takes place in the bright sunlight as the spectators cheer in the very plaza where Carmen will meet her fate.

"Les voici! Voici la quadreille!" (**"Here they come! Here's the quadrille!"**). The chorus of onlookers captures the excitement of the crowd

in the square in front of the building. The chorus hails the arrival of the toreadors and picadors by tossing their sombreros and commenting on their attractive appearance.

Les voici! Voici **la quadreille**!
La quadrille des **toréros**!
Sur les **lances** le soleil brille!
En l'air toques et **sombreros**!

Here they come! Here's **the quadrille**!
The **bullfighters**' quadrille!
The sun flashes on their **lances**!
Up in the air with your hats and **som-
breros**!

Voyez les **picadors**!
Comme ils sont beaux!
Comme ils vont du fer de leur lance,
harceler le **flanc** des taureaux!

Look at the **picadors**!
How handsome they are!
How they will **harass** the bulls' **flanks**,
with the tips of their lances!

"Carmen, il est temps encore" ("Carmen, there is still time"). Carmen
has accepted her destiny and she waits patiently for José to emerge from the
shadows of the bullring. In this duet, he makes one last effort to win back Carmen. By deserting the military, his career is finished and his character tar-
nished. Carmen is his only salvation. He begins by pleading in a humble and
quiet voice to a heartbreaking and tender melody. José pleads with her for
another chance and tells her there is still time, but she dismisses him coldly.
In the background, we hear the toreador's song darkened by the lower strings
suggesting tragedy. The tension rises as his agony turns to anger. She taunts
him by singing the same melody back to him. The tension reaches a peak as
José stabs her in an outburst of rage and jealousy.

DON JOSÉ
Carmen, il est **temps** encore.
O ma Carmen, laisse-moi
te sauver, toi que j'**adore**;
ah! laisse-moi te **sauver**
et me sauver avec toi!

Carmen, there is still **time**,
O my Carmen, let me
save you, you whom I **adore**;
ah! let me **save** you
and save myself with you!

CARMEN
Pourquoi t'**occuper** encore
d'un **coeur** qui n'est plus à toi?
Non, ce coeur n'est plus à toi!
En vain tu dis "Je t'**adore**,"
tu n'obtiendras rien, non, rien de moi.

Why still **occupy** yourself
with a **heart** that's no more yours?
No, this heart no more belongs to you!
In vain you say "I **adore** you,"
you'll get nothing, no nothing, from me.

Les Contes d'Hoffmann
(The Tales of Hoffmann)
by Jacques Offenbach

Pursued three ladies—each ending in a hopeless affair
Courted an automated doll with speech quite rare

First performed in Paris, February 10, 1881
Based on three tales by E.T.A. Hoffmann

Libretto by Jules Barbier
Translation by Mary-Ann Stadtler-Chester

*J*acques Offenbach was born in Cologne in 1819 and died in Paris in 1880. His father took him to France to study music. He played the cello at the Opéra Comique in Paris and later gave solo recitals. Over the next 30 years, he wrote more than 80 operettas that received great popularity. He was known to compose at lightning speed. It was said that he could compose music with a party going on around him. He even had a special table designed for his carriage where he composed during his trips to and from a small theater he owned in Paris. Artists drew comic drawings of Offenbach because he was known as the "thinnest man in Paris" with a face always "lit up by a smile."

As he got older, he became determined to write a serious opera that would be his crowning glory. He was already in poor health when he began working on *The Tales of Hoffmann* (Fr. *Les Contes d'Hoffmann*). He was afraid he wouldn't live long enough to see his opera performed. He worked on it for several years and it premiered in 1881 at the Opéra Comique four months after Offenbach died at 61. The opera is based on the fantastic tales of the German medieval author, E.T.A. Hoffmann. He was a prominent author during the Romantic Movement in Germany. His fantastic tales may be compared to Edgar Allan Poe's *Tales of Mystery and Imagination*. Offenbach was attracted to these imaginary and fantastic tales as a youth in Germany. He decided to use the author's last name as the main character in his opera.

Synopsis of Offenbach's Les Contes d'Hoffmann

Main Characters

Hoffmann, a poet	Tenor
Olympia, a mechanical doll	Soprano
Nicklausse, Hoffmann's friend	Mezzo-soprano
Dappertutto, an evil magician	Baritone
Antonia, a singer	Soprano
Giulietta, a courtesan	Soprano
Coppelius, an inventor	Baritone or Bass
Franz, a servant	Tenor

Prologue

Hoffmann and his friend Nicklausse are joined by a group of students in a tavern. They persuade Hoffmann to sing a lively ballad about a deformed dwarf named Kleinzach (Song: **"Il était une fois à la cour d'Eisenach!"**). The students ask Hoffmann to tell them the stories of three different women he fell in love with but lost.

Act I

The first story is about Olympia, the mechanical doll. After entering an inventor's ballroom, Hoffmann falls in love with the sleeping Olympia. Hoffmann's friend, Nicklausse, tries to warn him that Olympia may not be for real (Song: **"Une poupée aux yeux d'émail"**). The inventor, Coppelius, introduces himself and sells Hoffmann some magic glasses that make Olympia look more human (Song: **"J'ai des yeux, de vrais yeux"**). After a large group of guests enter the inventor's ballroom, he introduces Olympia, the mechanical doll. He winds her up and she sings a charming song (Song: **"Les oiseaux dans la** charmille"). After the guests depart for dinner, Hoffmann sings a passionate song and declares she loves him based on her only vocabulary, "Oui!, Oui!, Oui!" (Song: **"Doux avec, gage de nos amours"**). He dances with her but she spins him about until he falls in a faint. After arguing with another inventor, Coppelius destroys the doll, and Hoffmann suddenly realizes that "she was a mechanism."

Act II

At a palace in Venice, the courtesan Giulietta sings the famous barcarolle with Nicklausse (Song: **"Belle nuit, ô nuit d'amour"**) before retiring to the card tables. The magician, Dappertutto, calls on the power of his diamond ring to place Giulietta under its spell so that she can steal Hoffmann's reflection or his soul (Song: **"Scintille, diamant"**). Hoffmann falls under her spell and is intoxicated by her beauty (Song: **"O Dieu! De quelle ivresse"**). Hoffmann begs one of Giulietta's admirers for a key to search Giulietta's room for his reflection. When he refuses, Hoffmann kills Giulietta's admirer in a sword fight while she glides away in a gondola with another admirer.

Act III

A young singer named Antonia sits at her clavichord (keyboard instrument) and regrets the loss of her pet dove (Song: **"Elle a fui, la tourterelle"**). She has been warned not to sing because she is weak and dying from tuberculosis. The servant Franz is alone and he reflects on his inability to sing (Song: **"Jour et nuit je me mets en quatre"**). Hoffmann accompanies Antonia at the clavichord in a romantic duet (Song: **"C'est une chanson d'amour"**). After Hoffmann leaves, Antonia hears the voice of her dead mother from a portrait on the wall (Song: **"Mon enfant! Ma fille! Antonia!"**). She responds to her mother by singing until she falls dying just as Hoffmann rushes in to find out that he is too late.

Epilogue

Hoffmann has just finished telling his friends at the tavern about his third unlucky love affair. He faints and falls on the floor just as his newest romance, an actress named Stella, enters the tavern. Stella is supposed to combine the fascinating qualities found in his three lost loves—Olympia, Giulietta and Antonia.

Songs

Prologue

"Il était une fois à la cour d'Eisenach!" (**"Once upon a time at the court of Eisenach!"**). Hoffmann and his friends are having drinks inside a tavern. The friends join in to sing this lively and amusing song about a dwarf named Kleinzach. They provide a chorus by repeating the final words in Hoffmann's lines. The song begins and ends with a grotesque image of the dwarf, Kleinzach. Midway in the song, Hoffmann drifts off into a romantic cantilena (flowing melodic line) as he describes the face of his lost love. This provides a glimpse into Hoffmann's romantic character. The students interrupt him and remind him to focus on the dwarf, Kleinzach. It is a swaying and lilting tavern song.

HOFFMANN
Il était une fois à **la cour** d'Eisenach!

Once upon a time at **the court** of Eisenach!

STUDENTS
...à la cour d'Eisenach!

...at the court of Eisenach!

HOFFMANN
un **petit** avorton qui se **nommait** Kleinzach!

there was a deformed **little** dwarf **named** Kleinzach!

STUDENTS
...qui se nommait Kleinzach!

...named Kleinzach!

HOFFMANN
Il était coiffé d'un colbac,
et ses jambes elles faisaient clic, clac!
Clic clac, clic clac!
Voilà, voilà Kleinzach!

A tall fur helmet crowned his head,
and clippety clop went his legs!
Clippety clop, clippety clop!
That was he. That was Kleinzach!

STUDENTS
Clic clac!

Clippety clop!

Act I

"Une poupée aux yeux d'émail" (**"A doll with enamel eyes"**). Nicklausse is Hoffmann's constant companion. Although Nicklausse is a boy, his role is sung by a mezzo-soprano dressed as a boy—a tradition in French romantic opera. Nicklausse is trying to warn Hoffmann not to fall in love with an enameled eyed doll named "Olympia." Nicklausse sings this teasing ballad but Hoffmann does not take the ballad or warning seriously.

Une poupée aux yeux d'**émail**
jouait au mieux de l'éventail
auprès d'un **petit cog** en cuivre.
Tous deux chantaient à l'**unisson**
d'une **merveilleuse** façon,
dansaient, caquetaient, semblaient vivre.
Ah, le petit cog luisant et vif,
avec un air rébarbatif,

A doll with **enamel** eyes
artfully fluttered her fan
close to a **little** copper **cockerel**.
Both would sing **marvellously**
together in **unison**, they would dance and
chat, and seemed to be alive.
Ah, the little cockerel, shiny and lively,
with a forbidding look,

tournait par trois fois sur lui-même;
par un rouage **ingénieux**,
la poupée, en **roulant** les yeux,
soupirait et disait: Je t'aime!

would turn round and round three times;
by an **ingenious** mechanism
the doll **rolling** her eyes,
would sigh and say, 'I love you!'

"J'ai des yeux, de vrais yeux" (**"I have eyes, real eyes"**). Coppelius is an evil inventor and was responsible for creating Olympia's enamel eyes. He tricks Hoffmann by selling him a pair of magic glasses. The glasses allow Hoffmann to see whatever he wants to see. They give Olympia the appearance of a real woman and more beautiful than ever. When Coppelius says, "I have eyes," he is referring to magic glasses that he carries in a bag.

J'ai des yeux, de vrais yeux,
des yeux vivants, des yeux de **flamme**,
des yeux **merveilleux** qui vont jusques
au fond de l'âme; et qui même en bien
des **cas** en peuvent prêter une à ceux
qui n'en ont pas.
J'ai des yeux, de vrais yeux
vivants, des yeux de **flamme**.
J'ai des yeux, de **beaux** yeux. Oui!
Veux-tu voir le **coeur** d'une **femme**?

I have eyes, real eyes,
living eyes, **flaming** eyes,
miraculous eyes which can see to the
depths of the soul; and in many **cases**
they can even lend a soul to those who
have none.
I have eyes, real **living** eyes, **flaming** eyes.
I have eyes, **beautiful** eyes. Yes!
Do you want to see a **woman's heart**?

"Les oiseaux dans la charmille" (**"The birds in the arbor"** or **"The doll's song"**). After being wound up by her inventor, Olympia sings a very charming song for the guests in the large ballroom. It requires a crystal-clear voice with great agility and physical ability to capture Olympia's mechanical personality. To the accompaniment of a harp, she sings a sentimental ballad with some difficult coloratura passages. At times, her voice must have a bird-like sound. As the springs begin to wind down, Coppelius must rewind her. After being rewound, she returns with new vitality and repeats her pro-grammed words. She must sound poised, cheerful and amusing. (See "Les oiseaux dans la charmille" in Part II for in-depth analysis.)

Les oiseaux dans la charmille,
dans les cieux **l'astre** du jour,
tout parle à la **jeune fille**,
tout parle à la jeune fille d'**amour**!
Tout ce qui chante et **résonne**
et soupire tour à **tour**,
émeut son **coeur** qui **frissonne**,
émeut son coeur qui frissonne d'amour!
Ah, voilà la chanson mignonne,
la **chanson d'Olympia**!

The birds in the arbor,
the star of day in the heavens,
everything speaks to the **young girl**,
everything speaks to the young girl of **love**!
Everything that sings and **resounds**,
and sighs in **turn**,
she excites his **fluttering heart**,
she excites his fluttering heart with love!
Ah, this is the sweet song,
Olympia's song!

"Doux avec, gage de nos amours" (**"With the sweet pledge of our love"**). Hoffmann is completely bewitched by Olympia and he sings a romantic song meant to tie their hearts together. When he touches her on the shoulder, she responds with a mechanical "Yes!" ("Oui!"). Hoffmann thinks that Olympia accepts his affection, but he does not realize that "Oui" is the only word in her vocabulary. Hoffmann is bewitched by Olympia because his magic glasses make her look human.

Doux avec, gage de nos **amours**, tu m'appartiens, nos **coeurs** sont **unis** pour toujours!	With the sweet pledge of our **love**, you belong to me, our **hearts** are for ever **united**!
Ah, **comprends**-tu, dis-moi, cette joie **éternelle** des coeurs **silencieux**?	Ah, tell me, do you **understand** this eternal joy of our **silent** hearts?
Vivants, n'être qu'une âme et du même coup d'aile nous élancer aux cieux!	To be alive with only one soul, and with the same wings, we soar to the heavens!
Laisse **ma flamme** verser en toi le jour.	Let the fire of **my passion** pour light into you.
Ah, laisse éclore ton âme aux **rayons** de l'amour! Oh, Olympia!	Ah, let your soul kindle in the **rays** of love! Oh, Olympia!

Act II

"Belle nuit, ô nuit d'amour" (**"Beautiful night, oh night of love"** or **"Barcarolle"**). Giulietta and Nicklausse sing this famous duet as they arrive in a gondola on the Grand Canal in Venice. It is a song of beauty and seduction on a moonlit night. The popular title, "Barcarolle," refers to a lilting boat song. Soon after she arrives, Hoffmann will fall in love with the courtesan Giulietta. This song opens Act II. The melody will also end the act when Giulietta abandons Hoffmann in her gondola with another lover.

NICKLAUSSE

Belle nuit, ô nuit d'amour, souris à nos ivresses; nuit plus douce que le jour, ô belle nuit d'amour!	**Beautiful night, oh night of love**, smile upon our ecstasy; night more sweet than day, oh beautiful night of love!

GIULIETTA AND NICKLAUSSE

Le **temps** fuit et sans retour emporte nos **tendresses** loin de cet heureux séjour; le temps fuit sans **retour**.	**Time** flies and carries off our **affection** far away from this cheerful sojourn, never to return; time flies without **returning**.
Zéphyrs embrasés, versez-nous vos **caresses**; zéphyrs embrasés, donnez-nous vos baisers. Ah!	Balmy breezes, pour your **caresses** upon us, balmy breezes, shower us with your kisses. Ah!

"Scintille, diamant" (**"Sparkle, diamond"**). In each of Hoffmann's ill-fated love affairs, there is an evil character present to help destroy his romantic adventures. In this act, an evil magician named Dappertutto likes to steal souls. His diamond ring represents a force of evil seduction. He praises the hypnotic power of his diamond ring to lure women as he holds it upward. After he hypnotizes Giulietta, she will use the diamond to capture Hoffmann's mirror reflection that symbolizes his soul. Dappertutto's voice must convey charm, elegance, poise and authority. The orchestra expresses the sparkle of the diamond. (See "Scintille, diamant" in Part II for in-depth analysis.)

Scintille, **diamant, miroir** où se prend l'alouette,	Sparkle, **diamond**, you the **mirror** by which the lark is caught,
scintille, diamant, **fascine, attire**-la!	sparkle, diamond, **fascinate, entice** her!
L'alouette ou la **femme**	The lark or **woman**
à cet appât vainqueur	both go to this triumphant bait
vont de l'aile ou du **coeur;**	by wing or by **heart;**
l'une y laisse la vie	one leaves its life here,
et l'autre y perd son âme!	and the other loses her soul!
Ah, scintille, diamant, miroir où se prend l'alouette,	Ah, sparkle, diamond, you the mirror by which the lark is caught,
scintille, diamant, attire-la, attire-la!	sparkle, diamond, entice her, entice her!
Attire-la, **beau** diamant, etc.	Entice her, **beautiful** diamond, etc.

"O Dieu! De quelle ivresse" ("**Oh God, with what ectasy**"). Hoffmann has just fallen in love with the lovely courtesan, Giulietta. He sings this passionate song not knowing that she is about to steal his soul. He must sing with a brilliant intensity. There is a feeling of growing desire, as Hoffmann sings of his passion. He speaks of an overwhelming and breathtaking enchantment. (See "O Dieu! De quelle ivresse" in Part II for in-depth analysis.)

O Dieu! De quelle ivresse embrases-tu mon âme?	**Oh God**, with what ectasy do you set my soul on fire?
Comme un **concert divin** ta voix m'a **pénétré,**	Your voice has **penetrated** me like a **heavenly concert,**
d'un feu doux et brûlant mon être est **dévoré.**	my whole being is **devoured** by a sweet burning fire.
Tes regards dans les miens ont épanché leur **flame**	Your eyes have poured forth their **flame**
comme des **astres radieux;**	into mine like **radiant stars;**
et je sens, ô ma bien-aimée,	and, oh my beloved, I feel
passer ton haleine **embaumée**	your **balmy** breath
sur mes lèvres et sur mes yeux!	**pass** over my lips and my eyes!

Act III

"Elle a fui, la tourterelle!" ("**She has fled, the turtle dove!**"). Antonia is thinking sadly about how she has been separated from Hoffmann. In French poetry, the turtledove is a symbol of a girl separated from her lover. Antonia has been advised to stop singing because of her frail health. She yields to her loneliness and sings this sad song while seated at the clavichord (keyboard instrument). She must convey a deep sincerity and sweet sadness. At the end of the song, there are signs of her weak condition and she falls exhausted into a chair. (See "Elle a fui, la tourterelle" in Part II for in-depth analysis.)

Elle a **fui, la tourterelle!**	She has **fled, the turtle dove!**
Ah, souvenir trop doux! **Image**	Ah, too sweet a memory! Too **cruel**
trop **cruelle!**	an **image!**
Hélas, à mes genoux, je l'entends,	**Alas**, I hear him, I see him at
je le vois!	my knees!
Elle a fui, la tourterelle,	She has fled, the turtle dove,
elle a fui loin de toi!	she has fled far from you!
Mais elle est toujours **fidèle**	But she is still **faithful**
et te garde sa foi.	and keeps her word to you.
Mon bien-aimé, **ma voix** t'appelle,	My beloved, **my voice** calls you,
oui, tout **mon coeur** est à toi.	yes, **my heart** is yours alone.
Elle a fui, la tourterelle,	She has fled, the turtle dove,
elle a fui, loin de toi!	she has fled far from you!

"Jour et nuit je me mets en quatre" ("Night and day, I go out of my way"). The servant Franz sings this short song in praise of his own patience and cheerfulness in spite of his unpleasant master. Singing is his way of escaping from his troubles, even though he knows his singing is poor. When he tries to dance, he slips and falls. The song has a comical ring as he expresses his unappreciated musical talents.

Jour et nuit je me mets en quatre,	**Night and day** I go out of my way,
au moindre **signe** je me tais;	at the slightest **sign** I keep quiet;
c'est tout comme si je chantais,	it's as if I were singing,
encore non, si je chantais,	but, no, if I were singing,
de ses mépris il lui faudrait rabattre.	he would have to hold back his scorn.
Je chante seul quelque fois,	Sometimes **I sing** when I am alone,
mais chanter n'est pas commode.	but singing isn't easy.
Tra la la! Tra la la!	Tra la la! Tra la la!
Ce n'est pourtant pas **la voix**,	And yet it isn't **the voice**,
la la la,	la la la,
qui me fait **défaut**, je crois.	that I am **lacking**, I believe.
Tra la la! Tra la la!	Tra la la! Tra la la!

"C'est une chanson d'amour" ("It is a song of love"). Hoffmann and Antonia sing this lilting love duet. Later she sings a reprise of this duet as she dies. It is a very sincere and sympathetic portraiture. Hoffmann has returned after a year absence. They sing a sweet duet to express their happiness. Hoffmann is alarmed to observe how tired she is at the end of their duet. It is one of the most outstanding songs in the opera. This time Hoffmann has fallen in love with a woman who shares his affection.

HOFFMANN

C'est une **chanson d'amour** qui
s'envole, triste ou folle,
qui s'envole triste ou folle...
Mon coeur m'avait bien dit que j'étais
regretté! J'ai le bonheur dans l'âme!
Demain tu seras **ma femme**.
Heureux èpoux, l'avenir est à nous.

It is a **song of love** that is floating
away, sad or delirious,
that is floating away, sad or delirious...
My heart had told me I was missed!
My soul is filled with happiness!
Tomorrow you will be **my wife**.
A happy couple, the future is ours.

ANTONIA

J'ai le bonheur dans l'âme!
Demain je serai ta femme.
Heureux époux, l'avenir est à nous.

My soul is filled with happiness.
Tomorrow I shall be your wife.
A happy couple, the future is ours.

"**Mon enfant! Ma fille! Antonia!**" ("**My child! My daughter! Antonia!**"). Antonia begins singing in spite of her father's warning when she hears her mother's voice calling to her from a portrait on the wall. The song combines a trio of voices, including the ghostly mother's voice, Antonia's feverish ecstasy, and the evil Dr. Miracle. He causes the picture to talk to Antonia and he urges her to sing. He accompanies Antonia with his wild violin until she collapses. As her voice reaches a high C, she falls dying on the couch.

The author, S. Kracauer, of *Jacque Offenbach and the Paris of His Time* wrote, "He (Offenbach) was deeply affected by the story of Antonia, who, if she sang, was bound to die." Offenbach concluded that there was a connection between Antonia and himself because he knew he was close to death. Offenbach died before this song was completed.

FATHER

Mon enfant! Ma fille! Antonia!

My child! My daughter! Antonia!

ANTONIA

Mon père!
Ecoutez, c'est ma mère, ma **mère**
qui m'appelle!
Et lui ... de **retour**!
C'est une **chanson d'amour**,
une chanson d'amour qui s'envole,
triste ou folle...
Ah, c'est une chanson d'amour!

My father!
Listen, it is my mother, my **mother**
calling me!
And he ... has **come back**!
It is a **love song**,
a love song that is floating away,
sad or delirious...
Ah, it is a love song!

FATHER

Non! Un seul mot! Un seul!
Ma fille! Parle-moi, ma **fille**!
Parle donc! Mort exécrable!

No! Just one word! Just one!
My daughter! Speak to me, **daughter**!
Speak then! Attrocious death!

Faust
by Charles Gounod

Seeking the devil to recover youth and attract a lady
Refusing to flee prison even with her steed standing ready

First performed in Paris, March 19, 1859
Based on Goethe's *Faust* (first book)

Libretto by Jules Barbier and Michel Carré
Translation by Mary-Ann Stadtler-Chester

Charles Gounod was born in Paris in 1818 and died in St. Cloud in 1893. He had a gift for memorable melodies and the opera *Faust* was an immediate success. He introduced a lyrical style to French opera that was characterized by beautifully shaped melodies—both sensual and sacred. *Faust* was the most popular lyric opera in the world for three-quarters of a century. Goethe's *Faust* and Dumas' *Camille* are the two most popular themes in opera. Many composers have written operas and instrumental music based on these themes. Gounod's *Faust* is by far the most successful effort and it is based on book one of Goethe's two-part masterpiece. Some critics argue that Gounod's *Faust* is not true to Goethe's *Faust*. This argument is often voiced by critics who don't take into account how great literature must be adapted to the theatrical stage; otherwise, the musical flow would be fragmented and the drama far less popular to opera audiences.

Gounod had a very religious temperament, played the organ, and even studied for the priesthood. He abandoned his religious studies because he was drawn to the secular world of the theater. Gounod wrote intellectual essays and reviews and based his second most popular opera on another famous literary work, Shakespeare's *Romeo and Juliet*. Gounod became interested in *Faust* as a young student in Rome. Like the aging philosopher, Faust, Gounod was also a scholar with secular and spiritual interests. As he grew older, Gounod composed a series of masses and died at his piano while composing a requiem.

Synopsis of Gounod's Faust

Main Characters

Faust, a philosopher	Tenor
Marguerite, Valentin's sister	Soprano
Mephistophélès, the devil	Bass
Valentin, a soldier	Baritone
Siebel, Marguerite's admirer	Mezzo-soprano

Act I

In his study, the aged philosopher Faust is ready to drink poison because he thinks his life has been wasted pursuing knowledge. In a state of torment, he calls forth the devil and reveals his desire for youth and pleasure (Song: **"A moi les plaisirs"**). After selling his soul to the devil, Faust is transformed into a handsome young man.

Act II

At a town fair, the army officer Valentin calls on the Lord to protect his sister, Marguerite, while he goes off to battle (Song: **"Avant de quitter ces lieux"**). Méphistophélès interrupts a student chorus to offer an improper song in praise of greed and gold (Song: **"Le veau d'or est toujours debout"**). A crowd of townspeople and students perform a waltz in an outburst of song and dance (Song: **"Ainsi que la brise légère"**). Faust approaches Marguerite and offers to escort her home but she charmingly declines.

Act II

Siebel, a young suitor, has brought some flowers to Marguerite's garden to show his affection (Song: **"Faites-lui mes aveux"**). After Siebel leaves, Faust enters and is inspired by Marguerite's pure and sacred dwelling (Song: **"Salut! Demeure chaste et pure"**). Méphistophélès leaves a casket of jewels in the garden to help Faust win Marguerite's affection. She enters her garden after singing a ballad in front of her spinning wheel (Song: **"Il était un roi de Thulé"**). When she discovers the treasure, she delights in seeing herself dressed in precious jewels (Song: **"Ah! je ris de me voir"**). Later, Faust joins Marguerite in the garden and declares his love for her (Song: **"Laisse-moi, laisse-moi contempler ton visage"**). Faust enters her house and seduces Marguerite with Méphistophélès' encouragement and magic spell.

Act III

After giving birth to an illegitimate child, Marguerite sits before a spinning wheel wondering why Faust has not returned. In the town square, Valentin and his fellow soldiers sing of the glory of battle (Song: **"Gloire immortelle"**). Méphistophélès decides to sing a sarcastic serenade beneath Marguerite's window about unwed women and their lovers (Song: **"Vous qui faites l'endormie"**). Valentin emerges from the house and fights a duel with Faust to defend his sister's honor. The devil intervenes and Valentin is mortally wounded. Marguerite attempts to pray in church while Méphistophélès curses her.

Act IV

Marguerite is condemned to die for the murder of her illegitimate child. Faust enters her prison cell and encourages her to escape. She calls on the angels to save her (Song: **"Alerte! Alerte!"** and **"Anges purs, anges radieux!"**) when she sees Méphistophélès urging them to leave before it is too late. As she dies, a choir of angels proclaims her salvation and her soul rises to heaven.

Major Song Sketches

Act I

"A moi les plaisirs" (**"Pleasures for me"**). In his duet with Méphistophélès, Faust has just signed a contract with the devil and he confesses that he seeks youth and pleasure above all else. The song has a swinging quality that Faust introduces after expressing his desires. It has an energetic and glorious melody. After Méphistophélès provides a vision of a young, innocent, and lovely Marguerite at a spinning wheel, both Faust and the devil sing a duet reprise of Faust's solo.

FAUST

A moi les **plaisirs**,	**Pleasures** for me

les jeunes maîtresses!	and young mistresses!
A moi leurs **caresses**!	For me their **kisses**!
A moi leurs désirs!	For me their desires!

MÉPHISTOPHÉLÈS

A toi les plaisirs,	Pleasures for you
les jeunes **maîtresses**!	and young **mistresses**!
A toi la jeunesse,	Youth is for you,
a toi ses **désirs**,	for you its **desires**,
a toi son ivresse,	for you its intoxication,
a toi ses plaisirs!	for you its pleasures!

"**Avant de quitter ces lieux**" ("**Before I leave these parts**" or "**Valentin's farewell**"). As Valentin is about to leave for a military assignment, he asks the Lord to protect his sister while he is gone. He holds a medallion that Marguerite gave him for protection. He is introduced with a solemn religious theme. In the first part, his voice has a touch of sadness and proud devotion. He entrusts his sister to the Lord because she has no mother to protect her. In the second part, a march has a ringing theme and expresses his determination and bravery. It is dignified and sung with pride and faith in the Lord. The final bars are slower and religious with a shadow of death in battle but lightened by faith. The final part of the song repeats the first part. (See "Avant de quitter ces lieux" in Part II for in-depth analysis.)

Avant de **quitter** ces lieux,	Before I **leave** these parts,
sol **natal** de mes aïeux,	**birthplace** of my forefathers,
a toi, **Seigneur** et Roi des cieux,	to Thy care, o **Lord** and King of the skies,
ma soeur je **confie**.	I **entrust** my sister.
Daigne de tout **danger**	Deign to **protect** her always
toujours la **protéger**,	from every **danger**,
cette soeur, si chérie.	my sister, so dearly loved.
Délivré d'une triste pensée	Freed from care and worry,
j'irai chercher la **gloire** au sein	I will go to seek **glory** in the
des **ennemis**,	bosom of the **enemy**,
le **premier**, le plus **brave** au fort	the **first**, and the **bravest** in the thick of
de la mêlée,	the fight,
j'irai **combattre** pour mon pays.	I shall go to **fight** for my country.

"**Le veau d'or est toujours debout**" ("**The golden calf is still standing**"). Méphistophélès sings this rousing and wicked song to a crowd of villagers. It opens with a devilish orchestral outburst. It has a brutal and assertive melody with strange chromatic changes in harmony that produce a diabolic sound or a gathering of witches. It is a serenade that depicts the devil as more a rogue than an evil demon. He stirs up their feelings and plays on their worst instincts by telling them that gold rules the day. There is a downward rush of strings as the devil calls on Bacchus to fill their cups with wine. The rhythmic song appeals to the villagers and they join as a chorus until they recognize Méphistophélès as the devil. When the crowd realizes the stranger is the devil, the men hold their swords upward with their crosses facing him.

Le veau d'or est toujours debout;	The golden calf is still standing;
on encense sa puissance	they shower praises on its strength
d'un bout du monde à l'autre bout!	from one end of the world to the other!
Le veau d'or est **vainqueur** des dieux;	The golden calf has **vanquished** the gods;
dans sa **gloire** dérisoire	in its mocking **glory**
le **monstre** abjecte **insulte** aux cieux!	the abject **monster insults** the heavens!

CROWD

Et **Satan** conduit le bal!	And **Satan** leads the dance!

"**Ainsi que la brise légère**" ("**Just as the light breeze**"). This lovely chorus is composed of a variety of characters, thirsty students, swaggering soldiers, young and old men, and women. They all contribute to the festivity. It is an irresistible waltz with the chorus singing a countermelody against the main one. The waltz takes on different colors as the circumstances change. In the midst of the dancing, Marguerite appears and declines Faust's offer to escort her. The waltz resumes and the rhythm increase in tempo. This highly animated scene brings the act to a close and ends on a whirl of gaiety.

Ainsi que la **brise légère**	Just as the **light breeze**
soulève en épais tourbillons	sweeps up the dust of the
la poussière des sillons,	furrows in thick swirls,
que **la valse** nous entraîne!	so let **the waltz** sweep us away!
Faites retentir **la plaine**	Make **the plains** resound
de l'éclat de vos **chansons**!	with the outburst of **song**!

Act II

"**Faites-lui mes aveux**" ("**Make my confession to her**"). A sweet clarinet introduces Siebel's flower song. The orchestral opening is marked agitato to convey Siebel's troubled frame of mind after his unpleasant encounter with Méphistophélès in the village square. As he sings inside Marguerite's garden, he gathers flowers to express his affection for her. Siebel expresses his youthful character in a light and buoyant manner. He leaves a bouquet of flowers in the garden. Méphistophélès intervenes by wilting the flowers before Marguerite discovers them. It was customary in French opera for a mezzo-soprano to sing the part of a male youth.

Faites-lui mes aveux,	Make my confession to her,
portez mes **voeux**,	bring her my **vows**,

fleurs écloses près d'elle.	freshly blossomed **flowers** near her.
Dites-lui qu'elle est **belle**,	Tell her that she's **beautiful**,
que mon coeur **nuit** et jour	that **night** and day my heart
languit d'**amour**!	**languishes** with **love**!
Faites-lui mes **aveux**,	Make my confession to her,
portez mes voeux,	bring her my vows,
révélez à son âme	to her soul **reveal**
le secret de ma **flamme**!	**the secret** of my **ardour**!

"Salut! Demeure chaste et pure abode" ("Greetings, chaste and pure abode" or "Faust's cavatina"). Faust sings this tender song of lyric beauty after entering Marguerite's garden. A violin obbligato (introduction solo) provides a lovely prelude and postlude. He expresses his enchantment with Marguerite's pure and simple surroundings. Faust regards the garden as a shrine for praising and worshipping Marguerite's purity. The garden is imbued with her divine presence. The voice is simple and devoid of technical complications. Faust marvels at the fact that a humble place has nurtured a divine woman. His voice conveys a feeling of gratitude toward nature. The voice grows stronger and expresses a warm and loving tone. (See "Salut! Demeure chaste et pure abode" in Part II for in-depth analysis.)

Salut! Demeure **chaste et pure** abode,	Greetings, **chaste and pure** abode,
où se **devine la présence**	where one **divines the presence**
d'une âme **innocente** et **divine**!	of an **innocent** and divine soul!
Que de **richesse** en cette **pauvreté**!	What **riches** in this **poverty**!
En ce réduit, que de félicité!	In this recess, what happiness!
Ô nature, c'est là que tu la fis si **belle**!	**O nature**, it is here you made her so **beautiful**!
C'est là que cette **enfant** a dormi	It is here this **child** slumbered beneath
sous ton aile, a **grandi** sous tes yeux.	your wing, **grew up** beneath your eye.
Là que, de ton haleine **enveloppant**	Here that, from your breath that **enveloped**
son âme, tu fis avec **amour** épanouir	her soul, with **love**, you made blossom the
la **femme** en cet **ange** des cieux!	**woman** within this heavenly **angel**!

"Il était un roi de Thulé" ("There once was a king of Thule"). This ballad is sung by Marguerite in front of her spinning wheel as she meditates on the handsome stranger she met in the village square. It is a simple ballad with an archaic flavor. She interrupts her song twice as she reflects on how she reacted to the encounter. It is a kind of reverie with a melody of rare beauty. She sings mechanically because her thoughts are more directed at her encounter than the ballad. The song serves to expose her innermost thoughts. The words of the song are not connected to the drama.

Il était un roi de Thulé,	There once was a king of Thule,
qui, jusqu'à la **tombe fidèle**,	who, **faithful** unto the **grave**,

eut en **souvenir** de sa belle,
une coupe en or **ciselé**!...
Nul **trésor** n'avait tant de **charmes**!
Dans les **grands** jours il s'en servait,
et chaque fois qu'il y buvait,
ses yeux se remplissaient de larmes.
Et puis, en l'**honneur** de sa **dame**,
il but une dernière fois...

in **memory** of his lady-love had
a vessel of **chiseled** gold...
No **treasure** had more **charm**!
He used it on **grand** occasions,
and every time he drank from it
his eyes would fill with tears.
And then, in **honour** of his **lady**,
he drank for a last time...

"Ah! je ris de me voir" (**"Ah, I laugh at seeing myself"** or **"Jewel Song"**). Méphistophélès has placed a casket of jewels in Marguerite's garden to help Faust seduce her. When she discovers the jewels, she sings with delight on seeing herself decked in beautiful gems. She becomes more excited and animated, as she tries on more jewels. She expresses the boundless joy of a girl putting on her first jewels and fancying herself as a princess. The song is youthful, innocent, charming and joyful. Each phrase is a legato (sweet and smooth expression). She sings with enthusiasm and free fluctuations, including crescendos, decrescendos, and a trill. Marguerite expresses a brilliant lyric quality. The song is a sparkling and charming vocal waltz. (See "Ah! je ris de me voir" in Part II for in-depth analysis.)

Ah! je ris de me voir
si **belle** en ce **miroir**!
Est-ce toi, Marguerite?
Réponds-moi, réponds vite!
Non! non! ce n'est plus toi!
Ce n'est plus ton visage!
C'est la fille d'un roi,
qu'on salue au **passage**!
Ah! s'il était ici! S'il me voyait ainsi!
Comme une **demoiselle** il me
trouverait **belle**!

Ah, I laugh at seeing myself
so **beautiful** in the **mirror**!
Is that you, Marguerite?
Answer me, answer me quickly!
No, no, it's no longer you!
It's your face no longer!
It's the daughter of a king,
to whom all bow as she **passes**!
Ah, if only he were here! If he saw
me like this! **Pretty** as a **lady** he would
find me then!

"Laisse-moi, laisse-moi contempler" (**"Let me, let me gaze upon your face"**). This love duet between Faust and Marguerite expresses their mutual admiration in a moonlit garden. The words and exquisite melody express a tenderness and sweetness of great lyrical beauty. She plucks a daisy to test his love, as Faust woos Marguerite with a passionate melody. The music rises to a B major that underlines the final "He loves me." She follows by confessing her love for him. His rising passion frightens her and she breaks away from his embrace. Before running away, she promises to see him the next day. Faust is subdued by her purity. The parting causes the lovers to sing faster with one more impassioned exchange before they part.

FAUST

Laisse-moi, laisse-moi contempler	Let me, let me gaze upon your face
ton visage sous la **pâle** clarté	beneath the **pale** light with which
dont l'astre de la **nuit**, comme dans	the **night**'s bright luminary, as
un nuage, **caresse** ta **beauté**!	in a cloud, **caresses** your **beauty**!

MARGUERITE

O silence! ô bonheur!	**Oh, silence!** Oh, happiness!
Ineffable mystère!	**Unexplicable mystery!**
Enivrante **langueur!**	Intoxicating **languor!**
J'écoute et je **comprends** cette	I listen, and I **understand** this
voix solitaire	**lonely voice**
qui chante dans **mon coeur!**	which sings in **my heart!**
Laissez un peu, de grâce!	Let me a bit, I beg you!

Act III

"**Gloire immortelle**" ("**Immortal glory**" or "**The Soldier's Chorus**").
Valentin and his fellow soldiers have returned in triumph and they sing about
the glories of battle. The song was very popular with audiences in the 1860's
after the opera premiered in Paris. Some critics think it is too loud and unre-
fined, while others think it is a rousing expression of victory in battle.

Déposons les **armes**;	Let's lay down our **arms**;
dans nos foyers enfin nous	here we are at last returned to hearth
voici revenus!	and home!
Nos **mères** en larmes,	Our **mothers** in tears,
nos mères et nos soeurs ne nous	our mothers and sisters will have to wait
attendront plus!	for us no longer!
Gloire immortelle	**Immortal glory**
de nos aïeux,	of our forbears,
sois-nous **fidèle**,	be **faithful** to us,
mourons comme eux	we will die as they have!

"**Vous qui faites l'endormie**" ("**You who pretend to be asleep**" or
"**Méphistophélès' serenade**"). In Méphistophélès serenade, he pretends to
be courting Marguerite, but he is really mocking her. He plays a guitar as he
delivers this satirical song beneath her window. It has a grotesque sound along
with the chromatic turns in the orchestra. He sings this "moral song" to
increase Marguerite's sense of guilt. He makes a reference to her misfortune.
Even though he addresses the song to Catherine, he really has Marguerite in
mind. He uses a seductive and irresistible voice as he warns her not to yield to
a lover without a wedding ring. His voice becomes more persuasive and more
legato, as he continues. At the close of the serenade, he bursts into derisive
laughter at three different pitches—high, middle and low G's. (See "Vous qui
faites l'endormie" in Part II for in-depth analysis.)

Vous qui faites l'endormie,	**You** who pretend to be asleep,
n'entendez-vous pas,	do you not hear,
ô **Catherine**, ma mie,	**oh Catherine**, my love,
ma voix et mes pas?...	**my voice** and my footsteps?
Ainsi ton galant t'appelle,	It is thus that your suitor calls you,
et ton **coeur** l'en croit!	and your **heart** trusts and believes him!
Ah! ah! ah! ah!	Ah! ah! ah! ah!

Act IV

"Alerte! Alerte!" and **"Anges purs, anges radieux!"** (**"Watch out, watch out!"** and **"Pure angels, radiant angels!"**). This is a trio and chorus beginning with Méphistophélès urging Marguerite to escape before it is too late. She is in prison and condemned to die for killing her illegitimate child. Faust also urges her to escape. After recognizing the devil, she sinks to her knees and repeats her prayer three times—each time in a higher key with a gleaming light. Three times she calls on the heavenly angels to save her. In the background, the orchestra produces the sound of horses' hoofs encouraging her to escape. She receives her redemption as the angel chorus bears her spirit heavenward (Apotheosis). The song and opera end on a very inspirational and uplifting religious note.

MÉPHISTOPHÉLÈS

Alerte! alerte!	**Watch out, watch out!**
Ou vous êtes perdus!	Or you will be forever lost!
Si vous **tardez** encor,	If you **delay** any more,
je ne m'en mêle plus!	I won't have anything more to do with you!

FAUST

Viens! Fuyons!	Come, let us flee!
Peut-être il en est **temps** encore.	Perhaps, there's still **time**.

MARGUERITE

Anges purs, anges radieux!	**Pure angels**, radiant angels!
Portez mon âme au sein des cieux!	Carry my soul to the bosom of the heavens!
Dieu juste, à toi je m'**abandonne**!	**Just God**, I **surrender** myself to you!
Dieu bon, je suis à toi **pardonne**!	Good God, I am yours! **Forgive** me!

Manon
by Jules Massenet

Loving him along with wealth, pleasure and attention
Finding her irresistible even when she faced deportation

First performed in Paris, January 19, 1884
Based on the novel, *Manon Lescaut*, by Abbé Prévost

Libretto by Henri Meilhac and Philippe Gille
Translation by Mary-Ann Stadtler-Chester

*J*ules Massenet was born in Montaud in 1842 and died in Paris in 1912. He studied at the Paris Conservatory under Gounod. He wrote nearly 30 operas in the romantic and lyrical style of the 19th century. *Manon* is considered the third most popular French opera after *Carmen* and *Faust*. Massenet's operatic compositions are characterized by flowing melodies and his skillful use of dramatic effect. He used motifs or melodic phrases to identify persons, ideas, and situations. For the two main characters, Massenet used a cello melody to depict Des Grieux's tender nature and a short flow of staccato notes to capture Manon's coquettish nature. *Manon* had a successful premiere at the Opéra Comique in Paris in 1884. It made Massenet the most popular opera composer in France. Later, his operas lost favor, especially with critics, because they were considered to be overly sentimental. However, *Manon* has survived as a popular opera in the standard repertory.

The story of *Manon* is taken from a semi-autobiographical novel by Abbé Prévost, titled *Manon Lescaut*. The author, like the main character in the novel, Des Grieux, spent some time in a seminary. It was a very popular novel in Europe for over 200 years. Puccini also composed a popular opera based on Prévost's novel. The story captures the romantic atmosphere of the 18th century French Rococo era. Massenet's opera tells the story of two young lovers in a society noted for elegant, formal, showy, and superficial values. Massenet actually completed his opera in the house in which Abbé Prévost had written his novel over 150 years earlier. The story of *Manon* has been described as a series of "romantic depictions of life."

Synopsis of Massenet's Manon

Main Characters

Manon, lady of leisure	Soprano
Des Grieux, Manon's lover	Tenor
Lescaut, Manon's cousin	Bass
De Bretigny, a rich nobleman	Baritone

Act I

Manon has just arrived by coach in a lively town courtyard on her way to a convent. After being greeted by her cousin, Lescaut, she describes the excitement of the journey (Song: **"Je suis encor tout étourdie"**). An older man is attracted to her and offers his carriage but she rejects his offer. Her cousin returns and warns her not to talk to strangers and protect her family honor (Song: **"Regardez-moi bien dans les yeux!"**). Manon is attracted to the women's fine clothes, jewelry, and joyful lifestyle. As she reflects on their life of pleasure, Manon reminds herself to stop dreaming and prepare for life at a convent (Song: **"Voyons, Manon, plus de chimères!"**). A handsome young man, Des Grieux, arrives and is immediately attracted to Manon. They quickly fall in love and decide to live together in Paris (Song: **"Nous vivrons à Paris tous les deux!"**).

Act II

Manon and Des Grieux are living happily in a modest apartment in Paris. He has just written a letter to his father describing his deep affection for Manon and asking for his consent to marry her. She looks over his shoulder and reads the letter (Song: **"J'écris à mon père"** and **"On l'appelle Manon"**). Manon has found a wealthy suitor, De Bretigny, and she has decided to leave Des

Grieux even though she loves him. While Des Grieux is posting his letter, sadly she bids farewell to the little table where they have so often dined (Song: **"Adieu, notre petite table"**). Des Grieux returns and shares his dream of a country cottage. He tells her that his dream of paradise cannot come true without her (Song: **"En fermant les yeux"**). He answers a knock at the door by his father's emissaries, and he is taken away against his will.

Act III

Manon is now living with her new suitor, the wealthy De Bretigny. She arrives in a coach, along a fashionable avenue, and enjoys the attention of onlookers. She tells them how much she enjoys exhibiting her beauty and jewels. She sings two closely connected songs in praise of youth, pleasure and then warns young people to not let love pass them by (Songs: **"Je marche sur tous les chemins"** and **"Obéissons quand leur voix appellee"**). Manon is upset when she learns that Des Grieux has entered a retreat to pursue a monastic life. Des Grieux's father, the Count des Grieux, visits his son's retreat and tries to convince him to marry a suitable girl rather than pursue a religious life (Song: **"Épouse quelque brave fille"**). Des Grieux rejects his father's advice and begins praying for the strength to resist his memories of Manon (Song: **"Ah! fuyez, douce image"**). As soon as the father leaves, Manon arrives and tries to convince Des Grieux to leave with her. She reminds him that her hands and eyes have not changed (Song: **"N'est-ce plus ma main que cette main presse?"**). He cannot resist his love for her, and they leave to begin a new life.

Act IV

Manon and Des Grieux visit a famous gambling house. He is very successful at cards, and Manon is delighted with his good fortune because she still desires a life of leisure. Des Grieux is falsely accused of cheating at cards. He and his mistress, Manon, are arrested.

Act V

Manon has been sentenced to deportation for serving as an accessory to Des Grieux's misconduct. Des Grieux finds her with a convoy of unfortunate women on the road to exile. She falls exhausted into his arms, asks for pardon, and dies as Des Grieux tries to rouse her. They sing two closely connected songs (Songs: **"Ah! Des Grieux! ... O Manon!"** and **"Je me hais et maudis"**). Her final words are "It must be! And there you have the story of Manon Lescaut."

Prelude and Major Song Sketches

"Prelude." The short prelude introduces us to three major themes in the opera. First, there is the jubilant and festive music associated with the merry-makers in the court scene beginning Act II. This is followed by the brief folk-like phrase sung by the guards who escort Manon along the dreary road to her exile in the final Act V. The final major theme is based on an impassioned melody of love with which Des Grieux addresses Manon in the gambling house in Act IV.

Act I

"Je suis encor tout étourdie" ("I'm still completely dizzy"). Manon has just arrived in a lively village, and she expresses her delight at all the new sights she has experienced on her first coach ride. She describes the lovely things she is experiencing in her new surroundings, with some country shyness in her voice. In her state of discovery, she is very willing to accept the attention of suitors. It is a charming expression of her excitement, and the appealing melody captures her shyness, confusion, and sense of wonder. The song is an excellent example of a musical characterization.

Je suis encor tout étourdie,	I'm still completely dizzy,
je suis encor tout engourdie!...	I'm still numb all over!...
Pardonnez à mon bavardage,	**Please** forgive my chattering,
j'en suis à mon **premier voyage!**	this is the **first trip** I've ever taken!
Le coche s'éloignait à peine,	**The coach** had scarcely started out
que j'**admirais** de tous mes yeux,	when I **admired** wide-eyed
les **hameaux**, les grands bois, **la plaine**,	the **hamlets**, the woods, **the plain**,
les **voyageurs** jeunes et vieux.	the **passengers**, both young and old.

"Regardez-moi bien dans les yeux!" ("Look me straight in the eyes!"). An older man attempts to get Manon's attention and offer the use of his carriage. Her cousin, Lescaut, warns her to protect her reputation and the family honor. He warns her to beware of talking to strangers. Lescaut has appointed himself the guardian of the family honor. The song captures his bragging nature and pompous advice. As a member of the royal guards, Lescaut is characterized by a martial and swaggering cadence (a rhythmic flow of sound). After offering his advice, he departs to drink with his fellow guards.

Regardez-moi bien dans les yeux!	**Look me** straight in the eyes!
Je vais tout près à la caserne,	I am going to the barracks near by,
discuter avec ces **messieurs**	to **discuss** with these **gentlemen**,
de **certain point** qui les **concerne**...	a **certain matter** that **concerns** them...
Si par hasard, quelque **imprudent**	If by any chance, some **brazen** rogue

vous tenait un propos **frivole**,	should make **frivolous** remarks to you,
dans la crainte de l'**accident**,	for fear of a **mishap**,
ne dites pas une parole.	don't utter a word.

"Voyons, Manon, plus de chimères!" ("Come now, Manon, no more day dreaming!"). Manon's parents have sent her to join a convent, but she is immediately attracted to the expensive clothes and jewels worn by the ladies of the village. The song has a graceful and charming pathos as she reflects on a life of pleasure as opposed to the simple life of a convent. This presents a conflict between her parents' intentions and the attraction to a fashionable lifestyle. The song is meant to capture her inner conflict, but it soon becomes clear that she will choose fashion over simplicity.

Voyons, Manon, plus de chimères!	Come now, Manon, no more day dreaming!
Où va ton **esprit** en rêvant?	Where does your **spirit** go in your dreams?
Laisse ces **désirs** éphémères	**Leave** these fleeting **desires**
à la porte de ton **couvent**!	at the door of your **convent**!
Voyons, Manon! Voyons, Manon,	Come now, Manon! Come now!
plus de désirs, plus de chimères!	No more desires, no more idle fancies!
Et cependant, pour mon âme ravie	And yet, when I let myself be carried away,
en elles tout est **séduisant**!	everything in those ladies seems **enticing**!
Ah! Combien ce doit être **amusant**	Ah! How very **amusing** it must be
de s'**amuser** toute une vie!	to have **fun** one's whole life!

"Nous vivrons à Paris tous les deux!" ("We shall live together in Paris"). Manon's conflict is quickly resolved when she meets a handsome young man by the name of Des Grieux. It's love at first sight and he immediately expresses his passion for her. His character is expressed by a tender cello cantilena (a flowing melodic line). A solo violin is used to represent the lovers' main motif. Manon decides that Paris sounds much more exciting than confining herself to a convent. They waste no time taking a carriage to Paris.

DES GRIEUX

Nous vivrons à **Paris** tous les deux!	We shall live together in **Paris**!
Et nos coeurs **amoureux**,	And our hearts **chained** to each other in
l'un à l'autre **enchaînés**,	**love**, united forever, will experience
pour jamais réunis,	only days that are **blessed**!
n'y vivront que des jours **bénis**!	We shall live together in Paris! etc.
Nous vivrons à Paris etc.	

MANON

Tous les deux! À Paris! À Paris!	Both of us! In Paris! In Paris!
Nous n'aurons que des jours bénis!	We'll have only days that are blessed!
Nous vivrons à Paris etc.	We shall live together in Paris! etc.

Act II

"J'écris à mon père" ("I'm writing to my father") and "On l'appelle Manon" ("Her name is Manon"). Manon and Des Grieux are living in a modest apartment in Paris. Des Grieux has written a letter to his father describing his love for Manon and asking for his approval. Manon looks over his shoulder and reads the letter in the form of a song. Her song conveys the thoughts and feelings he wants to convey to his father. He's fearful that his father may not approve because he wants his son to marry a woman of high social standing. The song must be sung with complete sincerity because it's designed to convey Des Grieux's deep love for Manon.

DES GRIEUX
J'écris à mon père;
et je **tremble** que cette **lettre**
où j'ai mis tout mon coeur
ne l'**irrite**.

I am writing to my father;
and I **tremble** with fear that this
letter, into which I have put all my heart
may make him **angry**.

MANON
On l'appelle Manon, elle eut hier
seize ans; en elle tout **séduit**, la **beauté**,
la jeunesse, la **grâce**! Nulle **voix** n'a
plus de doux **accents**, nul regard plus
de **charme** avec plus de **tendresse**!

Her name is Manon, she was just
sixteen years old yesterday; everything
about her **is seductive**, her **beauty**, her
youth, her **grace**! No **voice** has a sweeter
sound, no glance has more **charm** with
more **tenderness**!

"Adieu, notre petite table" ("Farewell, our little table"). Manon is alone in the apartment because Des Grieux has left to post his letter. Even though she still loves him, she has decided to leave him and their poor existence for an older man who can provide a more luxurious lifestyle. This is Manon's nostalgic farewell to the little table they have shared. It is a very sentimental song with a simple accompaniment. She expresses her changing moods in a soft tempo. She must convey the beauty and simplicity of the song in a sustained tone. (See "Adieu, notre petite table" in Part II for in-depth analysis.)

Adieu, notre **petite table**,
qui nous **réunit** si souvent!
Adieu, adieu, notre petite table,
si **grande** pour nous cependant!
Un même verre était le nôtre,
chacun de nous, quand il buvait,
y cherchait les lèvres de l'autre...
Ah! **Pauvre** ami, comme il m'aimait!
Adieu, notre petite table, adieu!

Farewell, our **little table**,
which **united** us so often!
Farewell, farewell, our little table,
so **big**, however, for the two of us!
We shared the same glass, the two of us,
and when each one of us drank,
we tried to find the other's lips.
My **poor** friend, how he loved me!
Farewell, our little table, farewell!

"En fermant les yeux" ("Closing my eyes"). Des Grieux has just returned to the apartment and notices tears in Manon's eyes. It is a moving and tender narrative of his dream and how empty his life would be without Manon. He expresses his affection in a soft, sweet, and warm voice. He dreamed of a little house in a rustic landscape that reminded him of paradise. In a sad voice, he says that his dream will not be paradise without Manon. It is a quiet, intense, and loving description of how they will live when they are married. There are soft and repetitive dream-like chords by the strings. (See "En fermant les yeux" in Part II for in-depth analysis.)

En fermant les yeux, je vois là-bas une **humble retraite**, une maisonnette toute blanche au fond des bois! Sous ses **tranquilles** ombrages, les **clairs** et **joyeux** ruisseaux, où se mirent les feuillages, chantent avec les oiseaux! C'est le **paradis!** ... Oh non! Tout est là triste et **morose**, car il y manque une chose: il y faut encor Manon!	Closing my eyes, I see far away a **humble retreat**, a little white cottage lost in the woods! In its **peaceful** shadows, **clear** and **joyous** brooks, sing with the birds, and reflect the foliage! It's **paradise!** Oh no, everything there is sad and **sullen**, because one thing is missing: it still needs Manon!

Act III

"**Je marche sur tous les chemins**" ("**I walk on all roads**") and "**Obéissons quand leur voix appellee**" ("**Let's obey when their voices beckon us**" or "**Gavotte**"). These two songs are closely connected and reflect Manon's new luxurious lifestyle. She has just arrived in her carriage on a fashionable avenue in Paris. In the first song, she expresses her joy, without sounding boastful, at attracting attention in front of a group of onlookers. It is an outstanding florid aria and outstanding example of operatic poetry. A sparkling orchestral fanfare helps to accent her words. Manon's voice rises in a cadenza (virtuoso passage) to a radiant high note. There is a burst of laughter when she anticipates her own death. The second song is more serious as she advises young people to respond to love before it is too late. The tempo increases and ends with the sound of her laughter. The songs capture her philosophy of life. (See "Je marche sur tous les chemins" and "Gavotte" in Part II for in-depth analysis.)

Je marche sur tous les chemins aussi bien qu'une **souveraine**; on s'**incline**, on baise ma main, car par la **beauté** je suis reine!	I walk on all roads, as well as does a **sovereign**; people **bow**, they kiss my hand, for because of my **beauty** I am queen!
Autour de moi tout doit **fleurir!** Je vais à tout ce qui m'**attire!** Et si Manon devait jamais mourir, ce serait, mes amis, dans un éclat de rire!	All **around** me everything should **flower!** I go towards all that **attracts** me! And if ever Manon should die, it would be, my friends, in a burst of laughter.

Obéissons quand leur voix appelle	Let's obey when their voices beckon us,
aux tendres amours toujours,	to tender loves, always; as long
tant que vous êtes belle,	as you are still beautiful, use up your
usez sans les compter tous vos jours!	days without counting them!
Profitons bien de la jeunesse,	Let's take full advantage of youth, of the
des jours qu'amène le printemps;	days that springtime brings; let's love,
aimons, rions, chantons sans cesse,	laugh, and sing without stopping,
nous n'avons encor que vingt ans!	while we're still only twenty!

"Epouse quelque brave fille" (**"Marry some fine girl"**). Des Grieux is now living a monastic life and trying to free his memory of Manon. His father has come to visit him at the monastery. The Count Des Grieux tries to dissuade his son from living a monastic life, and encourages him to marry a proper woman. He sings a lovely and persuasive phrase urging his son to find a girl worthy of him and his family. The scene moves from dialogue to melodrama and back again in a carefully designed passage.

Epouse quelque brave fille,	Marry some fine girl,
digne de nous, digne de toi,	worthy of us and worthy of you,
deviens un père de famille	become the father of a family,
ni pire, ni meilleur que moi.	neither better nor worse than I.
Le ciel n'en veut pas davantage,	Heaven wants no more of you,
c'est là le devoir, entends-tu?	that is your duty, do you understand?
La vertu qui fait du tapage	Virtue that makes an uproar
n'est déjà plus de la vertu!	is no longer virtue!

"Ah! fuyez, douce image" (**"Ah! flee sweet memory"**). After his father leaves, Des Grieux is left to his own thoughts. As he meditates, he tries to free his thoughts from Manon so that he can fulfill his religious vows. At first, he speaks with confidence, but his voice grows more intense and reveals his suffering. The orchestra plays descending notes that suggest love and repeat Manon's motif (melodic phrase to identify her character), as he struggles with his memories. The middle part is dramatic against distant religious sounds. The sound of the chapel organ provides him with support, but he still can't free his thoughts of her. At the end, the aria fades into a diminuendo to create a softer and calmer mood, as he walks away. (See "Ah! fuyez, douce image" in Part II for in-depth analysis.)

Ah! fuyez, douce image	Ah! flee sweet memory too dear
a mon âme trop chère; respectez	to my heart; respect the peace and
un repos cruellement gagné,	quiet cruelly earned,
et songez si j'ai bu dans une coupe	and remember that if I have tasted
amère, que mon coeur l'emplirait	of a bitter cup, my heart could fill it up
de ce qu'il a saigné!	with the blood it has shed!
Ah! fuyez! fuyez! loin de moi!...	Ah! flee, flee, far from me!...

Mon, Dieu, de votre **flamme purifiez** mon âme, et **dissipez** à sa lueur l'ombre qui passe encor dans le fond de mon coeur!	Heavenly Father! **Purify** my soul and with your **fire**, and by its light **dispel** with your fire, the shadow that still lurks in the depths of my heart!

"N'est-ce plus ma main que cette main presse?" (**"Is this no longer my hand that yours is pressing?"**). After his father has left, Manon appears and tries to convince Des Grieux that she is still devoted to him. She sings a melody that is seductive and irresistible when she asks whether her hand, voice and eyes still hold the charm they once possessed. Massenet resorts to sparkling violins as their hands touch each other. The orchestra will play the same melody when Manon dies in the last act. Des Grieux finds that his physical desire for Manon is greater than his religious convictions. He decides to leave the monastery to be with Manon.

N'est-ce plus ma main que cette main **presse**? N'est-ce plus ma **voix**? N'est-elle pour toi plus une **caresse**, tout comme autrefois? Et ces yeux, jadis pour toi pleins de **charmes**, ne brillent-ils plus à travers mes larmes? Ne suis-je plus moi? N'ai-je plus **mon nom**? Ah! **regarde-moi**, regarde-moi!	Is this no longer my hand that yours is **pressing**? Is this no longer my **voice**? Is it no longer for you a **caress**, just as it used to be? And these eyes, long ago full of **charm** for you, do they no longer sparkle through my tears? Am I no longer myself? Have I no longer **my name**? Ah! **Look at me**, look at me!

Act V

"Ah! Des Grieux! ... O Manon!" and **"Je me hais et maudis"** (**"I hate and curse myself"**). These two brief closing duets recall themes and melodies from earlier scenes. Des Grieux has just caught up with Manon on her escorted journey to exile. He tries to convince her that they can still find happiness, but she is close to death and seeking his forgiveness. She expresses a touching and child-like delight at the sight of an evening star that she likens to a sparkling diamond. As she dies in his arms, her last words express a self-reproach: "You see, I am still a coquette."

MANON
Ah! Des Grieux!	Ah! Des Grieux!

DES GRIEUX
O Manon! Manon! Manon! Tu pleures! Manon! **Lève** la tête et ne songe qu'aux **heures** d'un bonheur qui revient!	Oh. Manon! Manon! Manon! You are crying! Manon! **Lift** up your head and think only on the **hours** of a happiness that is coming back to us!

MANON

Je me **hais** et maudis en pensant
à ces douces **amours** par ma
faute brisées, et je ne paierai pas
assez de tout mon sang la moitié
des douleurs que je vous ai **causées**!
Pardonnez-moi! Ah! pardonnez-moi!

DES GRIEUX

Ô Manon! Mon amour, ma femme,
oui, ce jour **radieux** nous **unit** tous
les deux! Voici les jours **heureux**!
Le ciel lui-même te pardonne! Je t'aime!

I **hate** and curse myself when I think
about the sweetness of our **love**, which I
destroyed, and I will not pay enough
with all my blood for even half
the pain I have **caused** you!
Forgive me! Ah! forgive me!

Oh Manon! My love, my lady,
yes, this **radiant** day **unites** us! Days
of **happiness** have come! Heaven itself
grants you forgiveness! I love you!

German Operas

Fidelio
by Ludwig van Beethoven

Served as a jailer to provide her husband protection
Received his freedom due to her love and devotion

First performed in Vienna, November 20, 1805
Based on a play by Jean Nicolas Bouilly
Libretto by Joseph Sonnleithner and Georg Friedrich Treitschke
Translation by Albert Richer

*L*udwig van Beethoven was born in Bonn in 1770 and died in Vienna in 1827. He believed that dedicated individuals who believed in the sacredness of human life could prevent injustice. This is the theme for *Fidelio* and it explains why Beethoven was willing to devote many years to completing his only opera. It is filled with insight into human nature and human feelings. It expresses his belief in the dignity of mankind and the sanctity of marriage. In Beethoven's time, Austrian state prisons were in need of reform, and *Fidelio* was a declaration against the inhumanity of state prisons. The story is based on a real event in the French Revolution, when a courageous woman rescued her husband from prison. Like Beethoven's *Ninth Symphony*, *Fidelio* was composed as an "Ode to Freedom."

The opera was a failure at its premiere in Vienna in 1805. The theater was only half full because Napoleon had invaded and occupied Vienna just one week earlier. Beethoven continued to labor over his opera by shortening and revising it for nearly a decade. The revised version became a great success in 1814. Beethoven only composed one opera because he was not a man of the theater and his temper often exploded during rehearsals. In his Will, he said of *Fidelio*, "before all others I hold it worthy of being possessed and used for the science of art."

Synopsis of Beethoven's Fidelio

Main Characters

Leonore, Florestan's wife	Soprano
Florestan, a state prisoner	Tenor
Marzelline, Rocco's daughter	Soprano
Rocco, chief jailer	Bass
Pizarro, prison governor	Baritone
Jaquino, a jailer	Tenor

Act I

In a Spanish prison, Marzelline, daughter of the jailer Rocco, has fallen in love with the new errand boy, Leonore (Song: **"O wär' ich schon mit dir vereint"**). She does not know that Leonore is really a woman dressed as a boy. She is disguised as a boy because she wants to locate and free her husband, who is being held as a political prisoner. Her real name is Fidelio. Leonore,

Marzelline, Rocco, and Jaquino sing the famous Canon Quartet (Song: **"Mir ist so wunderbar"**). When Rocco describes a prisoner dying in the vault beneath them, Leonore suspects that it must be her husband, Florestan. In a trio, Marzelline and Rocco support Leonore's request to visit the prisoner (Song: **"Gut, Söhnchen, gut"**). Pizarro, the prison governor, learns that the Minister of State is on way to inspect the prison. He vows to murder Florestan before the Minister's arrival (Song: **"Ha! Welch ein Augenblick!"**). In a duet, Pizarro orders Rocco to quickly prepare a grave (Song: **"Jetzt, Alter, jetzt hat es Eile!"**). Leonore overhears Pizarro's plan to murder her husband. She expresses her contempt for Pizarro, but she is hopeful that she can rescue her husband (Song: **"Abscheulicher! ... Komm, Hoffnung"**). Leonore and Marzelline persuade Rocco to give the prisoners some exercise and fresh air in the courtyard. The prisoners express their gratitude for the open air and hope for freedom (Song: **"O welche Lust!"**). Leonore begs Rocco to allow her to accompany him to the dungeon without telling him that she is looking for her husband.

Act II

Florestan sits in his cell and laments over his terrible fate. He is chained to a wall in a dark cell for having spoken out against injustice. He has a vision of freedom and his faithful wife (Song: **"Gott! Welch Dunkel hier! ... In des Lebens Frühlingstagen"**). He fails to recognize his disguised wife when she enters his cell because he is in a very weak and delirious condition. Leonore and Rocco begin to dig the grave. In a trio, Florestan thanks Rocco for offering him a drink while Leonore expresses her joy and sadness (Song: **"Euch werde Lohn in besser'n Welten"**). When they have finished digging the grave, Pizarro approaches the cell with a drawn dagger, Leonore intercepts Pizarro with a pistol and he withdraws. Florestan and Leonore fall into each other's arms and thank God for their joy (Song: **"O namenlose Freude!"**). When the Minister of State arrives, Rocco pleads for mercy for Florestan and describes Leonore's courage and devotion to her husband. Florestan is granted his freedom and Pizarro receives the punishment he deserves. The prisoners and crowd rejoice as the faithful wife removes her husband's chains and they hail Leonore's virtues and fidelity (Song: **"O Gott! O welch' ein Augenblick!"**).

Overture and Major Song Sketches

"Overture." Beethoven composed four overtures for *Fidelio* before selecting the last one to introduce the opera. It introduces a pleasant opening to the first scene in act one. The overture is structured to foreshadow the opera's two themes—the first joyful and uplifting and the second more dark and foreboding. The overture ends with the first theme on a triumphant note—the victory of goodness over evil.

Act I

"O wär' ich schon mit dir vereint" (**"Oh I wish I were united with you"**). Marzelline's song captures the homespun, middle class world that Beethoven worshipped. It has a simple, song-like structure with short conversational vocal lines. It is introduced and ornamented by an oboe and then supported by a bassoon. Marzelline expresses her desire to be married to Leonore, but she does not know that Leonore is a woman in disguise. She paints an intimate little picture of their life together. It has a formal structure with a romantic ending to each verse (solo passage). It is innocent and straight from the heart. It expresses Beethoven's high regard for the values of the middle class.

O wär' ich schon mit dir vereint,	Oh I **wish** I were united with you,
und dürfte **Mann** dich nennen!	**and** call you **husband** now!
Ein **Mädchen** darf ja, was es meint,	A **maiden** may only **half** confess
zur **Hälfte** nur bekennen.	that what it means.
In Ruhe **stiller** Häuslichkeit	In peaceful and **quiet** domesticity
erwach' ich jeden **Morgen,**	I will wake up each **morning,** and
wir **grüßen** uns mit Zärtlichkeit,	we will exchange tender **greetings;**
der Fleiß verscheucht die Sorgen.	diligent work will chase away all trouble.

"Mir ist so wunderbar" (**"I feel so wonderful"**). This is considered one of the greatest operatic quartets and the most famous song from *Fidelio*. It is called a canon quartet because each of the four singers repeats the same melody in succession, note for note. It has been compared to the slow movement of a string quartet in its clarity and intensity. The single melody serves to merge rather than separate the characters, even though each singer is expressing very different thoughts. The introductory bars have a profound religious quality. Beethoven creates an elevated mood and a profound communion of spirit. It begins with a sad melody in the lower strings. After a string introduction, the singers enter one-by-one expressing different feelings—Marzelline, Leonore, and the jailers Rocco and Jaquino. It has a wonderful quietness as all four characters sing softly. Leonore blends her voice with the others to conceal her true identity.

MARZELLINE

Mir ist so **wunderbar,**	I feel so **wonderful**
es engt das **Herz** mir ein;	it grips my **heart;**

er liebt mich, es ist klar,
ich werde glücklich sein!

LEONORE
Wie **groß** ist die Gefahr,
wie schwach der **Hoffnung** Schein!
Sie liebt mich, es ist klar,
o namenlose **Pein!**

ROCCO
Sie liebt ihn, es ist klar,
ja **Mädchen,** er wird dein!
Ein **gutes,** junges **Paar,**
sie werden glücklich sein!

JAQUINO
Mir sträubt sich schon das **Haar,**
der **Vater willigt** ein,
mir wird so **wunderbar,**
mir fällt kein Mittel ein!

he is in love, there is no doubt,
and happiness will be mine!

How **great** the danger,
and how weak the ray of **hope!**
She loves me, there is no doubt,
oh unspeakable **pain!**

She loves him, there is no doubt,
yes, **maiden,** he becomes yours!
A **nice** young **pair,**
happiness will be theirs!

My **hair** already stands on end,
the **father** is **consenting,**
I feel so **wonderful,**
and I see no remedy!

"Gut, Söhnchen, gut" ("**Good, dear son, good**"). The violins signal the beginning of this sympathetic trio. After Leonore declares her courage to free her husband, Rocco and Marzelline express their moral support and encouragement. It depicts their differing personalities in a lively way. Rocco expresses paternal kindliness; Leonore conveys gentle anxiety, and Marzelline expresses a strong resolve. The middle section of the trio suggests a symphonic development. Beethoven was the greatest symphonic composer of his day.

ROCCO
Gut, Söhnchen, gut, hab immer Mut,
dann wird's dir auch gelingen;
das **Herz** wird **hart** durch Gegenwart
bei fürchterlichen Dingen.

Good, dear son, good, keep up your
courage, and you will achieve your goal;
the **heart** will **harden** when awful
things are present.

LEONORE
Ich habe Mut!
Mit **kaltem Blut**
will ich hinab mich wagen;
für hohen Lohn
kann Liebe schon
auch hohe Leiden tragen.

I have courage!
In **cold blood**
I will risk and go down there;
love can also support
great **pains,**
if the reward is high.

MARZELLINE
Dein **gutes Herz**
wird **manchen** Schmerz
in diesen Grüften leiden...

Your **good heart**
will suffer **many** a pain
down in these dungeons...

"Ha! Welch ein Augenblick!" ("**Ha! What a moment!**"). The strings produce a frantic and furious accompaniment as the evil prison governor,

Pizarro, makes his entrance. He wants to murder Fidelio's husband. He spews his words in a robust manner with each note serving as an exclamation. The rhythms (note arrangements) keep changing with his hateful and disturbing words. The music captures his vile and corrupt personality. The ferocious pace never relaxes in this vengeful aria.

Ha! **Welch** ein Augenblick!	Ha! **What** a moment!
Die Rache werd' ich kühlen,	I shall still my vengeance!
dich rufet dein Geschick!	Fate is calling you!
In seinem **Herzen** wühlen,	To burrow into his **heart**,
o Wonne, **großes** Glück!	oh **great** joy! What bliss!
In seiner **letzten** Stunde,	In his **last** hour,
den **Stahl** in seiner **Wunde**,	the **steel** in his **wound,**
ihm noch ins Ohr zu schrei'n:	to shout into his ear
Triumph! Der Sieg **ist mein!**	**triumphantly!** "Victory **is mine!**"

"**Jetzt, Alter, jetzt hat es Eile!**" ("**Now, my old man, it is urgent!**"). In this duet, the prison governor, Pizarro, calls on Rocco, the chief jailer, to prepare a grave for the prisoner. The strings produce a sinister sound. Rocco is horrified by the request. It is a great study in contrasting characters—the cunning and evil governor and the pleasant jailer. Pizarro is clever enough to appear as Rocco's benefactor. He tries to bribe Rocco by promising to make him a wealthy man. Every thought is expressed with clarity and there is not a wasted note.

PIZARRO

Jetzt, Alter, jetzt hat es Eile!	Now, my old man, it is urgent!
Dir wird ein **Glück** zu Teile,	Good **luck** is yours,
du wirst ein **reicher Mann**;	you will become a **wealthy man**;
das geb' ich nur daran.	this is just an advance.

ROCCO

So sagt doch nur in Eile,	Well then, hasten to tell me,
womit ich dienen kann!	how I may be helpful!
Die Glieder fühl' ich beben,	I feel my limbs trembling,
wie könnt' ich das besteh'n?	how could I stand all that?
Ich nehm' ihm nicht das **Leben**,	**I** will not take his **life**,
mag, was da will, gescheh'n.	whatever may occur.

"**Abscheulicher! ... Komm, Hoffnung**" ("**Monster! ... Come, hope**"). In the recitative, Leonore expresses her anger at the evil Pizarro because she has just overheard his plan to murder her husband. She compares her peaceful soul to his raging soul. After releasing her anxiety, she reaffirms her unyielding faith and hope to save her husband. The song represents Beethoven's high regard for an ideal marriage built on fidelity and devotion. The tempo becomes more vigorous as she expresses her determination. (See "Abscheulicher! ... Komm, Hoffnung" in Part II for vocal skills.)

Abscheulicher! Wo eilst du hin?	Monster! Where to so fast?
Was hast du vor in **wildem** Grimme?	What are your **wild** and furious plans?
Des Mitleids Ruf, der Menschen	Compassion calling, the voice of
Stimme, rührt nichts	humanity, does nothing move
mehr deinen **Tigersinn**!	your **tiger's mind**?
Doch toben auch wie Meereswogen	Even though like ocean waves
dir in der **Seele** Zorn und Wut,	fury and hatred storm in your **soul**,
so leuchtet mir ein Farbenbogen,	in me shines a rainbow,
der hell auf **dunkeln** Wolken ruht.	resting bright on **dark** clouds.
Komm, Hoffnung, laß den **letzten**	**Come, hope**, do not let fade the **last**
Stern der Müden nicht erbleichen!	**star** of the weary!
O komm, erhelle **mein Ziel**,	**Oh come**, light up **my goal**,
sei's noch so fern,	however distant it may be,
die **Liebe** wird's **erreichen**.	and **love** will **reach** it then.
Ich folg' dem **inner'n** Triebe,	**I** follow my **inmost** instinct,
ich **wanke nicht**, mich stärkt die Pflicht	I do **not waver**, strengthened by the duty
der treuen Gattenliebe!	of faithful marital love!

"**O welche Lust!**" ("**Oh what joy!**"). This prisoners' chorus begins with the grave sound of the strings followed by a rising motif (short theme) of the woodwinds that symbolizes the prisoners climbing toward the light. The chorus represents Beethoven's compassion for those who suffer from inhuman treatment and suffering. The orchestra carries the major theme. One young prisoner sings in praise of freedom while an older one cautions restraint. These two brief solos interrupt the chorus. As they approach the light, their distant voices gradually become shouts of joy as they welcome the sunlight and fresh air.

O welche Lust! In **freier** Luft	**Oh what delight** in the **free** air
den Atem leicht zu heben!	to breathe with ease!
Nur hier, nur **hier ist Leben**,	Only here, only here **there is life**,
der Kerker eine Gruft.	and the prison a tomb.
Sprecht leise, **haltet** euch zurück!	**Speak** love, **refrain**!
Wir sind belauscht mit Ohr und Blick.	**We** are heard by watchful ears and eyes.
Sprecht leise, ja leise!	**Speak** in a whisper, yes!
O welche Lust! In freier Luft	Oh what delight! In the free air
den Atem leicht zu heben!	to breathe with ease!

Act II

"**Gott! Welch Dunkel hier! ... In des Lebens Frühlingstagen**" ("**My God! What darkness here! ... In the springtime of my life**"). Florestan's only solo begins the second act. He is alone and chained to a wall in a dark dungeon. After a prolonged orchestral introduction, Florestan must begin with a cry of despair. He then relates how he was imprisoned for telling the truth but content that he did what was right. He confirms his faith in God's

Will. His agitation grows as he has a vision of an angel (Leonore) coming to free him, but does not realize that she is about to discover his location. Beethoven rewrote this song 18 times before he was satisfied with the results. (See "In des Lebens Fruhlingstagen" in Part II for vocal skills.)

Gott! Welch Dunkel hier!	My **God! What darkness here!**
O grauenvolle **Stille!**	**Oh** most dreadful **silence!**
Öd' ist es um mich her;	Desolation is all around me;
nichts lebet außer **mir.**	**nothing** alive beside **me.**
In des Lebens Frühlingstagen	In the springtime of my life,
ist das Glück von mir **gefloh'n.**	happiness has **flown away.**
Wahrheit wagt' ich kühn zu sagen,	I dared to boldly speak the truth,
und die Ketten sind mein Lohn.	**and** chains are my reward.
Willig duld' ich alle Schmerzen,	**Willingly** I endured all pain,
ende schmählich meine Bahn;	and **end** my life in misery;
süßer Trost in **meinem Herzen:**	**sweet** consolation of **my heart:**
meine Pflicht hab' ich getan!	I have done **my** duty!

"**Euch werde Lohn in besser'n Welten**" ("**May your reward be in better worlds**"). In this trio, Florestan, Rocco and Leonore arrive at Florestan's dungeon and comfort him. The music pauses as Leonore gives him bread in this gentle song of compassion. He thanks her for her kindness without realizing she is his wife, due to his delirious condition. Leonore, Florestan, and Rocco join voices to sing a glorious ensemble. There are some lingering final notes before he eats the bread.

FLORESTAN

Euch werde Lohn in **besser'n Welten,**	May your reward be in **better worlds,**
der **Himmel** hat euch mir geschickt. **O**	**Heaven** has brought you to me. **Oh**
Dank! Ihr habt **mich** süß erquickt;	**thanks!** You gave **me** sweet refreshment;
ich kann die Wohltat nicht vergelten.	this good deed, I cannot repay.

ROCCO

Ich labt' ihn gern, den armen **Mann,**	I gladly gave him a drink, poor **man.**
es ist ja bald um ihn getan.	He will so soon be done.

LEONORE

Wie heftig **pochet** dieses **Herz!** Es	How strongly this **heart** is **pounding;**
wogt in Freud' und **scharfem** Schmerz!	it heaves with joy and **sharp** pain!
Wie heftig pochet dieses Herz,	How strongly this heart is pounding,
die hehre, bange Stunde winkt,	the glorious dreaded hour beckons
die Tod mir oder Rettung **bringt.**	that **brings** me death or salvation.

"**O namenlose Freude!**" ("**Oh unspeakable joy!**"). Leonore has just saved her husband's life by preventing Pizarro from killing him. He was about to kill Florestan with a dagger, but Leonore stepped in front of her chained husband and pointed a pistol at Pizarro. After he backed off, Leonore and

Florestan sing this duet to celebrate an end to their suffering and thank God for their togetherness. It has a florid (a highly ornamented musical passage) vocal line as they release their repressed feelings in pure rapture. Their voices overlap in this joyful duet. This duet ends the prison scene and, after a brief silence, is linked to the final celebration.

FLORESTAN

O, **meine Leonore**, was hast du für mich getan?	Oh, **my Leonore**, what have you done for me?

LEONORE

Nichts, nichts, mein Florestan!	**Nothing**, nothing, my Florestan!

LEONORE AND FLORESTAN

O **namenlose** Freude! Nach unnennbaren Leiden so übergroße **Lust**!	Oh **nameless** joy! After untold suffering such unsurpassed **delight**!

LEONORE

Du wieder nun in **meinen Armen**!	You are once more in **my arms**!

FLORESTAN

O **Gott**! Wie **groß** ist dein Erbarmen!	Oh God, how **great** is thy compassion!

LEONORE AND FLORESTAN

O **Dank** dir, Gott, für diese Lust!	Oh **thank** Thee, God, for this joy.

"O Gott! O welch' ein Augenblick!" ("Oh God! Oh what a moment!").
The finale is a grand celebration featuring six characters and chorus. This glorious ending reminds the listener of the finale from Beethoven's *Ninth Symphony* known as the "Ode to Joy." In a brief recitative, the Minister of State honors Leonore for her nobility. After she frees her husband, the song begins with a solo oboe and husband and wife singing a gentle melody. The quintet, chorus, and orchestral accompaniment follow this. It reflects Beethoven's faith in justice, reason, and his belief in the dignity of man. The opera ends on a glorious note as the chorus praises Leonora's wifely devotion.

MINISTER OF STATE

Du schlossest auf des Edlen **Grab**, jetzt nimm ihm seine Ketten ab! Doch **halt**! Euch, edle Frau, allein, euch ziemt es, ganz ihn zu **befrei'n**.	You who opened up the noble man's **grave**, now remove his chains! But **stop**! Yours alone, noble lady, is the right to entirely set **him free**.

CHOIR AND QUINTET

O Gott! O welch' ein Augenblick! O **unaussprechlich süßes** Glück! Gerecht, o Gott! ist dein Gericht, du prüfest, du verläßt uns nicht.	**Oh God**! Oh **what** a moment! Oh **unspeakably sweet** happiness! Righteous, oh God, is Thy judgment. Thou dost test, but not forsake us.

CHOIR

Wer ein holdes Weib errungen,	He who has won a lovely wife

stimm' in unsern **Jubel** ein.	let him join in our **jubilation**.
Nie wird es zu hoch besungen,	Never can we sing with enough praise
Retterin des Gatten sein.	the saviour of her husband's life.

Der Fliegende Holländer
(The Flying Dutchman)
by Richard Wagner

Cursed to sail forever until a woman sets him free
Convinced she's untrue until she follows him to the sea

First performed in Dresden, January 2, 1843
Based on a sea legend set forth by Heinrich Heine

Libretto by Richard Wagner
Translation by Albert Richer

*R*ichard Wagner was born in Leipzig in 1813 and died in Venice in 1883. He began writing plays in his early teens and musical works when he was 16. He credited von Weber for instilling in him "a passion for music." He began his theatrical career when he was appointed choirmaster in Wurzburg.

He soon became the most famous composer of German Romantic opera. Wagner's concept of "music-drama" emerges with *Die Fliegende Holländer* (*The Flying Dutchman*). It brought together several themes of his future operas, such as the synthesis of text and music, emphasis on mood and color, and motifs (short musical units) to identify characters and themes. Wagner had a personal experience on a small schooner across the Baltic and North Seas. His four-week voyage and encounter with stormy seas inspired his music. The sailors on board told the tale of *Die Fliegende Holländer*. The story is derived from literary sources, but Wagner reshaped the tragic tale to make it suitable for the operatic stage.

Die Fliegende Holländer is considered Wagner's first mature opera. It was his first attempt to achieve a complete unity of music and drama. In a symphonic sense, he referred to it as "the most precise correlation of music and action." Wagner regarded *Die Fliegende Holländer* as a romantic opera, in the tradition of von Weber's *Der Frieschütz*. He commented that the Dutchman, who has been cursed to roam the seas for eternity, must be capable of arousing the deepest sympathy. He should exhibit "...a certain terrible peace in his external manner even in the most passionate expression of inner pain and anguish..." By the end of his opening solo, he should create an image of a distressed individual who "...in the grip of the most frightful torments, proclaims his rage at eternal justice...."

Synopsis of Wagner's Die Fliegende Holländer

Main Characters

Dutchman, a cursed sea captain	Baritone
Daland, Norwegian sea captain	Bass
Senta, Daland's daughter	Soprano
Eric, a huntsman	Tenor
Mary, Senta's nurse	Contralto
Steersman	Tenor

Act I

Daland, a ship's captain, and his sailors are trying to bring their ship under control during a terrible storm. While the ship is at anchor, a young steersman keeps watch at night and tries to keep himself awake by singing a love song (Song: **"Mit Gewitter und Sturm aus fernem meer"**). The Dutchman's ship with blood red sails and black masts appears nearby. The Dutchman goes ashore and tells how he was condemned by the devil to sail forever and come ashore once every seven years to find a faithful wife (Song: **"Die Frist ist um"**).

The Dutchman asks Daland if he can share the same Norwegian harbor until the storm subsides. He offers Daland his large treasure if he can marry his daughter. According to the legend, the only way for the Dutchman to receive salvation is to marry a faithful woman (Song: **"Hast du eine Tochter?"**). Daland agrees when he realizes that the Dutchman will make him a rich father-in-law.

Act II

The act begins in Daland's house as a group of young girls sing as they sit at their spinning wheels (Song: **"Summ und brumm, du gutes Rädchen"**). They are waiting for the young sailors to return with gifts. Mary, the maid, scolds Senta for spending too much time admiring a painting of the Dutchman. Senta sings a ballad (Song: **"Johohoe! Traft ihr das Schiff im Meere"**) based on the legend of the cursed Dutchman. At the end of the ballad, she announces that she would like to be the woman who saves the Dutchman from the devil's curse. Her boy friend, Erik, is upset to hear Senta's declaration and he rushes out of the house. Daland enters the house with the Dutchman. He tells Senta how he met the Dutchman, about his wealth, and that he will be staying with them (Song: **"Mögst du, mein Kind"**). While the Dutchman and Senta stare at each other, her father announces that the stranger has agreed to be her husband. Their love duet consists of three sections (Song: **"Wie aus der Ferne langst vergangner ... Wirst du des Vaters Wahl nicht schelten? ... Ein heil'ger Balsam meinen Wunden"**). The Dutchman tells Senta that she appeared in his dreams and Senta marvels at seeing the man in the painting standing before her. In section two, Senta states that she will fulfill her father's request and be faithful to her husband. In the final section, they rejoice at the thought that she will heal his wounds.

Act III

The act begins with a scene of the two ships anchored in the harbor. The crew of the Norwegian vessel is celebrating and singing while the crew on the Dutchman's vessel is silent (Song: **"Steuermann, laß die Wacht!"**). Suddenly, the Dutchman's crew begins to sing as the water surrounding the ship begins to get turbulent (Song: **"Johohoe! Johohoe!"**). Outside Daland's house, Erik begs Senta to explain what is going on (Song: **"Willst jenes Tags du nicht dich mehr entsinnen"**), and reminds her of a vow of devotion she once made to him and their former happiness together. The Dutchman has been hiding nearby and listening to their conversation. He bursts forth in frustration (Song: **"Verloren! Ach, verloren!"**) and announces that he is releasing her from the oath she swore to him. Senta desperately attempts to convince him that she will be faithful, but he boards his ship and sails away. She leaps into the ocean, as a sign of her fidelity. Immediately, the ship sinks and Senta and the Dutchman are seen ascending to heaven.

Overture and Major Song Sketches

"**Overture.**" The overture is meant to be a summary of the plot in the form of a symphonic poem. It gives the impression of a vessel caught in a stormy and angry sea. We hear the whistling wind and the wild cries of the sailors. Two contrasting themes emerge—the curse motif placed on the Dutchman and the lovely motif that captures Senta's devotion and desire to redeem the Dutchman. The final section is largely a joyous outburst on the theme of redemption with the Dutchman's motif sounding triumphantly. The overture ends softly and slowly to suggest the spiritual transfiguration of the Dutchman and Senta.

"**Mit Gewitter und Sturm aus fernem meer**" ("**In storm and gale from distant seas**"). A young steersman has been assigned the night watch, and he sings this song to keep him awake. He prays that a south wind will help bring him home to his girlfriend. The song is interrupted when the ship is struck by a sudden surge of water. The bassoons introduce the song. It has a lovely folk-like melody. String instruments depict the sea. The steersman begins to fall asleep after the first stanza (set of lines). He awakens at the sound of the Dutchman's ship dropping anchor nearby. He murmurs the beginning of the song before falling asleep once more.

Mit Gewitter und **Sturm** aus fernem
Meer—**mein Mädel**, bin dir nah!
Über **turmhohe** Flut vom **Süden** her—
mein Mädel, ich bin da!
Mein Mädel, wenn nicht **Südwind** wär,
ich **nimmer** wohl **käm'** zu dir!
Ach, lieber Südwind, **blas** noch mehr!
Mein Mädel verlangt nach mir.
Hohoje! Halloho! Jolohohoho!

In **storm** and gale from distant seas—
my maiden, I am near you!
Over **towering** breakers from the **south**,
my maiden, I am here!
My maiden, where there's no **south wind**,
I could **never come** to you!
Ah, dear south wind, **blow** harder still!
My maiden longs for me!
Hohoye! Halloho! Jolohohoho!

"**Die Frist ist um**" ("**The time is up**"). The Dutchman's aria is a self-portrait of a man in agony that combines narrative and an outburst of despair. In the opening recitative, he explains why he is allowed to come on land once every seven years. After a recitative about his gloomy life at sea, there is a vigorous account of his rovings at sea. In the next section, he sees deliverance against a stormy orchestral accompaniment. The strings paint a picture of the swirling sea. He ends his rage against his fate to the sound of outbursts from the brass section. A quieter section follows when he asks to be released from his fate. The Dutchman's narrative ends by crying out for Judgment Day as the only answer to his curse. (See "Die Frist ist um" in Part II for vocal skills.)

Die Frist ist um, und abermals	The time is up and **seven**
verstrichen sind **sieben** Jahr.'	more years have gone by.
Voll Überdruß wirft **mich** das Meer	Weary of it all, the sea throws **me**
ans **Land** ... Ha, stolzer **Ozean!**	towards **land** ... Ha, proud **ocean!**
Da, wo der **Schiffe** furchtbar Grab,	There, in the dreaded tomb of **ships**,
trieb **mein** Schiff ich zum Klippengrund:	I drove **mine** on the rocks:
Nirgends ein **Grab!** Niemals der Tod!	nowhere a **grave!** Never death!
Dies der **Verdammnis** Schreckgebot.	This is **damnation**'s awful command!

"**Hast du eine Tochter?**" ("**Have you a daughter?**"). The Dutchman's rugged individuality is in sharp contrast to Daland's greedy desire for wealth. His personality is depicted in the jaunty rhythms. The pair sways together in rounded lyrical (smooth and melodic) lines urged on by the strings ending with the sound of horns. Daland's tune is lively and hopeful that he has made a profitable deal by pledging his daughter in marriage. The duet has a pleasant and easy melody to follow.

DUTCHMAN

Hast du eine **Tochter?**	**Have** you a **daughter?**
Ach, ohne **Weib**, ohne **Kind** bin ich,	Alas, I have no **wife**, no **child**,
nichts fesselt **mich** an die **Erde!**	**nothing** binds **me** to this **Earth!**
Rastlos verfolgte das Schicksal mich,	An unrelenting fate has chased me,
die Qual nur war mir Gefährte.	and agony has been my sole companion.

DALAND

Die ihn an diese Küste brachten,	You **winds** who landed to these shores,
ihr **Winde**, sollt gesegnet sein!	I bless you!
Ha, wonach alle **Väter** trachten,	Yes, what all **fathers** seek,
ein reicher Eidam, er **ist mein.**	a **rich** son-in-law, **is mine!**

Act II

"**Summ und brumm, du gutes Rädchen**" ("**Hum and buzz, my good wheel**"). The young maidens are seated behind their spinning wheels as they anticipate the return of their sweethearts from sea. The repetitive melody and accompaniment of the chorus depicts the ceaseless turning of the wheels and the tiresome routine of spinning. The string instruments accompany the spinning wheels while the oboe continues to repeat the melody. The girls take up the simple and repetitive melody to suggest the nature of their work.

Summ und brumm, du **gutes** Rädchen,	Hum and buzz, my **good** wheel,
munter, munter, dreh dich um!	gaily, turn and turn!

Spinne, spinne **tausend** Fädchen,
gutes Rädchen, sunn und brumm!
Mein Schatz ist auf dem Meere drauß,'
er **denkt** nach **Haus** ans fromme Kind;
mein gutes Rädchen, braus und saus!

Spin and spin a **thousand** threads,
my good wheel, hum and buzz!
My dear love is out at sea,
he **thinks** of **home** and his loyal maid;
my good wheel, whizz and turn!

"Johohoe? Traft ihr das Schiff im Meere?" (**"Yohohoe! Have you met the ship at sea?"** or "Senta's Ballad"). Wagner described this song as the thematic heart of the music. It consists of two motifs—one of damnation and one of redemption. To begin the ballad, a horn call suggests the Dutchman's motif and a ghostly atmosphere. Senta's excitement increases with each stanza. The ballad is a combination of dramatic intensity and melodic beauty against a rich accompaniment. In a short cadenza (closing passage), Senta stands up to announce that she will be the faithful woman to rescue the Dutchman from his curse. (See "Johohoe! Traft ihr das Schiff im Meere?" in Part II for vocal skills.)

Johohoe! Traft ihr das **Schiff** im Meere
an, **blutrot** die **Segel**, schwarz der **Mast**?
Auf hohem Bord der bleiche **Mann**,
des Schiffes Herr, **wacht** ohne **Rast**.

Yohohoe! Have you met the **ship** at sea
with **blood-red sails** and black **mast**?
High on deck, the pale **man**, master
of the ship, keeps **watch** without **rest**.

Bei bösem **Wind** und **Sturmes** Wut
umsegeln wollt' er einst ein **Kap**;
Er flucht' und schwur mit tollem Mut:
"In Ewigkeit lass' ich nicht ab!"

In vicious **wind** and **storm**,
he once attempted to go round a **cape**;
he cursed, in mad bravery and swore:
"I will give up nevermore!"

Vor **Anker** alle **sieben Jahr**,'
ein Weib zu frei'n, geht er ans **Land**:
er freite alle sieben Jahr,'
noch nie ein **treues** Weib er **fand**.

At **anchor** every **seven years**,
a **wife** to woo, he goes on **land**:
every seven years he wooed,
but never a **true** wife he **found**.

"Mögst du, mein Kind" (**"My child, do welcome this stranger"**). The strings provide a sweet melody and yearning sound to accompany Daland as he introduces the Dutchman. He is in a merry mood because of the treasure he will receive when Senta marries the Dutchman. Daland's aria is lighthearted and designed to impress his daughter with the Dutchman's wealth. He is unaware that his daughter has already committed herself to redeeming the Dutchman. He leaves the room when Senta and the Dutchman stand motionless gazing at each other. We hear the Dutchman's theme on the horns and then Senta's on the woodwinds.

Mögst du, **mein Kind**, den
fremden Mann willkommen heißen;
seemann ist er gleich **mir**,
das **Gastrecht** spricht er an.

My child,
do welcome this stranger;
a **seaman** he is, like **me**,
he asks to become our **guest**.

Sieh dieses **Band**, sieh diese Spangen!
Was er besitzt, macht dies gering. Muß,
teures Kind, dich's nicht verlangen?
Dein ist es, wechselst du den **Ring**.

See this **bracelet**, see these clasps!
This is little to what he owns. For sure,
don't you want them, my dear child?
It is all yours, when you exchange **rings**.

"Wie aus der Ferne längst vergangner" (**"As from mist of long gone times"**) … **"Wirst du des Vaters Wahl nicht schelten?"** (**"Will you not disapprove your father's choice"**) … **"Ein heil'ger Balsam meinen Wunden"** (**"A holy balm for my wounds"**). This extended song is considered Wagner's first great love duet. It consists of three sections and begins with two monologues. The Dutchman and Senta are absorbed in their own thoughts as they gaze at each other. In the first section, the voices gradually come together in a somewhat traditional cadenza (virtuoso passage). In section two, Senta accepts his proposal and promises to obey her father's wishes. Nervous sounding strings accompany his question and soft chords on the horns reflect her consent. She pledges her faithfulness until death with an accompaniment that suggests a heavenly chorus. In the final section, their voices rise to a joyful level as they commit themselves to a faithful bond. They express their happiness in a more florid (highly ornamented) vocal line with the redemption motif in the form of heavenly music.

(1) DUTCHMAN
Wie aus der Ferne **längst** vergangner
Zeiten **spricht** dieses Mädchens Bild zu
mir: wie ich's geträumt seit bangen
Ewigkeiten, vor meinen Augen **seh'
ich's hier.**

As from the mist of **long** gone times
this girl's image **speaks** to me: as I
dreamt of her for troubled endless years,
I see her now before my eyes.

(1) SENTA
Versank ich jetzt in **wunderbares Träu-
men**, was ich erblicke, ist's ein Wahn?
Weilt' ich bisher in trügerischen Räumen,
brach des **Erwachens** Tag heut an?

Have I sunk into a **wonderful dream**?
What I see, is it an illusion? Have
I been till now in a deceptive world,
is this the dawn of my **awakening**?

(2) DUTCHMAN
Wirst du des **Vaters** Wahl nicht schelten?
Was er versprach, wie?—dürft' es gelten?
Du könntest dich für ewig mir ergeben,
und deine **Hand** dem Fremdling
reichtest du?

Will you not disapprove your **father's**
choice? What he promised, I beg you,
may I count on it? Could you give
yourself forever and offer your **hand**
to me, a stranger?

(2) SENTA
Wer du auch seist und **welches** das
Verderben, dem grausam dich dein
Schicksal konnte weihn—was auch das
Los, das ich mir sollt' erwerben,
gehorsam stets werd' ich dem **Vater** sein!

Whoever you may be, **whatever** the evil
life which cruel fate has reserved for you—
whatever the destiny that is meant for me,
I will aways owe obedience to my **father**!

(3) DUTCHMAN

Ein heil'ger **Balsam** meinen **Wunden**	A holy **balm** for my **wounds**
dem Schwur, dem hohen **Wort** entfließt.	flows from this oath, these solemn **words**.
Hört es: mein Heil hab' ich **gefunden**,	**Hear** this: my salvation I have **found**,
mächte, die ihr zurück mich stießt!	you powers that have repelled me!

(3) SENTA

Von **mächt**'gem Zauber **überwunden**,	By **mighty** magic **overwhelmed**,
reißt mich's zu seiner Rettung fort:	I am swept away to his rescue:
hier habe Heimat er **gefunden**,	**here** may he **find** a home,
hier ruh' sein **Schiff** in sichrem Port!	here may his **ship** lie safe at anchor!

Act III

"Steuermann, laß die Wacht!" (**"Steersman, leave your watch!"**). Wagner said the inspiration for this chorus resulted from echoing calls of sailors on his voyage to a Norwegian harbor. The orchestra introduces the choral melody. The sailors on the Norwegian ship celebrate their return while the Dutchman's crew remains silent. Young women bring baskets of food and drink on deck to join the sailors. The women sing a variation on the sailors' chorus, and then join the sailors to call out to the Dutchman's crew to join them. Their loud calls are followed by long silences. The men and women take turns crying out louder and louder to the silent crew.

Steuermann, laß die **Wacht!**	**Steersman**, leave your **watch!**
Steuermann, her zu uns! Ho! He! Je! Ha!	Steersman, come join us! Ho! He! Ye! Ha!
Hißt die Segel auf! **Anker fest!**	**Hoist the sails! Anchor fast!**
Fürchten weder **Wind** noch bösen Strand,	We fear nor **wind** nor dangerous coast.
wollen heute mal recht lustig sein! Jeder	Today we'll make merry!
hat sein Mädel auf dem **Land**, herrlichen	Each has his girl on **land**,
Tabak und **guten Branntewein**.	great **tobacco** and fine **brandy!**

"Johohoe! Johohoe!" (**"Yohoehoe! Yohohoe!"**). The cellos and basses suggest a rising storm with tempest winds. As the storm begins to rock the Dutch ship, the crew appears on deck. They sense that the Dutchman has been unable to secure a bride by voicing the curse motif (short musical theme). They sing as they prepare the rigging for sailing out to sea. The sailors on both ships appear to be engaged in a choral contest. The Norwegian sailors try to renew their joyful song, but the Dutchman's ghostly crew manages to drown out the Norwegian crew. They leave the deck and go below. The scene is one of tense dramatic contrast between voices of joy and voices of terror.

Johohoe! Johohoe! Hoe! Hoe!	Yohohoe! Yohohoe! Hoe! Hoe!
Hoe! Hui-ßa!	Hoe! Hui-ssa!
Nach dem **Land** treibt der **Sturm**.	The **storm** wind whips on **land**.

In die Bucht laufet ein!	Run for the bay!
Schwarzer Hauptmann, geh ans Land,	Dark captain, go on land,
sieben Jahre sind vorbei!	**seven** years are over!
Frei um **blonden Mädchens Hand!**	Ask the **blonde maid's hand!**
Blondes Mädchen, sei ihm **treu!**	Blonde maid, be **true** to him!

"Willst jenes Tags du nicht dich mehr entsinnen" ("Won't you remember the day you called me to you"). Erik demands to know why Senta has broken her pledge to him, in the form of a cavatina (short entrance aria). The broken-hearted Erik makes his case to Senta to remain true to her commitment. Wagner wanted Erik to sound stormy and impulsive rather than sentimental. The song is presented in a typical Italian style as a separate piece. In his future operas, Wagner would reject this format by integrating text and music.

Willst jenes Tags du nicht dich mehr	Won't you remember the day when
entsinnen, als du zu dir mich riefest	you called me to you in the valley?
in das Tal?	
Gedenkst du, wie auf **steilem Felsenriffe**	Do you recollect how on a **steep cliff**
vom Ufer wir den **Vater** scheiden sahn?	we saw your **father** leave the shore?
Er zog dahin auf weißbeschwingtem	He sailed away on a white-winged **ship**,
Schiffe, und meinem Schutz vertraute	and to my protection he entrusted you.
er dich an. Als sich dein **Arm** um **meinen**	When you **slung** your **arms** around
Nacken schlang, gestandest du mir Liebe	**my neck**, didn't you confess your love
nicht aufs neu?' Was bei der **Hände**	again? The bliss I felt at the touch of
Druck mich hehr durchdrang...	your **hands**...

"Verloren! Ach, verloren!" ("Lost! Lost alas!"). The Dutchman has overheard Erik's claim that Senta has not honored her commitment to him. He suddenly appears and tells Senta that he is releasing her from her vow to him. She pleads that she will remain faithful to him. The Dutchman, Senta, and Erik express their conflicting emotions in the form of an impassioned trio. While Senta tries to convince the Dutchman that she will remain faithful, Erik tries to convince her to run away with him. It has a theatrical sound that resembles Italian opera.

DUTCHMAN

Verloren! Ach, verloren!	Lost! Lost alas!
Ewig verlornes Heil!	Salvation lost forever!
In **See!** In See—für ew'ge Zeiten!	To **sea!** To sea—forever!
Um deine Treue ist's getan,	Your pledge is ended,
um deine Treue—um mein Heil!	and with your pledge, so is my
Leb wohl, ich will dich nicht	salvation gone! Farewell, I will
verderben!	not ruin you!

SENTA

Zweifelst du an meiner **Treue?**	Do you doubt my **faithful** love?

Unsel'ger, was verblendet dich?	Unhappy man, why are you so blinded?
Halt ein! Das Bündnis nicht	**Stay!** Do not regret our bond!
bereue! Was ich gelobte, halte ich!	My promise, I'll fulfill!

ERIK

Was hör' ich! **Gott**, was muß **ich sehen!**	What do I hear! Oh **God**, what is this **I see?**
Muß ich dem Ohr, dem Auge traun?	Am I to trust my ears, my eyes?
Senta! Willst du zugrunde gehen?	Senta! Do you want to perish?
Zu mir! Du bist in **Satans Klau'n!**	Come to me! You are in **Satan's clutches!**

Der Freischütz (The Free Shooter)
by Carl Maria von Weber

Feared for his safety and prayed for their togetherness
Returned victorious over evil to assure their happiness

First performed in Berlin, June 18, 1821
Based on a story by Apel and Laun

Libretto by Friedrich Kind
Translation by Albert Richer

*C*arl Maria von Weber was born in Eutin in 1786 and died in London in
1826. He was a leading pioneer of German Romantic music, was born
in Germany. He studied music in Vienna and served as Director of the Prague
Opera. *Der Freischütz* premiered in 1821 and became very popular throughout
Europe. The title seems to suggest a very good marksman who never fails to
hit his target. The story is taken from German folklore and music and is considered the first pure German opera. Weber came across *Der Frieschütz* (*The
Free Shooter*) in a collection of stories called the *Ghost Book*. The theme is
based on the struggle between the natural and supernatural, light and darkness,
and good versus evil. Weber highlights these conflicts at the beginning of the
final act by using orchestral sounds to depict a haunted "Wolf's Glen." Ghostly
apparitions and demons appear in the forest during this frightening scene.

Weber created a national German opera to rival the dominance of Italian
opera. He used musical motifs (short musical expressions to identify characters,
ideas, and themes) and orchestral color to explore the relationship between
the natural and supernatural worlds. Weber used major keys to symbolize light
and hope, minor keys for dark and gloom, and different instruments to represent characters. Weber set the stage for German romantic composers like
Beethoven and Wagner. Wagner was very influenced by Weber. He also based
his operas on folklore and made extensive use of motifs in his operas. After
Weber died in London at the early age of 39, Wagner gave a eulogy and composed music to accompany the funeral in Dresden.

Synopsis of Weber's Der Freischütz

Main Characters

Agathe, forester's daughter	Soprano
Max, an assistant forester	Tenor
Ännchen, Agathe's cousin	Soprano
Caspar, an assistant forester	Bass
Killian, a wealthy peasant	Baritone

Act I

Before the act begins, the orchestra plays the famous overture. It includes
melodies from the "Huntsman's Chorus" and Agathe's prayer aria, "Leise,
leise." "Fromme Weise." A chorus of peasants has just congratulated Kilian,
in front of a tavern in the Bohemian Forest, for his victory in a shooting competition. They make fun of Max's failure and join Kilian in a mocking song
with laughter (Song: **"Schau der Herr mich an als König!"**). Max is reminded

that he must win the shooting contest the next day to become the new chief forester and marry Agathe, the chief forester's daughter. When he is left alone, Max wonders why he has suddenly lost his ability to shoot straight (Song: **"Durch die Wälder, durch die Auen"**). Another huntsman, Casper, also wants to marry Agathe and has acquired some magic bullets from the devil. Casper offers to give Max seven magic bullets when they meet in the haunted Wolf's Glen at midnight. After Max leaves, Casper sings about Max's approaching danger and his own victory (Song: **"Schweig, schweig, damit dich niemand warnt!"**).

Act II

In the chief forester's house, the serious Agathe and the carefree Ännchen sing a duet that reflects their different personalities (Song: **"Schelm, halt fest!"**). Agathe and Max want to get married, but she is worried that he may lose the contest. To cheer and lift Agathe's spirit, Ännchen sings a lively song about the attraction between young men and women (Song: **"Kommt ein schlanker Bursch gegangen"**). After her cousin leaves, Agathe expresses her religious faith and confidence that Max will be successful (Song: **"Leise, leise, fromme Weise"**). Max enters the house and tells Agathe and Ännchen that he must visit the Wolf's Glen at midnight. Both women are horrified and they warn Max that the Wolf's Glen is a dangerous place and to look out for the evil black huntsman (Song: **"Wie? Was? Entsetzen!"**).

Act III

Before this act begins, the orchestra creates a scary atmosphere for the Wolf's Glen, including supernatural sounds and a chorus of invisible spirits. Max is testing the magic bullets without knowing that Caspar plans to offer him to the devil. The next scene shows Agathe dressed in her wedding gown and kneeling in front of a religious altar. She had a bad dream that her life was in danger because she appeared as a dove in the forest. She affirms her trust in God (Song: **"Und ob die Wolke sie verhülle"**). Ännchen entertains Agathe with a scary tale followed by a reminder that a bride-to-be should be cheerful (Song: **"Trübe Augen"**). At an outdoor hunting camp, the huntsmen sing about the pleasure of tracking wild game (Song: **"Was gleicht wohl auf Erden"**). In the forest, Max shoots at a white dove and both Caspar and Agathe fall to the ground. Caspar dies but Agathe lives because a hermit protected her. Max is about to be punished for the shooting, but the hermit intervenes on behalf of Max and prevents his banishment. He may marry Agathe if he proves himself worthy for one year. The opera ends with a hymn of praise for God's mercy (Song: **"Wer rein ist von Herzen"**).

Overture and Major Song Sketches

"**Overture.**" The famous overture captures the drama and several lovely melodies of the opera. Weber was a great musical dramatist and orchestral colorist who used instruments to depict characters and scenes. No earlier overture had captured such depth and variety of themes. It begins by creating the spirit of the romantic German forest. Violins suggest a soft rustling sound followed by the cheerful sound of horns and clarinets to suggest wildlife. The double basses and kettledrums (timpani) create a sinister sound that rises to a climax and then fades away. The clarinets provide the melody of the hero's major aria. The melody merges with a full orchestra scene from the evil Wolf's Glen. A solo clarinet produces a shaft of light penetrating the darkness. The violins and clarinets sing the heroine's song of happiness as her hero returns. Finally, the full orchestra makes a triumphant statement.

Act I

"**Schau der Herr mich an als König!**" ("**Sir, now look at me, the king!**). As the title suggests, this is a very boastful song. Killian is a rich farmer who is teasing Max for losing a shooting contest. The village tradition calls for the winner to tease and taunt the loser. Killian must sound confident, boastful, and somewhat arrogant because he has defeated the best marksman in the village. As he asks Max to honor him, Killian interrupts his singing with a mocking laugh. The chorus of villagers echoes him and adds a lyrical (melodic) note to the song. The chorus honors Killian and, as they circle Max, they tease and laugh at him. They add a bright, jolly, and rustic sound.

Schau der **Herr mich** an als **König!**	**Sir**, now look at **me**, the **king!**
Dünkt Ihm **meine** Macht zu wenig?	Do you deem **my** power too small?
Gleich zieh Er den **Hut**, Mosje!	Take off your **hat** to me right now!
Wird Er, frag' ich, he, he, he?	**Will** you, I say? ha, ha, ha?
Darf ich etwa Euer Gnaden	May I perhaps invite your Highness
's **nächste** Mal zum Schießen laden?	to a shooting match **next** time?
Er gönnt andern was, Mosje!	You owe it to the others, dear sir!
Nun, Er **kommt** doch, he, he, he?	**Come** now, won't you? Ha, ha, ha!

"**Durch die Wälder, durch die Auen**" ("**Through woods and through fields**"). Max wants to marry the Head Ranger's daughter, Agathe, and become his successor. He is depressed because he has just lost a shooting contest. The song begins with a gloomy outburst at his misfortune. The shadows change to light as he recalls his former happy days. Flutes and clarinets combine to produce a sunny forest scene. Max reminisces about his happiness as a hunter and Agathe's love. In the second part, he becomes more somber and nervous as he tries to shake off the evil spell he is under. The changes of mood are not subtle because he is under the influence of an outside force. He conveys his contrasting emotions with deep conviction. (See "Durch die Wälder, durch die Auen" in Part II for vocal skills.)

Durch die **Wälder**, durch die Auen	Through **woods** and through fields
zog ich **leichten** Sinn's dahin;	I roamed with a **light** mind;
alles, was ich konnt' erschauen,	whatever I could behold
war des sichern Rohrs Gewinn.	**was the sure** barrel's prize.
Jetzt ist wohl ihr Fenster **offen**	Now her window must be **open**
und sie horcht auf **meinen** Tritt,	and she harkens for **my** steps,
läßt nicht ab vom treuen **Hoffen:**	does not stop her faithful **hoping:**
Max **bringt gute** Zeichen mit.	Max **brings good** omens with him.
Doch mich **umgarnen** finst're Mächte!	But I am **ensnared** by obscure powers!
mich fasst Verzweiflung, foltert Spott!	I am seized by despair, and tormented
O dringt kein Strahl durch diese **Nächte,**	by mockery! Oh, does no ray penetrate
herrscht **blind** das Schicksal,	this **darkness**, does Fate reign **blindly,**
lebt kein **Gott?**	is there no living **God?**

"**Schweig, schweig, damit dich niemand warnt!**" ("**Hush, hush, that none may warn you!**"). Caspar pretends to be sympathetic to Max's misfortune, and he promises Max some magic bullets if he comes to the Wolf Glen at midnight. After Max leaves to bid Agathe good night, Caspar sings his evil drinking song. It is a song of evil triumph over his rival's approaching destruction because Caspar wants to win Agathe and become the Head Forester. He sold his soul to the devil for seven magic bullets. He hopes to escape damnation by giving them to Max. It is a difficult song to sing because it contains a series of difficult vocal scales. Weber uses minor keys to represent darkness and evil.

Schweig, schweig, damit dich **niemand warnt!**	Hush, hush, that **none** may **warn** you!
Schweig, damit dich niemand warnt!	Hush, that none may warn you!
Der **Hölle** Netz hat dich umgarnt!	**Hell** has ensnared you in its net!
Nichts kann vom tiefen **Fall** dich retten.	Nothing can save you from a precipitous **fall.**
Nichts kann dich retten vom tiefen Fall!	**Nothing can** save you from the precipice.
Umgebt ihn, ihr Geister, **mit Dunkel** beschwingt!	Surround him, you spirits, winged **with darkness!**
Schon trägt er knirschend eure Ketten!	Already he is held down, dragging your chains!
Triumph, triumph, triumph, die Rache gelingt!	**Triumph**, triumph, triumph! Revenge will succeed!

Act II

"**Schelm, halt fest!**" ("**You scoundrel, hold fast!**"). Ännchen and Agathe sing a charming duet. The song reflects each girl's character. Weber uses major keys to symbolize brightness and purity. Ännchen is in a cheerful mood as she hangs a picture that fell off the wall. Her personality is reflected in her carefree and bright passage. Agathe is concerned about Max and her voice is more serious. Her slower moving phrases indicate her more serious nature. In spite of her more somber phrases, Agathe joins her cousin in this charming duet.

ÄNNCHEN

Schelm, halt **fest**! Ich will dich's lehren!	You scoundrel, hold **fast**! I'll teach
Spukereien kann man entbehren	you! Ghoulish foolery we can do
in solch altem **Eulennest**.	without in this old **owl's nest**.

AGATHE

Alles wird dir zum **Feste**,	For you, everything becomes a **party**,
alles beut dir **Lachen** und Scherz!	everything is a pretext for **laugher** and
O wie anders fühlt **mein Herz**!	jokes! Oh! how different **my heart** feels!

ÄNNCHEN

Grillen sind mir böse **Gäste**!	Whims are unwanted **guests** for me!
Immer mit **leichtem** Sinn **tanzen** durchs	Always with a **light** heart to **dance**
Leben hin, das nur ist Hochgewinn!	through life, that is the road to success!

"**Kommt ein schanker Bursch gegangen**" ("**When a slim boy comes along**"). This charming song is sung by Ännchen. She is trying to cheer up Agathe who had a frightening dream that she changed into a dove and was fatally shot. Ännchen prefers to dwell on a more cheerful subject, and her song reveals a young woman's longing to find a husband and become his faithful bride. The song has a rustic sound, a joyful melody, and pictures the charm of a happy domestic life. An oboe creates a dance-like rhythm, and a viola provides a romantic theme to ornament the song. Ännchen sings with a youthful, innocent and carefree voice. It has a waltz-like rhythm that reflects Ännchen's light-hearted, high spirited and teasing nature.

Kommt ein **schlanker** Bursch gegangen,	When a **slim** boy **comes** along,
blond von **Locken** oder **braun**,	with **blonde locks** or **brown**,
hell von Aug' und **rot** von Wangen,	clear-eyed with **rosy** cheeks,
ei, nach dem kann man wohl schau'n.	well, it's worth having a look at him.
Bald heißt's **Bräutigam und Braut**.	Soon they're called **bridegroom and bride**.
Immer näher, liebe Leutchen!	Draw closer, my dear people!
Wollt ihr mich im Kranze sehn?	Do you want to see me with a bridal wreath?
Gelt, das ist ein nettes Bräutchen,	Isn't this a pretty bride,
und der Bursch nicht minder schön?	**and the** lad no less handsome?

"**Leise, leise, fromme Weise**" ("**Softly, softly, pious melody**"). Agathe is alone when she sings a prayer for her beloved Max. A clarinet introduces this slow and sweet song with a string backing. She steps out on the balcony and raises her hands in prayer and seeks protection from Heaven. The orchestra creates a magical scene of rustling and sighing forest sounds. This theme was introduced in the overture. The music gets faster as Agathe sees Max returning. She returns to her room and sings of her joy and thankfulness. (See "Leise, leise, fromme Weise" in Part II for vocal skills.)

Wie nahte mir der **Schlummer** **bevor** ich ihn geseh'n?	How **sleep** would overcome me **before** I met him!
Ja, **Liebe** pflegt mit Kummer stets **Hand in Hand** zu geh'n!	Yes, **love** with sorrow always go **hand in hand**.
Leise, leise, fromme Weise, schwing'dich auf zum **Sternenkreise**.	Softly, softly, pious melody, rise up to the **starry sky**.
Lied, erschalle! Feiernd walle mein Gebet zur **Himmelshalle**.	Song, ring out, let in celebration my prayer flow up the **heavenly vault**.
Konnt'ich das zu **hoffen** wagen?	**Could** I dare **hope** this?
Ja, es wandte sich das Glück zu dem teuren Freund zurück.	Yes, fortune has turned around to my dear love again.
Will sich's **morgen** treu bewähren?	Will it prove faithful **tomorrow**?

"Wie? Was? Entsetzen!" ("What? Where? Oh horror!"). Max informs Agathe that he will visit the Wolf's Glen at midnight. A trio of voices is heard as Agathe and Ännchen try to dissuade him from visiting such an evil place while Max insists upon going. Agathe and Ännchen express their horror beginning in a minor key. Again, Weber uses a minor key to depict dark and gloom. At the end of the trio, Ännchen has recovered her usual light-hearted nature in a major key.

AGATHE
Wie? Was? Entsetzen! Dort in der Schreckensschlucht?	What? Where? Oh horror! There in the glen of terror?

ÄNNCHEN
Der **wilde** Jäger soll dort hetzen, und wer ihn hört, ergreift die **Flucht**.	The **wild** hunter rages there, it's said, and he who hears him, **flees**.

MAX
Darf Furcht im **Herz** des Waidmanns hausen?	Can fear dwell in a huntsman's **heart**?

AGATHE
Doch sündigt der, der **Gott** versucht!	But he who tempts **God**, sins!

MAX
Ich bin vertraut mit jenem Grausen, das **Mitternacht** im Walde webt, **wenn** sturmbewegt die Eichen sausen, der Häher **krächzt**, die **Eule** schwebt.	I am acquainted with such horror, at **midnight** murmuring in the forest, **when** oaktrees rustle in the storm, and jay **squawks**, and the **owl** hovers.

Act III

"Und ob die Wolke sie verhülle" (**"And though hidden by a cloud"**). In her wedding dress and kneeling in front of the house altar, Agathe affirms her trust in God. Agathe has just had a disturbing dream. She prays to heaven for protection because she dreamed she was a white dove and shot by Max. A cello introduces Agathe's serene cavatina (short entrance aria) and accompanies her prayer. It has a hymn-like melody and expresses a spirit of hope and trustful resignation. As she raises her eyes to God, her voice changes to a major key. She rises from the altar and sings about her confidence. (See "Und ob die Wolke sie verhülle" in Part II for vocal skills.)

Und ob die Wolke sie verhülle,	And though hidden by a cloud,
die **Sonne** bleibt am Himmelszelt;	the **sun** remains on the firmament;
es waltet dort ein heil'ger **Wille**,	there reigns a sacred **will**,
nicht **blindem** Zufall dient die **Welt**.	the **world** does not serve **blind** chance.
Für mich auch wird der **Vater** sorgen,	Of me too, **Father** will take good care in
dem **kindlich Herz** und Sinn vertraut,	whom my **heart** and mind puts **childlike**
und wär' dies auch **mein letzter Morgen**,	trust, though this be **my last morning**,
rief mich sein **Vaterwort** als **Braut**.	though his **fatherly word** calls me, the **bride**, away.
Sein Auge, ewig rein und **klar**,	His eye, eternally pure and **clear**,
nimmt meiner auch mit **Liebe** wahr!	bestows me, too, his **loving** care.

"Trübe Augen" (**"Sad eyes"**). In an attempt to cheer Agathe, Ännchen sings a scary song about an old cousin who had a nightmare about a ghost coming into her room. It turned out to be a dog dragging its chains. This tale is designed to relieve Agathe's anxiety. A solo viola introduces Ännchen's romanza with some heroic sounds from the orchestra. After the scary introduction, she changes to a merry and carefree tone and tells Agathe that tears are inappropriate for a bride-to-be. There is a touch of coloratura (a decorative passage with rapid trills) at the end.

Einst träumte meiner sel'gen Base,	My late cousin once dreamed
die kammertür eröffne sich,	that her bedroom door opened,
und kreideweiß ward ihre **Nase**,	and her **nose** became as white as chalk
denn näher, furchtbar näher schlich	because nearer, and terribly nearer
ein Ungeheuer...	there crept a monster...
Trübe Augen, liebchen, taugen	Sad eyes, my dear, don't suit
einem holden **Bräutchen** nicht.	a blissful **bride**.
Daß durch Blicke sie erquicke	With her glances may she refresh
und **beglücke** und bestricke...	and **delight** and captivate...

"Was gleicht wohl auf Erden" (**"What pleasure on earth"**). This popular song is also known as the **"Huntsmen's Chorus."** It begins with a sudden explosion in a major key. The sound of horns is associated with the German forest. The forest becomes both an idyllic image and an image of approaching anxiety and conflict.

Was gleicht wohl auf **Erden** dem Jägervergnügen? Wem sprudelt der Becher des **Lebens** so reich? Beim Klange der **Hörner** im Grünen zu liegen, den Hirsch zu verfolgen durch **Dickicht** und teich, ist fürstlishe Freude, ist **männlich** Verlangen, erstarket die Glieder und würzet das Mahl. **Wenn Wälder** und Felsen uns hallend umfangen, tönt **freier** und freud'ger der volle Pokal!	What on **earth** can compare with a hunter's pleasure? Whose cup of **life** sparkles so abundantly? To lie in the pasture at the sound of **horns**, to follow the stag through **thicket** and pond, is joy for a prince, is a **man**'s desire, it strengthens the limbs and spices the food. **When** echoing **woods** and rocks surround us all, a full goblet sings a **freer** and happier song!

"**Wer rein ist von Herzen**" ("**Whoever is pure of heart**"). Six happy soloists are joined by a happy chorus in a hymn of praise for God's mercy. The words celebrate the unfailing power of virtue and submission to the will of God. It includes a triumphant theme from Agathe's aria, "Softly, softly, pious heart." The chorus is based on the motive of uplifting love. The song ends with a joyful chorus when Max is given the right to marry Agathe after a year's probation. The ensemble ends in a bright major key with the chorus praising God's mercy.

Wer rein ist von **Herzen** und schuldlos im Leben, darf **kindlich** der **Milde** des **Vater** vertrau'n!	Whoever is pure of **heart** and free of guilt in life may, **childlike,** trust in the **gentleness** of the **Father**!
Ja, laßt uns die Blicke erheben und fest auf die Lenkung des **Ewigen** bau'n, fest der Milde des Vaters vertrau'n! Wer rein ist von Herzen und schuldlos im **Leben**, darf kindlich der Milde des Vaters vertrau'n!	Yes, let us raise our eyes and firmly rely on the guidance of the **Eternal**, trust firmly in the gentle Father! Whoever is pure of heart and guilt free in **life**, may, trust in the gentleness of the Father.

Die Zauberflöte
(The Magic Flute)
by Wolfgang Amadeus Mozart

Falling in love with the Queen of the Night's daughter
Passing trials to enter a Kingdom of Light and be together

First performed in Vienna, September 30, 1791
Based on a variety of sources, including a play by Wieland

Libretto by Emanuel Schikaneder
Translation by Albert Richer

*W*olfgang Amadeus Mozart was born in Salzburg in 1756 and died in Vienna in 1791. His last and most successful opera was *Die Zauberflöte*. It was composed and first performed in 1791—the year Mozart died at age 34. Even though several of Mozart's most famous operas were written in Italian, *Die Zauberflöte* (*The Magic Flute*) was written in German and Mozart referred to it as his "German opera." Spoken dialogue (Singspiel) instead of sung dialogue was used to link the songs. It contains some of Mozart's most glorious and uplifting music. Beethoven considered *Die Zauberflöte* to be

Mozart's greatest, most inspirational and noblest opera. It's reported that Mozart loved *Die Zauberflöte* and said on his deathbed, "If only I could hear my *Zauberflöte* once more." *Die Zauberflöte* was the forerunner of the Age of Romanticism in music. Romantic composers, like Beethoven, Weber and Wagner, were inspired by Mozart's final opera.

The opera is full of magic, symbolism, mythology and nobility. Mozart belonged to a Masonic lodge (a fraternal order believing in fellowship and religious toleration) in Vienna that was opposed by the Imperial Court and Catholic Church. In a show of defiance, Mozart wanted his opera to appeal to the common folk rather than the aristocracy. It was meant to be popular entertainment with a comic and storybook theme. The symbolism revolves around the number three, including Three Ladies, Three Boys, three doors to Three Temples, and three rituals to enter the Brotherhood. The Three Temples represent the three virtues of Reason, Nature, and Wisdom. The opera has a strong humanitarian message that focuses on love, honor, truth, mercy and wisdom. Most of the story takes place either in Egyptian-Masonic temples or in the palm groves that surround them.

Synopsis of Mozart's Die Zauberflöte

Main Characters

Tamino, a prince	Tenor
Pamina, Queen's daughter	Soprano
Queen of the Night	Soprano
Papageno, a birdcatcher	Baritone
Sarastro, priest of the sun	Bass

Act I

After being chased by a dragon and falling unconscious, Prince Tamino awakens and hides on sight of Papageno, a bird catcher dressed in feathers. Papageno, who catches birds for the Queen of the Night, describes his lonely life (Song: **"Der Vogelfanger bin ich ja"**). He is punished by the Three Ladies to the Queen of the Night for not telling the truth. They give Tamino a portrait of the Queen's daughter, Pamina. He immediately falls in love with her portrait and praises her beauty (Song: **"Dies Bildnis ist bezaubernd schön"**). The Queen appears and tells Tamino her daughter is being held prisoner by Sarastro, whom she describes as an evil sorcerer (Song: **"O zittre nicht, mein lieber Sohn!"**). If he rescues her daughter, she will give him Pamina's hand in marriage. The Three Ladies tell Papageno that he must accompany Tamino on his mission to save Pamina. They give each of them a magic instrument to protect them from harm—bells for Papageno and a magic flute for Tamino. Papageno discovers Pamino at Sarastro's temple and tells her why he has come. He explains Tamino's mission, and she joins him in marveling at the nature of human love (Song: **"Bei Männern, welche Liebe fühlen"**). Meanwhile, Tamino arrives at the Three Temples of Wisdom, Reason and Nature. The speaker for the Temple of Wisdom tells him of the Queen's deception and how Sarastro is protecting Pamina from her evil mother. Tamino expresses his relief by playing his magic flute that pacifies and attracts wild animals (Song: **"Wie stark ist nicht dein Zauberton!"**). When Tamino and Pamina see each other for the first time, they rush into each other's arms. Sarastro blesses the young couple and bids them to submit to the trials of purification as his followers praise the high ideals that will transform earth into paradise (Song: **"Es lebe Sarastro, Sarastro soll leben!"**).

Act II

A solemn procession of Priests enter a sacred grove where Sarastro informs them that Tamino and Papageno must undergo several rituals (trials) to join their brotherhood. Sarastro and the Priests offer a prayer to the gods and ask them to strengthen Tamino and Papageno (Song: **"O Isis und Osiris"**). Two Priests lead them blindfolded into the courtyard of the temple to prepare them for the trials. As Pamina sleeps in the temple garden, the Queen of the Night arrives, shrieks with fury, and seeks vengeance on Sarastro (Song: **"Der Hölle Rache kocht in meinem Herzen"**). Just as a servant tries to seduce Pamina, she is rescued by the intervention of Sarastro who tells her he will forgive her mother's hostility (Song: **"In diesen heil'gen Hallen"**).

Two priests lead Tamino and Papageno to the temple crypt where they undergo the test of silence. When Tamino does not answer Pamina's question, she fears that his indifference means that he no longer loves her (Song: **"Ach, ich fühl's, es ist entschwunden"**). Sarastro hears about how Tamino adhered to his vow of silence. He summons the lovers and tells them that they must face two more trials—the caverns of fire and water. Meanwhile, Papageno has failed the test of silence, but he pleads for a sweetheart to fulfill his earthly desires (Song: **"Ein Mädchen oder Weibchen"**). The lovers pass through fire and water to the flute's music. In an exotic garden, Papageno whistles for his mate and a young lady appears and they sing about their future family. At the temple, Sarastro hails the victory of light over darkness and blesses Tamino and Pamina as his followers offer a hymn of praise to the gods (Song: **"Heil sei euch Geweihten!"**).

Overture and Major Song Sketches

"**Overture.**" The famous overture begins with three solemn chords that suggest the Masonic symbolism and temple rites that reappear throughout the opera. The trombones help create this somber atmosphere. The symbolism of the number three is expressed in a major key. A lively chatter that spreads follows this from the violins to other strings and woodwinds. This liveliness suggests the fairy tale nature of the drama about to unfold. Three chords produced by the wind instruments halt the chatter. The orchestra returns to a more quiet tone in the original key of E-flat major.

Act I

"**Der Vogelfänger bin ich ja**" ("**Yes, I am the birdcatcher**"). The first character to appear is the bird catcher Papageno. He is a strange looking character covered with feathers and carrying a large birdcage on his back. His folk-like song tells of his lonely life. He's tired of catching birds for the Queen, and he would rather catch a young sweetheart. Each verse has the sound of panpipes or a bell-like sound for luring birds. It's a comic, robust, and cheerful song because Papageno is an earthly man of pleasure.

Der Vogelfänger bin ich ja,	Yes, I am the birdcatcher,
stets lustig, heißa hopsasa!	and ever merry—hop hopsasa!
Ich Vogelfänger bin **bekannt**	As bird catcher I am well **known**
bei alt und **jung** im ganzen **Land**.	by old and **young** throughout the **land**.
Ein **Netz für Mädchen** möchte ich,	I wish I had a **net for girls**—for me
ich fing sie **dutzendweis'** für mich!	I'd catch them **by the dozen** then!
Dann sperrte ich sie bei mir ein,	I'd lock them in a cage at home,
und alle Mädchen wären **mein**.	**and all** the girls would be **mine**.

"**Dies Bildnis ist bezaubernd schön**" ("**This portrait is ravishingly beautiful**"). Tamino has just been given a portrait of the Queen's daughter and he is filled with wonder and rapture and overcome by her beauty. Without waiting to meet her, he is convinced that she is a woman of great beauty and purity. The song is sung on a high poetic level and expresses his respect, admiration and devotion. In a slow tempo and lyric voice, Tamino creates a dream-like atmosphere. It's a very demanding aria that requires great control in linking the notes in a flowing sound. (See "Dies Bildnis ist bezaubernd schön" in Part II for vocal skills.)

Dies Bildnis ist bezaubernd schön,	This portrait is ravishingly beautiful,
wie noch kein Auge je gesehn!	such as no eyes have ever seen!
Ich fühl' es, wie dies Götterbild	**I feel** how this divine picture is
mein Herz mit **neuer** Regung füllt.	filling **my heart** with **new** emotion.

Dies Etwas kann ich zwar nicht **nennen**,	This "something" I cannot **name**;
doch fühl' ich's hier wie **Feuer brennen**.	but feel it **burn** like **fire**.
Soll die Empfindung **Liebe** sein?	Can this sensation be **love**?
Ja, ja! Die Liebe ist's allein.	**Yes, yes!** It can only be love.

"O zittre nicht, mein lieber Sohn!" (**"Oh tremble not, my dear son!"**). After the sound of thunder, the Queen of the Night appears in the moonlight as if descending from the stars. Her song begins slow and grave as she regrets the loss of her daughter. The Queen must disguise her evil nature. She tells how a wicked magician kidnapped her daughter. She pours out her grief to Tamino to enlist his support in rescuing her daughter. After arousing Tamino's sympathy, the Queen follows with a fiery ending and expresses her anger in a rising coloratura (a series of high notes). (See "O zittre nicht, mein lieber Sohn!" in Part II for vocal skills.)

O zittre **nicht, mein** lieber **Sohn!**	Oh tremble **not, my** dear **son!**
Du bist unschuldig, weise, fromm.	You are innocent, reasonable, good.
Ein Jüngling, so wie du, vermag	A young man like you
am **besten**, dies tiefbetrübte	is **best** able to console this
Mutterherz zu trösten.	**mother's** deeply saddened **heart**.
Zum Leiden bin ich auserkoren;	I am destined to grieve;
denn **meine Tochter** fehlet mir.	for I am longing for **my daughter**.
Du wirst sie zu **befreien** gehen,	You will go and **set** her **free**;
du wirst der Tochter Retter sein!	you will be my daughter's savior!
Und werd' ich dich als Sieger sehen,	**And** if I see you victorious,
so sei sie dann auf ewig dein!	then will she be yours forever!

"Bei Männern, welche Liebe fühlen" (**"In men who know the feeling of love"**). Papageno has agreed to help Tamino rescue the Queen of the Night's daughter. He locates Pamina inside an exotic palace where she is being held prisoner. After consoling her, they both sing the praises of married life. It's a simple and beautiful duet between two innocent and idealistic people. It is a moment of great tenderness and humanity sung by two people with very different personalities but similar ideals. The duet takes the form of a hymn as they wonder at the spiritual nature of marital love. Pamina's serene ornamentation distinguishes her voice from his more earthly voice. It has a very simple orchestral accompaniment and ends with several highly decorated farewells.

PAMINA

Bei **Männern**, welche **Liebe fühlen**,	In **men** who know the **feeling of love**,
fehlt auch ein **gutes Herze** nicht.	**good hearts** cannot be missing.
Die Lieb' versüßet jede Plage,	Love sweetens every trouble;
ihr opfert jeder **Kreatur**.	all **creatures** sacrifice to it.

PAMINA AND PAPAGENO

Ihr **hoher** Zweck zeigt deutlich an,	Its **higher** purpose makes it clear
nichts Edlers sei als **Mann und Weib**.	that nothing is nobler than **man and**
Mann und Weib, und Weib und Mann	**woman**. Man and woman, and woman
reichen an die Gottheit an.	and man, attain the level of divinity.

"Wie stark ist nicht dein Zauberton!" (**"How powerful is your magic sound!"**). Tamino has just learned of the Queen's deception and that her daughter was kidnapped to protect her from her evil mother. He expresses his relief by playing his magic flute and attracting a variety of odd birds and stray animals. According to the stage directions: "Various birds of every hue and plumage appear amongst the branches of the trees, and carol in concert to his music; various wild beasts, apes, etc., also appear, and draw around Tamino, soothed and charmed by the magic spell of his flute." More than any other song, this charming aria gives the opera a storybook and magical setting. After playing the melody on his flute, he sings the same melody. The flute solo is interspersed throughout the song.

Wie stark ist nicht dein Zauberton!	How powerful is your magic sound,
weil, holde **Flöte**, durch dein Spielen	for through your play, sweet **flute**,
selbst **wilde** tiere Freude fühlen.	even **wild** beasts feel joy.
Doch, nur Pamina bleibt davon.	Yet Pamina stays away.
Pamina. Pamina, **höre mich!**	Pamina, Pamina, will you **hear me!**
Ha! das ist Papagenos Ton!	Ha! that is Papageno's call!
Vielleicht sah er **Pamina schon**,	Perhaps, he has already **seen Pamina**,
vielleicht eilt sie mit ihm zu mir,	perhaps, she hurries to me with him,
vielleicht führt mich der Ton zu ihr!	perhaps, the sound will lead me to her!

"Es lebe Sarastro, Sarastro soll leben!" (**"Long live Sarastro—Sarastro, hail to you!"**). Act I ends with an uplifting Masonic chorus of priests in honor of Sarastro. The message is similar to the final chorus in Fidelio—virtue and justice will make a paradise on earth. The chorus is accompanied by the sound of solemn trumpets and trombones. Sarastro appears in a chariot drawn by tame lions—perhaps, an example of Mozart's sense of humor. He is determined to break the power of the evil Queen. After comforting Pamina, he leads her to the temple door. The majestic chorus resembles a coronation or a grand mass.

Es **lebe Sarastro**, Sarastro soll leben!	Long **live Sarastro**—Sarastro, hail to you!
Er ist es, dem wir uns mit Freuden	To him it is we dedicate ourselves
ergeben!	with joy!
Stets mög er des Lebens als **Weiser**	May he forever, in his **wisdom**, enjoy
sich freun!	life's pleasure!
Er ist unser Abgott, dem alle sich	He is the idol to whom we dedicate
weihn!	ourselves!

Wenn Tugend und Gerechtigkeit	If virtue and righteousness strew
den **Großen Pfad** mit Ruhm bestreut,	the **Great Path** with fame,
dann ist die **Erd'** ein **Himmelreich**,	then the **Earth** will be a **heavenly kingdom**
und Sterbliche den **Göttern** gleich.	and mortals will be like **Gods**.

Act II

"O Isis und Osiris" ("O Isis and Osiris"). At the opening of Act II, the priests march solemnly from the temple to a palm grove accompanied by flutes, horns and trombones. The trombones add a solemn note to the song. Sarastro announces Tamino's candidacy for the Brotherhood. Sarastro and the priests pray to the Egyptian gods Isis and Osiris that Tamino and Papageno will endure the rituals of initiation. Sarastro's rich and deep bass voice provides majesty while the men's chorus echoes each of his thoughts. It is a grand, simple, and dignified song with a male chorus. The second half is especially melodic.

O Isis und Osiris, schenket	O Isis and Osiris, grant the spirit of
der **Weisheit** Geist dem **neuen Paar!**	**wisdom** to the **new pair!** You that
Die ihr der **Wandrer** Schritte lenket,	guide the **wanderers'** footsteps,
stärkt mit Geduld sie in Gefahr!	patiently **strengthen** them in danger!
Laßt sie der Prüfung **Früchte** sehen;	Let them see the **fruits** of their trial;
doch **sollten** sie zu **Grabe** gehen,	but **should** they go to their **grave**, reward
so lohnt der Tugend kühnen Lauf,	them the bold course of their virtue, and
nehmt sie in euren Wohnsitz auf!	take them up into your dwelling place!

"Der Hölle Rache kocht in meinem Herzen" ("The vengeance of Hell boils in my heart"). The Queen is in a hysterical rage and she is calling for vengeance. She instructs her daughter to kill Sarastro. It is an intense display of dramatic expression and a sensational coloratura (rapid runs and trills) aria. It is a very difficult aria requiring a very high but controlled voice. It requires a strong voice with a wide range and forceful and dramatic delivery. It requires a very high pitch throughout that many sopranos cannot perform. The outstanding and flexible coloratura passages provide a great display of passionate anger and strong conviction.

Der **Hölle** Rache kocht **in meinem Herzen**; Tod und Verzweiflung **flammet** um mich her!	The vengeance of **Hell** boils **in my heart**; death and despair **flame** around me!
Fühlt nicht durch dich Sarastro Todesschmerzen, so bist du **meine Tochter** nimmermehr!	If you do not make Sarastro feel a painful death, you will be **my daughter** no more!
Verstoßen sei auf ewig, verlassen sei auf ewig, zertrümmert sei auf ewig alle	Outcast forever and abandoned, destroyed forever be all **bonds** of **nature**—

Bande der **Natur**—wenn nicht durch
dich Sarastro wird erblassen! **Hört!**
Rachengötter! Hört der **Mutter** Schwur!

if Sarastro does not perish through you!
Hear me, gods of vengeance! Hear a
mother's vow!

"In diesen heil'gen Hallen" ("In those sacred halls"). In this sacred and hymn-like song, Sarastro tells Pamina that he forgives her mother's call for vengeance. As he puts it, "A helping hand, rather than revenge, is what distinguishes man." Sarastro's deep bass voice conveys paternal warmth in a very stately and noble sound. It expresses his humanistic creed that love can overcome vengeance. It is a song of great beauty, reflection and dignity. The final notes require Sarastro to reach for his lowest register. The strings provide elegant support in counterpoint (combining musical lines at the same time) to his voice, and take over the melody when his voice reaches its lowest depth.

In diesen heil'gen **Hallen**
kennt man die Rache nicht,
und ist ein **Mensch gefallen,**
führt Liebe ihn zur Pflicht.
Dann wandelt er an **Freundes Hand,**
vergnügt und froh ins **bessre Land.**

Wen solche Lehren nicht erfreun,
verdienet nicht, ein Mensch zu sein.

In those sacred **halls**
we know no revenge,
and when a **man has fallen,**
love comes to his rescue.
Then a **friend's hand** will lead him
satisfied and happy into a **better land.**

Who is not joyed by such teaching
is not worthy to be called man.

"Ach, ich fühl's, es ist entschwunden" ("Alas, I feel that all is vanished"). Tamino has taken a vow of silence as a test of his worthiness. Pamina, who is unaware of his vow, feels rejected when Tamino will not answer her. She is overcome with sorrow and contemplates death because she thinks that Tamino no longer loves her. The delicate orchestra accompaniment helps to express her grief. She repeats her plea several times to the silent Tamino before expressing her yearning for peace in death. (See "Ach, ich fuhl's, es ist entschwunden" in Part II for vocal skills.)

Ach, **ich fühl**'s, es ist entschwunden,
ewig hin der **Liebe** Glück, mein ganzes
Glück. **Nimmer kommt** ihr,
Wonnestunden, **meinem Herzen** mehr
zurück! **Sieh,** Tamino, **diese Tränen
fließen,** Trauter, dir allein;
fühlst du nicht der Liebe Sehnen,
so wird Ruh' im Tode sein.

Alas, **I feel** that all is vanished, finished is
love's happiness, my total bliss. **Never**
will you **come,** hours of enchantment,
back again unto **my heart!**
See, Tamino, see **these tears
flow,** beloved, for you alone;
if you do not feel love's longing,
then my peace must be in death.

"Ein Mädchen oder Weibchen" ("A maiden or a little wife"). Papageno has just learned from the High Priest that he failed to pass the Brotherhood rituals. He's prepared to settle for a sweetheart or wife. After a glass of wine, Papageno bursts into a song in praise of love. A glockenspiel (an instrument

with a series of graduated metal bars) in the orchestra creates the sound of
Papageno's magic bells. It is a pretty song with the bell-like sounds occurring
between the verses. At the end, Papageno shakes his bells and discovers, much
to his disappointment, that his reward is not a young sweetheart but an ugly
old woman.

Ein Mädchen oder **Weibchen**	**A maiden** or a little **wife**
wünscht Papageno sich!	is Papageno's **wish!**
O, so ein sanftes Täubchen	Oh such a gentle dove
wär' Seligkeit für mich!	would be my bliss!
Wird keine mir **Liebe** gewähren,	If none will grant me **love**, then **the**
so muß mich **die Flamme** verzehren,	**flame** of desire will consume me;
doch küßt' mich ein weiblicher Mund—	but if I get a woman's kiss,
so bin ich schon wieder gesund.	I shall be happy and well again.

   "Heil sei euch Geweihten!" ("Hail to the initiated!"). Tamino and
Pamina have passed their trials of fire and water and are about to be united in
marriage. As they stand inside the Temple of the Sun, Sarastro tells how the
rays of the sun have driven away the night—meaning the Queen of the Night.
The final chorus is in the form of a noble hymn of thanks to Isis and Osiris.
The fairy tale ends with a triumphal chorus announcing the forces of good
have defeated the forces of evil. Tamino and Pamina are congratulated by the
cheerful chorus for achieving wisdom by exhibiting courage, fidelity and virtue.

Heil sei euch Geweihten!	**Hail** to you initiated!
Ihr dranget durch **Nacht**.	You pressed through the **night**.
Dank sei dir, Osiris.	**Thanks** to thee, Osiris,
Dank dir, Isis, gebracht!	Thanks to thee, oh Isis!
Es siegte die **Stärke**,	**Strength** has triumphed,
und **krönet** zum Lohn	and **crowns** as reward
die Schönheit und **Weisheit**	beauty and **wisdom**
mit ewiger Kron!'	with a crown eternal

PART II

Arias by Composer

The main purpose of Part II is to develop the listener's appreciation for memorable songs and the remarkable vocal skills required to express them. For example, many listeners can recognize the aria, "O mio babbino caro" from a commercial or the movie *A Room with a View*. However, few listeners could tell what the song is about or identify the vocal skills required to perform this lovely aria. In the song, Lauretta is pleading with her daddy (babbino) to receive his consent to marry; otherwise, she threatens to jump off a bridge and drown her sorrows. A skilled lyric soprano knows that she must produce a smooth and flowing (legato) melody ending on a soft (pianissimo) note so that Lauretta can win her father's sympathy. Knowledge of the setting and vocal skills helps the listener to appreciate the singer's performance.

This part provides an in-depth analysis of 62 outstanding arias by the 14 composers in Part I. The aria sheets are designed to help listeners develop a greater understanding and appreciation for the vocal skills required to sing these demanding arias. Each aria sheet is divided into three sections. The "Dramatic setting" explains the circumstances that motivated the character to express his or her thoughts and emotions. This section should help the listener to develop a contextual understanding and a sense of empathy for the character. The "Vocal requirements" describe the technical skills required of the singer to successfully convey the nuances of the song.

The "What to listen for" section focuses on how the singer should express certain words, phrases, and passages. This section also includes the original libretto text in an abbreviated form and the English translation. The libretto and translated passages have been condensed and selected to illustrate the

131

vocal demands required during each part of the aria. As in Part I, certain words are boldfaced to help the listener connect the English translation with the native language of the libretto.

It is advisable to read an aria page just prior to listening to the song. Listeners often find it difficult to listen for the words, especially in a foreign language, as they are being sung. Sung words are generally more difficult to recognize than spoken words, especially if the singer does not enunciate carefully. After reviewing the aria sheet, the listener may prefer to put it aside and concentrate on the vocal skills and character portrayal. Having studied the aria sheet in advance, the listener is now prepared to anticipate and appreciate the vocal artistry that distinguishes operatic voices. For example, after reviewing the aria page for *Celeste Aida*, the listener should be prepared to hear soft and vibrant high notes and frequent crescendos and diminuendos. The listener will also know when to expect these vocal fluctuations and what message they are meant to convey.

Note: CD opera highlights or complete recordings are ideal for accompanying the aria sheets. Numbered CD indexes make it easy to locate individual songs.

Verdi Arias

"Celeste Aida"
("Celestial Aida")
from *Aida*

Performed by Radamès (Commander)

Dramatic setting: Radamès, an army officer, has just been informed by the Egyptian High Priest that a commander will be chosen to fight the Ethiopians. He is alone in a large room of the palace when he sings about his desire to be chosen commander. If he can achieve military glory, it will serve as an offering of love for Aida, the Ethiopian slave.

Vocal requirements: This very demanding song is composed for a spinto tenor with lyric and dramatic ability. It requires the voice to be both brilliant and melodious at the same time. He must respond to dramatic trumpet sounds followed by legato sounding woodwinds and strings. His heroic notes express his wish for glory, and his soft notes are a desire for love. His voice must have the flexibility to respond to crescendos and diminuendos. He must be able to make a quick transition from a dazzling high note to a tender pianissimo.

What to listen for: The first section opens with Radamès dream-like wish to be chosen "warrior." After the call of trumpets, he speaks with growing enthusiasm of leading valiant men to victory. His voice will become softer and more tender when he refers to sweet Aida. The first section will end on a triumphal note of achieving victory for Aida.

Se quel **guerrier** io fossi!	If I were that **warrior**!
Se il **mio** sogno si avverasse!	If **my** dream could come true!
Un esercito di prodi	An army of valiant men

133

da me guidato ... e la **vittoria**...	led by me ... and **victory**...
e il **plauso** di Menfi tutta!	and the **approval** of all Memphis!

After the violins set the mood, Radamès will sing his love song *Celeste Aida*. This part is sung legato and piano to suggest her noble beauty. It also requires frequent crescendos and diminuendos. His reference to "light and flowers" calls for a pianissimo. His voice must suddenly blend with the sweet sounding woodwinds and strings.

Celeste Aida, **forma divina**,	**Celestial** Aida, **divine form**,
mistico serto di **luce** e **fior**;	**mystic** garland of **light** and **flowers**;
del mio pensiero tu sei **regina**,	you are the **queen** of my thought,
tu di mia vita sei lo **splendor**.	you are the **splendor** of my life.

Radamès expresses his tender love with the words "your beautiful blue skies..." He then links love to glory by referring to Aida's "royal crown" and "royal throne." After a vibrant high note, his voice must begin fading away to express a diminuendo with the words "in the sun." The "Celeste Aida" section is repeated. The ending suggests a dream-like ecstasy with soft sounding high notes. It is a difficult task and many tenors prefer to end on a heroic high note.

Il tuo bel cielo vorrei ridarti,	I would like to give you once more your
le dolce **brezze** del patrio **suol**,	beautiful blue skies, the sweet **breezes**
un **regal** serto sul crin posarti,	of your native **soil**, a **royal** crown
ergerti un **trono** vicino al **sol**.	to deck your brow, a royal **throne**
	for you, in the **sun**!

"Ritorna vincitor!"
("Return a victor!")
from *Aida*

Performed by Aida (Ethiopian slave)

Dramatic setting: The priests have led Radamès to the temple to receive his new title as Commander of the Egyptian army. The crowd and Aida cheer him on his way with the words "Return a victor!" She is horrified with her dilemma. If she supports Radamès and the Egyptians, she will betray her father's army and her Ethiopian homeland.

Vocal requirements: The song requires a large spinto soprano voice. It requires a very flexible voice with comfortable high and low ranges. Aida must express extreme intensity and violent contrasts, ranging from bliss to anguish.

The soprano must have a talent for conveying deep emotion and a skilled legato. Her large voice must express despair and a feeling of helplessness. Her melodious sound must blend with the orchestral accompaniment.

What to listen for: Aida sings the words "Ritorna vincitor" with horror and agitation as she realizes that she has committed an act of betrayal. The words "Victorious over my father" cause her to become more intense and horrified. The following phrases become faster and louder as she contemplates the blood of her countrymen and her father in chains.

Ritorna **vincitor**!	**Return** a victor!
E dal mio labbro	My lips have spoken
uscì l'empia parola!	the traitorous words!
Vincitor del **padre mio**,	Victorious over **my father**,
di lui che impugna l'**armi** per me...	who takes up **arms** for me...

In the second section, Aida prays to the gods to forgive her words and to support her father's enemies. As soon as she prays for the oppressors to be destroyed, she retreats and condemns her own words. The third section introduces a beautiful melody with "And my love." The voice is legato and ascends on the high notes. The words "this fervent love" rise to an intense crescendo. Aida sings a pure love song as she recalls Radamès.

E l'amor mio?	And my love?
Dunque scordar poss'io	Can I forget then
questo **fervido amore**	this **fervent love**
che, **oppressa** e **schiava**	which, **oppressed** and **enslaved**
come **raggio di sol**	so I was, like a **ray of sunshine**
qui mi beava?	made me happy here?

The fourth section is a feeling of hopelessness broken into anguished fragments. It is sung legato with animation. The words "in deep darkness..." express Aida's extreme misery. She asks the gods to "have pity on my suffering!" The final section is soft and requires a pure and clear tone. She surrenders herself and is ready to die. As in Radamès' aria, "Celeste Aida," her voice must seem to fade away in a prayer-like sound.

In notte cupa la **mente** è perduta	My **mind** is lost in deep darkness
e nell'ansia **crudel** vorrei morir.	and because of this **cruel** anguish I wish to
Numi, **pietà** del **mio soffrir**!	die. Gods, have **pity** on **my suffering**!

"O patria mia"
("Oh my homeland")
from *Aida*

Performed by Aida (Ethiopian slave)

Dramatic setting: Aida is waiting for Radamès along the moonlit Nile River. If he does not appear, she plans to drown herself in the river and never again see her beloved homeland. She expresses her anguish and yearning before singing a lovely hymn to her beloved homeland.

Vocal requirements: The song requires a soprano voice capable of expressing sensitive and shining vocal lines. The voice should resemble a light vibrating string. It should sound light and tender, sweet and sad, and convey a mood of nostalgia and hopelessness. The high but soft pianissimos are sung tenderly in a mood of sweet resignation. The vocal lines call for great beauty and tenderness.

What to listen for: The opening recitative is very important for setting the mood for the song. In a somber voice, Aida expresses her willingness to drown herself in the Nile if Radamès bids her farewell. The oboe introduces the title line "O patria mia..." with a pastoral melody. A violin motif creates a moonlit scene along the Nile. The title sets the aria's somber mood of yearning without hope. The words "mai più" are almost murmured with a sense of despair. Aida's voice takes on a serene and weightless sound as she describes her homeland.

O patria mia, mai più ti rivedro.	Oh my homeland, I shall never see you again.
O cieli azzuri,	Oh blue skies,
o **dolce** aure **native**	oh **soft native** breezes,
dove **sereno**	where shone the
il mio matin brillò...	**serene** morning of my life...

In the second verse, Aida expresses her longing for her homeland more strongly. Her voice remains tender and light, but the tempo and intensity increase slightly by referring to the day of return she was promised. This brief verse gives her a chance to express a peaceful longing after her initial words of despair in the first verse.

O **fresche valli**,	Oh **fresh valleys, blessed,**
o **queto** asil beato,	**peaceful** haven,

che un dì **promesso**	which one day **promised** me
dall'**amor** mi fu...	by **love**...

There is a soft sadness with the words "the dream of love is gone..." The orchestra helps to create a sensitive touch with a return reference to "oh my homeland." The voice shows great emotion and rises to a crescendo followed by a pianissimo with the words "mai più." The voice must ascend to a high C without changing the mood of tender hopelessness. The final phrase consists of two pure high A pianissimos. She must now express a somber belief in approaching death with no hope of returning to her homeland.

Or che d'**amore** il sogno	Now that the dream of **love**
è dileguato, **o patria mia,**	is gone, **oh my homeland,**
mai più ti rivedrò...	I shall never see you again...

"Caro nome"
("Dear name")
from *Rigoletto*

Performed by Gilda (Rigoletto's daughter)

Dramatic setting: Rigoletto tries to protect his innocent daughter by keeping her at home. She recently observed a young man in church who was attracted to her. He has managed to enter Gilda's secluded garden and declare his love. After he leaves, she sings a song of adoration and devotion dedicated to his "dear name."

Vocal requirements: This famous song is very demanding because it requires exceptional coloratura (decorative and high pitched trills) ability. It calls for a young, innocent, and crystal clear sounding soprano voice. The high notes and coloraturas are meant to express a young girl's ecstasy at discovering her first love. The cadenzas (highly skilled passages) must be sung with a radiant beauty and legato (smooth and melodic) voice.

What to listen for: The song begins with Gilda's radiant voice against a background of soaring flutes. The first few lines are expressed with pleasure and like a long sigh. A young man has just declared his love for her and revealed his name.

Gualtier Maldè—	Gualtier Maldè—
nome di lui si amato,	**name** of the one so loved,
ti scolpisci nel core innamorato.	you engraved yourself on my lovesick heart.

The title of the song, "Caro nome," is sung piano (softly) and legato with the violins providing a short motif (theme) to express the ecstasy of her first love. The word "caro" is sung with a crescendo of expression. The following trills call for a very light and bright voice.

Caro nome che il **mio cor**	Dear name which first
festi primo **palpitar,**	made **my heart palpitate,**
le **delizie** dell'amor	you will always **remind** me
mi dêi sempre **rammentar.**	of love's **delights.**

The phrases become longer as Gilda refers to her "desire." The cadenza ends with a diminuendo (voice becomes softer) suggesting Gilda's sweet devotion to the dear name. The last cadenza reaches a high C. Gilda must express the high notes with a radiant beauty without changing her pure character. The crescendo and decrescendo (vocal ascent and descent) require a clear and legato sound.

Col pensier il mio **desir**	With every thought my **desire**
a te sempre volerà,	will always fly to you,
e fin l'**ultimo** sospir	and even my **last** breath,
caro nome, tuo sarà.	dear name, shall be yours.

"La donna è mobile"
("Woman is [women are] fickle")
from *Rigoletto*

Performed by Duke of Mantua (seducer of women)

Dramatic setting: After seducing Gilda in his palace, the Duke is no longer interested in her. He is spending the night in an assassin's inn. The Duke is attracted to the assassin's sister. He sings about the faithlessness of women before going to bed. It is his way of justifying his own libertine (a person of loose morality) and irresponsible behavior.

Vocal requirements: This very popular song requires a lyric tenor with exceptional agility. He must be able to express a cheerful and carefree personality. He must be skilled at legato, bravura (passage of exceptional agility) and ornamental passages. At the end, he must sing a rapid and light cadenza (highly skilled passage) ending on a high B.

What to listen for: The first verse is cheerful, carefree, and elegant. After a short introduction to the melody, the tenor picks up the melody. In both verses of the song, the opening bars are sung almost staccato (pauses between notes) and bravura. The following bars are warmer and more legato. The voice bounces on the words "woman" and "feather." The voice becomes lighter and humorous when he refers to a woman's "thoughts." When he repeats the word, he will sing it with greater strength and vigor.

La **donna** è mobile,	The **women** are fickle,
qual **piuma** al vento	as a **feather** in the wind
muta d'**accento** e di pensiero.	she changes **speech** and thoughts.
Sempre un amabile, leggiadro viso,	A sweet, pretty face, in tears
in pianto o in riso è menzognero.	or in laughter is always untruthful.

The second verse has less boldness and is sung with a somewhat deeper voice and less bounce. The Duke is more restrained as he reflects on the fickleness, power, and danger of women. After the opening bars, the phrases become warmer and more melodious. The line referring to "who has not tasted her love" is sung pianissimo (very softly) and with some sympathy. The song ends with a carefree and cheerful cadenza. It should be sung rapidly and lightly and end on a high B note.

E sempre **misero**	He is always **miserable**
chi a lei s'affida	who trusts in her,
chi le **confida** mal **cauto** il **core!**	who **confides** his **cautious heart** to her!
Pur mai non sentesi felice appieno	Yet nobody feels fully contented
chi su quel seno non liba **amore!**	who has not tasted her love!
La donna è mobil...	The women are fickle...

"Ah, fors'è lui"
("Ah, perhaps he is the one")
from *La Traviata*

Performed by Violetta (courtesan)

Dramatic setting: Violetta lives a carefree life of pleasure, but suffers from consumption (tuberculosis). She faints at a party she is giving and a young admirer comes to her assistance. He offers her love and companionship. After her guests leave, she reflects on the young man's offer and weighs his love against her freedom.

Vocal requirements: The first part of the song calls for a beautiful lyric (smooth and melodic sound) soprano voice with great sensitivity and flexibility. The second part requires coloratura (ornamental and light passage) skill for the many runs and ringing high notes. The song has a dramatic dimension that expresses a variety of deep emotions, such as hope, hesitation, and sorrow. She must color and shape the inflections.

What to listen for: In the opening recitative, Violetta reflects on her emotions after encountering a young admirer. She starts softly as she contemplates her troubled soul. She expresses her uncertainty as she wonders whether a serious love would "be unfortunate for me?" Her voice grows in intensity as she considers love to her carefree lifestyle.

È **strano**! È strano!	It's **strange**! It's strange!
In core scolpiti ho quegli **accenti**!	In my heart, those words are **accented**!
Saria per me sventura un **serio amore**?	Would a **serious love** be unfortunate for me?
Che risolvi, o **turbata** anima mia?	What do you decide, my **troubled** soul?

The title line is expressed in a clear voice like an uplifting dream. Violetta's voice grows in confidence and reaches high A-flats on the words "tumulti" and "occulti." In the following lines, the joy of her new love reaches a crescendo of intensity. The second part of the aria begins with a reversal of thoughts as she views her fateful illness as a rejection of her dream. The coloratura runs that follow reflect the fast pace of her life.

Ah, fors'è lui che l'anima,	Ah, perhaps he is the one whom my soul,
solinga ne'**tumulti**,	lonely in **tumultuous** crowds,
godea sovente **pingere**	often imagined **painting**
de suoi **colori occulti**.	in **concealed colors**.

In the final part, she celebrates her freedom ("libera") to seek joy and pleasure. The singing is elegant and impulsive, consisting of alternating staccato and legato notes, light voiced trills and high C's. She has decided that a light-hearted lifestyle offers less risk.

Sempre **libera** degg'io	Forever **free** I shall frolic
follegiare di **gioja** in gioja,	from **joy** to joy,
vo'che scorra il viver mio	I want my life to run forever
pei sentieri del **piacer**.	in the paths of **pleasure**.

"Di Provenza il mar, il suol"
("The sea, the soil of Provence")
from *La Traviata*

Performed by Germont (father of Violetta's lover)

Dramatic setting: Germont has succeeded in ending the romance between Violetta, whom he regards as a dangerous woman, and his son Alfredo. He tries to relieve Alfredo's grief with radiant memories of his childhood home in Provence. It begins like a father's lullaby.

Vocal requirements: This aria requires a baritone with a smooth, warm and legato (smooth and melodic) sound. Germont's intervention was the cause of his son's broken romance, and now he must convey a sympathetic, sincere, and a very intense desire to relieve his son's suffering. The song has a beautiful melody but, after the father leaves, it fails to relieve his son's sorrow.

What to listen for: The soft and brief orchestral introduction creates a nostalgic mood. The opening lines emphasize a vocal softness and lightness in their reference to Provence. There is a strong accent on the words "heart" and "destiny" as he addresses his grieving son.

Di Provenza il mar, il **suol**,	The sea, the **soil** of Provence,
chi dal cor ti cancellò?	who has removed them from your heart?
Al **natio** fulgente sol,	From your **native** land and splendid sunshine,
qual **destino** ti furò?	what **destiny** stole you away?

In a soft voice, he reminds him peace "can still shine upon you." The voice becomes more majestic with the word "splendere." The line "God guided me here!" is repeated religiously and triumphantly.

Oh **rammenta** pur nel duol	Oh, **remember** in your sorrow
ch'ivi gioja a te brillò,	that there joy shone for you,
e che **pace** colà sol	and that there alone can you find **peace**
su te **splendere** ancor può.	and can still **shine** upon you.
Dio mi guidò!	**God guided** me here!

The third stanza follows the same pattern as the second. Germont tries to reach his son's heart by expressing strong sincerity and a crescendo (vocal climax) of emotion. He hopes that his plea will succeed when he refers twice to his son's "voice of honor." His closing reference to God is repeated slowly in a warm voice descending to a soft ending (diminuendo).

Ma se al fin ti trovo ancor,	But if at last I have found you again,
se in me speme non **fallì**,	if my hope did not **fail** me,
se la **voce** dell'**onor**	if the **voice** of **honor**
in te appien non ammutì,	is not totally silent in you,
Dio m'esaudì.	God has answered my prayer.

"Il balen del suo sorriso" ("The radiance of her smile")
from *Il Trovatore*

Performed by Count di Luna (young noble)

Dramatic setting: The Count di Luna is in love with Leonora, but she loves the knight Manrico. After a battle with the Count, Leonora assumes Manrico is dead, and she enters a convent dressed in robes. The Count confesses his love for Leonora to his faithful captain and sings a tribute to her beauty.

Vocal requirements: The song calls for a large Verdi baritone voice. The Count should have a full and resounding voice, especially in the upper range. He must demonstrate flexibility and a command of soft, high tones and lightness in the staccato (brief pauses) notes. It is a romantic cantilena (flowing and sustained) of great beauty that expresses admiration, devotion, and affection.

What to listen for: After a short string prelude, the Count begins his recitative (introductory lines) in a silent and empty cloister. In a slow voice, he tells how the death of his rival seemed to have removed every obstacle to winning Leonora. He expresses anger and scorn to find she has devoted herself to a convent altar. With an outburst of lyrical determination and passion, he announces, "Leonora is mine!"

Spento il **rival**,	With the dead **rival**,
caduto ogni **ostacol** sembrava	every **obstacle** to my wishes
a'miei desiri.	appeared to have been removed.
Novello e più **possente**	A **new** and more **powerful** one

ella ne appresta,	she is preparing,
l'**altare**...	the **altar**...

The aria is introduced by repeating the string prelude followed by a silence. This provides a mood of devotion and affection. The slow tempo (speed) helps the Count to express his deep feelings in an elegant and legato (smooth and melodic) voice. He refers to her radiant smile and beautiful face with vocal flexibility and control of the soft and high tones.

Il balen del suo sorriso	The radiance of her smile
d'una **stella** vince il raggio;	could capture the rays of a **star**;
il fulgor del suo **bel** viso	the radiance of her **beautiful** face
novo infonde a me **coraggio**.	inspires me with **new courage**.

The final part calls for a strong and resounding voice, especially in the upper range. He expresses the calming effect of her glance with a diminuendo. The final lines are repeated with increased accentuation, a full-voiced cadenza (highly skilled passage), and forceful release of his passion.

Ah! l'**amor** ond'ardo	Ah! may the **love** which burns within me
le favelli in **mio favor**,	plead to her in **my favor**,
sperda il sole d'un suo **sguardo**	may the sunshine of one **glance** of hers
la **tempesta** del mio cor!	calm the **tempest** in my heart!

"D'amor sull'ali rosee" ("On love's rosy wings")
from *Il Trovatore*

Performed by Leonora (noble lady)

Dramatic setting: Leonora is at the base of a castle tower where her lover is being held prisoner. She pledges her love, and hopes that her voice will reach and comfort him. She seeks to awaken him to memories of their love without revealing the pain in her heart.

Vocal requirements: This song requires a lirico-spinto soprano with an excellent legato (smooth flowing and melodic sound) and great dramatic strength. Leonora must express trill phrases with crescendos and decrescendos (vocal increases and decreases in volume). She must demonstrate vocal flexibility, refinement, and a variety of feelings, including sweetness and sadness. A crystal-clear pianissimo (very soft sound) will introduce her high A note.

What to listen for: To introduce her aria, Leonora's recitative states that she is close to her lover in the dark night. In a slow and somber voice, she adds that he doesn't know she is near. In a gentle and sweet tone, she asks the "plaintive breeze" to carry her sighs to her lover. Her voice is crystal-clear with her pianissimo as she makes her request.

In quest'**oscura notte** ravvolta presso a te son io, e tu nol sai! Gemente aura, che intorno spiri, deh, **pietosa** gli arreca i miei sospiri!	Wrapped in this **dark night,** you do not know that I am close to you! Plaintive breeze that sighs around me, ah, bring to him my **pitiful** sighs!

The aria is adagio (slow) and the notes are often tied together to create a flow and continuity. The opening lines have a gentle continuity. Trills are integrated early in the aria to add expression to the words. For example, the words "sorrowful sigh" contain a trill and end on a pianissimo (the voice diminishes to a soft tone). A pianissimo is used to introduce the high note in "conforta..."

D'**amor** sull'ali **rosee** vanne, sospir dolente, del **prigioniero misero** **conforta** l'egra **mente**...	On **love's rosy** wings fly, sorrowful sigh, **comfort** the **miserable prisoner's** ailing **mind**...

Leonora turns more hopeful. In addition to a bright trill, each phrase contains a crescendo and decrescendo. The phrase "to the dreams of love" concludes with an excellent legato. The song ends with Leonora telling the breeze not to reveal "the pains of my heart!" to her lover. There is a feeling of sorrow in her voice, but her beauty of tone is present to the end.

...com'aura di speranza aleggia in quella stanza, lo desta alle **memorie,** ai sogni dell'**amor!**	...like a breeze of hope that lingers in that room, awaken him to the **memories,** to the dreams of **love!**

Rossini Arias

"Largo al factotum della città!" ("Make way for the handyman of the city!") from *Il Barbiere di Siviglia*

Performed by Figaro (town barber)

Dramatic setting: On his way to work, Figaro pauses to express the beautiful nature of his occupation. With the accompaniment of his guitar, he celebrates his ability to provide an important daily service to the residents of his town. He ends by applauding his success.

Vocal requirements: This song calls for a lyric baritone with a ringing sound and the ability to sing rapid passages. Dramatic baritones also sing this aria. It expresses an outburst of happiness that must capture Figaro's cheerful, lighthearted, and self-congratulatory nature. The rapid tempo (speed) should not obscure the diction or the cheerful spirit.

What to listen for: Figaro expresses his joyful and humorous nature with his opening words "Make way for the factotum (a person with many skills) as he walks down an empty street. He sings about his "lovely life" and "great pleasure" with elegance. "Ah, Bravo..." is sung in full voice and reaches a high A note on bravo (an expression of praise).

Largo al factotum della **città**!	Make way for the handyman of the **city**!
Ah che bel vivere,	Ah what a lovely life,

che bel **piacere**,	what great **pleasure**,
per un **barbiere di qualità**!	for a **barber of quality**!
Ah bravo, Figaro, bravissimo!	Ah bravo, Figaro, bravissimo!

Figaro's reference to "razors and combs" reflects the precise efficiency of a skilled barber. He often adds a sequence of "lala ran la..." to keep the song moving at a fast pace and to express his enthusiasm.

...vita più **nobile**, no, non si dà.	...a more **noble** life can indeed not be found.
Rasori e pettini, **lancette** e forbici,	**Razors** and combs, **lancets** and scissors,
al **mio comando** tutto qui sta.	everything is here at **my command**.

There is a joy in his voice as he speaks of his profits as a messenger between lovers, ladies and gentlemen. In the next section, Figaro impersonates the different callers who seek his assistance. He lists them in rapid succession without taking a breath and finally calls his own name. He even pleads for mercy pretending to be overcome by their demands.

Figaro su, Figaro giù!	Figaro up, Figaro down!
Figaro qua, Figaro là!	Figaro here, Figaro there!
Pronto, prontissimo,	**Fast, faster**,
son come il fulmine...	I am like a thunderbolt...

His voice becomes stronger and more sustained when he repeats the words "I am the factotum of the city." The words are sung with pride and brilliance with a high G note.

"Una voce poco fa"
("A voice just now")
from *Il Barbiere di Siviglia*

Performed by Rosina (clever young woman)

Dramatic setting: Rosina is alone in her guardian's house reflecting on the voice that serenaded her and touched her heart. She speaks of her suitor's love and how she will outsmart and escape from her elderly and jealous guardian. She holds a letter she will try to send to her suitor. The song reveals her charming personality and determination to succeed.

Vocal requirements: The song calls for a young sounding soprano with sparkle and wit. Rosina must reveal two faces: charm and a sweet legato in the first part and a strong will power in the second half. The coloraturas and cadenzas (highly skilled passages) should not detract from the elegance and beauty of tone. She must convey good humor and a friendly sympathy.

What to listen for: Rosina begins in a warm and intimate mood as she thinks aloud. She sings piano (softly) and a lovely legato (a smooth melodic phrase). She is pleased and somewhat puzzled by the new emotion in her heart. There is a sigh of delight before referring to how the voice "touched my very heart." She mentions her suitor, who sang beneath her balcony, with deep affection and some timidity.

Una voce poco fa	**A voice** just now,
qui nel cor mi risuonò,	has touched my very heart.
il **mio cor** ferito è già,	**My heart** has already been pierced,
e Lindor fu che il piagò.	and it was Lindor who hurled the dart.

There is a quiet firmness and a feeling of love when she repeats Lindor's (her suitor's) name. Rosina expresses great confidence when she states that she has sworn to succeed. At this point, there is a change of notes as Rosina expresses her ability to handle her guardian.

Il tutor ricuserò,	My guardian won't consent,
io l'ingegno aguzzerò,	but I will sharpen my wits,
alla fin s'accheterà,	and at last, he will relent,
e **contenta** io resterò.	and I shall be **content**.

A moderato interlude precedes the second part. Rosina begins by sounding obedient and submissive. She is no longer sentimental as she dedicates herself to preparing her freedom and a happy ending. Suddenly, Rosina's second face appears as she warns that she can become a viper and lay a hundred traps. She relies on coloraturas and cadenzas to express her wit and charm. The song ends with an outstanding bravura (vocal brilliance).

Io sono **docile**, son **rispettosa**,	I am **docile**, I am **respectful**,
son **obbediente**, dolce, **amorosa**.	I am **obedient**, gentle, **loving**.

"La calunnia è un venticello" ("Slander is a little breeze")
from *Il Barbiere di Siviglia*

Performed by Don Basilio (music teacher)

Dramatic setting: Rosina's elderly guardian, Doctor Bartolo, hopes to marry her. He is worried about a young man who has attracted her attention. He has asked Rosina's music teacher, Don Basilio, to help get rid of Rosina's suitor. Basilio explains how he will use slander (calumny) to destroy the young man's reputation.

Vocal requirements: The song calls for a bass-baritone with the ability to speak very rapidly. He must be able to imitate the frightening power of slander, including an explosion of hatred at the end. This skillful composition requires pianissimos, crescendos and fortissimos (very loud passages). The song also requires legato and staccato (brief pauses between notes) passages.

What to listen for: The song builds suspense by beginning piano and slowly reaching a crescendo. The title "La calunnia" is sung legato followed by short staccato interruptions in the second line. The first five lines are meant to blend and suggest a gentle breeze. The short pauses after "insensibly" and "subtly" suggest pauses in the breeze, and the words "commences to whisper" are sung staccato.

La **calunnia** è un venticello,	**Slander** is a little breeze,
un'auretta assai **gentile**,	a **gentle** breeze,
che **insensibile, sottile,**	which **insensibly, subtly,**
leggermente, dolcemente,	lightly and sweetly
incomincia a susurrar.	**commences** to whisper.

The following short phrases are instrumentally accompanied to create the sound of spreading gossip. This leads to the first crescendo (increase in volume). A series of waves follow with a legato flow. The expectation of gossip returns with the words "From the mouth..." A growing crescendo reaches a climax as the gossip flies "from place to place..."

Dalla bocca fuori uscendo	From the mouth it emerges,
lo schiamazzo va **crescendo**,	the noise grows in **crescendo**,
prende **forza** a poco a poco,	gathers **force** little by little,
vola già di **loco** in **loco**...	runs it course from **place** to **place**...

The sound should be very rhythmical with a sense of legato. The music seems to explode in strength with two fortissimos on a "canon shot." References to "a tremor" and "a thunderstorm" should have a legato sound. Don Basilio expresses scorn for the victim of slander. There is a sound of cruelty and satisfaction as the victim has been trampled and destroyed.

Alla fin trabocca e scoppia,	In the end it overflows and breaks out,
si propaga, si **raddoppia**	it spreads, it **redoubles**
e **produce un'esplosione**	and **produces an explosion**
come un colpo di **cannone,**	like a **cannon** shot,
un **tremoto**, un temporale...	a **tremor**, a thunderstorm...

Puccini Arias

"Che gelida manina!"
("What a cold little hand!")
from *La Bohème*

Performed by Rodolfo (romantic poet)

Dramatic setting: Rodolfo is alone in his cold attic when his neighbor, Mimì, knocks on the door. She needs a light for her candle. She drops her key in his cold and dark room. He pretends to be looking for it when he touches her cold hand. As he tries to warm her hands, he tells her about his dreams and how her eyes have made his dreams disappear.

Vocal requirements: The song requires a strong lyric tenor with a compassionate and poetic personality. Rodolfo must convey a youthful, cheerful, somewhat boastful and romantic character. The dynamics will require transitions from piano to forte (soft to loud) and forte to an affectionate pianissimo (a very soft note). The building tension will require a famous high C note.

What to listen for: The first part begins pianissimo as Rodolfo offers to help warm Mimì's cold hand. His voice ascends to an A note as he questions the need to keep searching for her key. In the moonlight interlude, he refers to the "moonlit night" to encourage their closeness.

Che gelida manina,	What a cold little hand,
se la lasci riscaldar.	let me warm it for you.
Cercar che giova?	What's the use of searching?
Al buio non si trova.	It can't be found in the dark.
Ma per **fortuna** è **notte di luna**...	But **fortunately** it is a **moonlit night**...

In the second part, Rodolfo reveals who he is and expresses his growing affection for Mimì. He tells her, with pride in his voice, that he is a poet with a "delight in poverty." But in his dreams, he has the soul of a millionaire. The word "milionaria" is expressed with a broad enthusiasm and warmth. As the melody becomes more passionate, he prepares to release his vocal tension on a high note.

In **povertà** mia lieta	I delight in **poverty**
scialo da **gran signore**	I pretend to be a **bold gentleman** of
rime ed inni d'**amore**.	**rhymes** and songs of **love**.
Per sogni e per chimere	When it comes to hopes and dreams
e per **castelli in aria**...	and **castles in air**...
l'anima ho **milionaria**.	I have the soul of a **millionaire**.

He flatters Mimì by comparing her beautiful eyes to two thieves who have stolen his jewels or dreams. He declares in a warm and close voice, "The theft does not discourage me." This line allows Rodolfo to prepare for his famous high C note in the following line. His voice becomes more radiant as he releases his high C note with the words "dolce speranza!" (sweet hope). This is followed by a friendly request for Mimì to tell who she is. The request ends the song with an affectionate pianissimo.

Ma il furto non m'accora poichè	But the theft does not discourage me because
v'ha preso stanza la dolce speranza!	the empty space is filled with sweet hope!

"Mi chiamano Mimì"
("They call me Mimì")
from *La Bohème*

Performed by Mimì (embroiderer)

Dramatic setting: In his cold attic, Rodolfo has just sung to Mimì about who he is, his dreams, and her beautiful eyes. After asking her to introduce herself, she sings about her simple and lonely life. She likes to embroider flowers and loves sunlight and spring flowers. They have fallen in love and they leave the attic arm-in-arm to join his friends.

Vocal requirements: This song requires a lyric (smooth and melodic) soprano who can convey a simple sincerity and modesty. In a sweet legato voice, Mimì expresses her cheerful and contented personality. After her shy introduction, Mimì becomes more vibrant, passionate, and charming as she looks forward to spring. She sings with simplicity and without adornment.

What to listen for: The tempo begins very slowly. In the opening lines, Mimì states that "They call me Mimì," but she stresses that her real name is Lucia. She describes her work with a simple sincerity and speaks of her embroidering with modesty. In an effort to impress Rodolfo, she becomes more lyrical as she describes herself as "happy."

Mi chiamano Mimì,	They call me Mimì,
ma il **mio nome** è Lucia.	but **my name** is Lucia.
La **storia** mia è **breve**.	My **story** is **brief**.
A tela o a seta	On canvas or on silk, I embroider
ricamo in **casa** e fuori.	at **home** or outside. I am **tranquil**
Son **tranquilla** e lieta,	and happy, and my pastime
ed è mio svago far gigli e **rose**.	is making lilies and **roses**.

The pace increases as she describes the things she likes. There is enjoyment and lightness in her voice when she mentions "primavere" (spring). To draw closer to Rodolfo, she reveals that she, too, has dreams of things "called poetry." The melody and her passion grow in intensity as she praises the beauty of spring.

Mi piaccion quelle cose	I like those things
che han si dolce malìa	that have such sweet magic,
che parlano d'**amor**,	that talk of **love**,
di **primavere**, che parlano	of **spring**, that talk
di sogni e di chimere,	of dreams and fancies,
quelle cose che han nome **poesia**.	those things that are called **poetry**.

Her words come more quickly and a sweet legato as she tells how she lives alone and often prays to the Lord. There is a silence as she looks at Rodolfo for the first time in their arias. Her shyness melts and her voice becomes more passionate as she mentions the approaching "thaw" and "the first sunrays are mine!" She repeats these words with intense emotion. She ends her aria with an apologetic good-bye for disturbing him.

Ma quando vien lo sgelo	But when the thaw comes
Il primo **sole** e **mio**!	the first **sunrays** are **mine**!

"Quando me'n vo soletta"
(When I walk alone)
from *La Bohème*

Performed by Musetta (flirtatious woman)

Dramatic setting: Mimì, Rodolfo and his three roommates, including the painter Marcello, are at a sidewalk café to celebrate Christmas Eve. Marcello's former girlfriend, Musetta, has arrived with an elderly admirer. She tries to regain Marcello's affection by misbehaving and then singing this famous waltz. She sings about how her beauty attracts attention.

Vocal requirements: This famous song requires a lyric soprano with an outstanding legato (sweet flowing) and velvety voice. She must use a variety of inflections from phrase to phrase to convey charm, warmth, sensuous appeal, seductiveness, and temptation. The singer must resort to constant shading, coloring, and changing of pace to reflect Musetta's many moods.

What to listen for: When her former lover ignores her, Musetta sings this famous waltz to make him jealous. The tempo (speed) changes many times to reflect her vocal inflections and seductive devices. The title line calls for a perfect legato and smooth voice. The next line is slower because "people stop and look." She refers to "my beauty" with legato and pride. Again, Musetta slows down when she refers to how people look for the beauty "in me."

Quando me'n vo **soletta**	When I walk **alone**
per la via,	on the street,
la gente sosta e **mira**,	people stop to **look**,
e la **bellezza mia**	and **my beauty**
tutta ricerca in me,	is looked for in me,
da capo al piè.	looked for from head to toe.

She sings about her irresistible charms and conquests. The words "desire surrounds me" are prolonged to prepare for a forte and repeat of "makes me happy." Marcello is listening but trying to ignore her with his back turned.

Così l'effluvio del **desio**	Thus the onrush of **desire**
tutta m'aggira	surrounds me completely,
felice mi fa.	and it makes me happy.

At this point, she directs her words to Marcello who has become more agitated. The line "And you who know" refers to her past affair with Marcello as she turns to look at him. The lines that follow and conclude the aria are meant to appeal and tempt Marcello. Musetta expresses her sensuous appeal with beauty and elegance without sounding shrill. Musetta succeeds in charming her audience and winning back her lover as they leave arm-in arm. The waltz melody is reprised after Marcello and Musetta decide to reunite.

E tu che sai	And you who know,
che **memorie** ti struggi	who **remember** and suffer,
da me tanto rifuggi?	do you avoid me so?

"Recondita armonia"
("Hidden harmony")
from *Tosca*

Performed by Mario Cavaradossi (painter)

Dramatic setting: Cavaradossi is painting a large picture of Mary Mag-
dalena in a church in Rome. He has painted her with blue eyes and golden
hair because of a woman who prays near his scaffold. He stops painting and
reaches into his pocket to look at a medallion of his lover, Tosca, who has dark
eyes and hair.

Vocal requirements: This song calls for a lyric tenor who can express a
youthful passion and enthusiasm. He must sing with vibrant and vital energy.
The song requires crescendo-decrescendo (growing-diminishing) pairings. It
must be sung as a reflection that expresses his love for Tosca. His pleasure and
happiness will peak with a B note.

What to listen for: Cavaradossi begins by expressing his happiness with
ease and without haste. The dynamics are marked pianissimo. To make the
words sound beautiful, the vowels are sung with love. Cavaradossi accents Flo-
ria Tosca's physical characteristics by stressing the consonants in "bruna" and
"ardente." Ardente is expressed with tenderness. His description of Magadalena
is expressed in lyrical and bright tones.

Recondita **armonia**	Hidden **harmony**
di **belleze diverse!**	of **contrasting beauties!**
E **bruna** Floria,	Floria is a **brunette**,
l'**ardente** amante **mia**;	**my ardent** mistress;
e te, beltade ignota,	and you, mysterious woman,
cinta di chiome **bionde!**	are crowned with **blond** hair!

When he compares their blue and dark eyes, he shifts from clear to darker
tones. He expresses this comparison with pleasure and delight. He sings of the
mystery of art in an easy voice and as a restful moment.

Tu azzuro hai l'occhio,	You have blue eyes,
Tosca ha l'occhio nero!	Tosca's eyes are dark!
L'**arte** nel suo **mistero**	By the **mysteries** of **art**
le diverse bellezze insiem confonde...	contrasting beauties are mixed together...

There are crescendos-decrescendos when he sings about "paint her portrait" and "my only thought." The line "my only thought is of you" is sung

forte (loud) with a sustained "you." There is a bravura (exceptional vocal agility) on the two notes of "Tos-ca" and the voice reaches a high B note. The last notes are sustained.

...ma nel ritrar costei	...as I paint her portrait
il **mio solo** pensiero	**my only** thought,
ah! il mio sol pensier	ah! my only thought
sei **tu**, Tosca, sei tu!	is of **you**, Tosca, of you!

"Vissi d'arte"
("I lived by art")
from *Tosca*

Performed by Tosca (singer)

Dramatic setting: Tosca is experiencing deep anguish because her lover has been led away in chains to be tortured. The cruel police chief is trying to seduce her in exchange for her lover's freedom. She is bewildered and distraught as to why she must endure this terrible injustice because she is a caring and religious person. She wonders why the Lord has abandoned her.

Vocal requirements: This song requires a dramatic soprano capable of expressing religious devotion and distress over her unjust situation. Tosca must progress from piano, legato (smooth and flowing passage) and intense feeling to a moment of great vocal power, including a majestic crescendo (voice rises to a climax) and an intense B note.

What to listen for: The beginning dynamics (volume) is pianissimo (very soft voice) with intense feeling and very legato. There is a feeling of sincere devotion in Tosca's voice because she has lived for art, love, and kindness toward others.

Vissi d'**arte**,	I lived by **art**,
vissi d'**amore**,	I lived by **love**,
non feci mai male	never did I harm
ad **anima** viva.	a living **creature**.

The song turns to her religious devotion and offerings. The voice should sound beautiful, melodic, and still very slow. The intensity reaches a majestic crescendo when she refers to putting "flowers at the altars..." In a more confidential tone and without sounding too bold, she questions why the Lord has not provided support in her hour of need. The last line expresses her broken spirit and ends abruptly with the last word of her question, "...why do you repay me thus?"

Sempre con fè **sincera**	Always in **sincere** faith
diedi **fiori** agli **altar**	I placed **flowers** at the **altars**
nell'ora del dolore	in the hour of sorrow,
perchè, perchè, **Signore**	why, why, **Lord**,
perchè me ne **rimuneri** così?	why do you **repay** me thus?

As she tells how she gave jewels to the Madonna and a song to the stars, she can no longer contain her sorrow and distress. She raises her voice in a great forte (loud voice) and very slow tempo (speed). In an outcry to the Lord, she reaches a B note in a powerful and beautiful climax. The song ends when she repeats the question, "..why do you repay me thus?"

Diedi gioielli	I brought jewels
della **Madonna** al **manto**,	for the **Madonna's mantle**,
e diedi il canto	and songs for the **stars** in
agli **astir**, al ciel,	heaven, to the sky,
che ne ridean più **belli**...	that they shone forth with more **beauty**...

"Oh! mio babbino caro" ("Oh! my dear daddy")
from *Gianni Schicchi*

Performed by Lauretta (Gianni's daughter)

Dramatic setting: Lauretta wishes to marry a young man whose family opposes the marriage because they consider themselves to be on a higher social level. Lauretta and her fiancé want her clever father to assist in their marriage plans by settling a family dispute over a rich cousin's will. Lauretta pleads with her father for his support and threatens to drown herself if she doesn't receive his consent. She refers to a bridge in Florence, the Ponte Vecchio, across the River Arno.

Vocal requirements: This song requires a lyric soprano with a youthful, tender, beautiful, and warm legato sound. Lauretta's pleas should sound completely sincere and full of affection. The word "babbino" refers to daddy and comes before dear. She resorts to high A flats, strong crescendos and a beautiful diminuendo and pianissimo to make her pleading more irresistible.

What to listen for: The dynamic level is piano. The word "caro" (dear) is full of affection. Lauretta's love adds intensity to the second line "I like him, he is beautiful, beautiful." The line includes a tender A-flat and a strong E-flat when "bello, bello" is repeated. In a firm but not loud voice, she expresses her desire to visit Porta Rosa to purchase a wedding ring.

Oh! mio babbino caro,	**Oh!** my dear daddy,
mi piace, è **bello**, bello;	I like him, he is **beautiful**, beautiful;
vo'andare in Porta Rossa	I want to go to Porta Rossa
a comperar l'anello!	to buy the wedding ring!

She becomes more affirmative and emotional when she declares, "I want to go there!" A strong crescendo accents her distress if she loves "him in vain." There is an intense and almost tearful sound to her voice when she shrewdly threatens suicide.

Sì, sì, ci voglio andare!	**Yes**, yes, I want to go there!
e se l'amassi indarno,	and if I should love him in vain,
andrei sul Ponte Vecchio	I'd go to the Ponte Vecchio,
ma per buttarmi in Arno!	only to throw myself in the Arno!

The loudest line occurs when Lauretta refers to "wasting away" and agonizing. It contains two A notes with the second one followed by a diminuendo (changing to a softer voice). The "O Dio" pianissimo has a beautiful and irresistible sound. The voice grows to a strong crescendo with an A note on the final words "pietà, pietà!" (mercy, mercy!). The last words are repeated as a soft prayer.

Mi struggo e mi **tormento**!	I am wasting away and **tormented**!
O Dio, vorrei morir!	**O God**, I want to die!
Babbo, **pietà**, pietà!	Dad, have **mercy**, mercy!

"Un bel dì vedremo" ("One beautiful day")
from *Madama Butterfly*

Performed by Cio-cio-san (Pinkerton's wife "Butterfly")

Dramatic setting: Butterfly has been waiting three years for her American lieutenant husband to return to Japan. Her maid prays for his return but no longer believes in it. Butterfly refuses to doubt his sincerity and tries to convince her maid that, on one beautiful day, he will return. She creates an imaginary scene and detailed description of his return.

Vocal requirements: The song calls for a lyric soprano with great vocal skill to express Butterfly's imagination, self-control, and unrelenting faith. The delivery must convey her simple, soft, patient, and modest character. Her more passionate expression requires more legato, limited crescendos, pianissimos, and a ringing B-flat at the end.

What to listen for: Butterfly's voice enters slowly and softly, as if from a distance. Her light and remote voice suggests that a "thread of smoke" is on the distant horizon. As the "ship appears" and enters the harbor, the voice becomes stronger and triumphant with the words "He has come!" She tries to sound convincing even though the picture she paints is imaginary.

Un bel dì vedremo	One fine day we will see
levarsi un fil di **fumo**	a thread of **smoke** rising
sull'**estremo confin** del mare.	at the **extreme confines** of the sea.
E poi la nave **appare**...	And then the ship **appears**...

Even with the ship in port, Butterfly maintains her self-control and passivity. The voice reveals some passion and perseverance concerning her long wait. The tempo increases as she describes a man advancing toward the hill, but the voice remains very light. Butterfly's voice becomes more legato (melodic flow of notes) and intense as she questions what he will say. She answers very slowly "He will call Butterfly from faraway."

Chiamerà "Butterfly" dalla lontana.	He will call "Butterfly" from faraway.
Io senza dar risposta	I without answering
me ne starò nascosta...	will remain hidden...

After a bit of teasing, she imagines his very words. She sings "My darling little wife" in a state of ecstasy. Butterfly's daydream returns to reality as she says to her maid "All this will come to pass..." She expresses these words in a legato voice with warmth and great passion. She ends on a ringing B-flat as she reaffirms her faith to wait for him.

"Piccina mogliettina, olezzo di **verbena**,"	"My darling little wife, fragrance of
i **nomi** che mi dava al suo venire.	**verbena**," the **names** he used to give me
	when he **arrives**.
Tutto questo **avverrà**...	All this will come to pass...

"Nessun dorma"
("Nobody sleep")
from *Turandot*

Performed by Calaf (secret prince)

Dramatic setting: After correctly answering Princess Turandot's three riddles, Calaf has given her the opportunity to win back her freedom. She must guess his real name by morning. She has ordered the whole city to stay awake and try to discover his secret. Late at night, Calaf expresses his confidence that by dawn he will be victorious.

Vocal requirements: This song requires a powerful tenor with a vibrant and far reaching lyricism (a melodic sound). A comfortable high range is required, including a line of high A's. The song requires a prolonged diminuendo (soft sound) and a loud B note at the end. Calaf must express confidence and a feeling of approaching happiness.

What to listen for: Tenors usually sing this famous aria very slowly. The opening words "Nessun dorma" are sung by a distant chorus and then repeated by Calaf. The words are sung firmly to create a mood of nocturnal silence. There is a cold sound to his voice as he visualizes the icy Turandot in her cold room looking to the stars for an answer. He raises his lyric (smooth and melodic) voice with the words "gaze at the stars..." and sounds warmer "...with love and hope."

Nessun dorma! Nessun dorma!	Nobody sleep! Nobody sleep!
Tu pure, o **Principessa**,	Even you, oh **Princess**,
nella tua **fredda** stanza	in your **cold** room
guardi le **stelle**	**gaze** at the **stars**
che **tremano** d'**amore** e di speranza.	which **tremble** with **love** and hope.

The "mystery is sealed within" should be sung with warmth and strength. A line of high A's introduces the words "on your mouth..." The words "la luce" (the light) have a mellow sound and "splenderà" (shine) has a delightful and prolonged diminuendo.

Ma il **mio mistero** è chiuso in me,	But **my mystery** is sealed within me,
il **nome** mio nessun saprà.	nobody shall know my **name**.
No, no, sulla tua bocca lo dirò,	No, no, on your mouth shall I say it,
quando la luce **splenderà**.	when the light will **shine**.

A short orchestral moment introduces the most intimate and sensuous lines. The choral interludes provide a lyric background to Calaf's ascending voice with an outstanding set of A notes. The final line "At dawn I will win!" is sung softly with confidence and serenity.

Ed il mio baccio scioglierà	And my kiss will release
il **silenzio** che ti fa **mia**!	the **silence**, which makes you **mine**!
Dilegua, o **notte**,	Fade away, oh **night**,
tramontate, stelle!	set, **stars**!
All'alba **vincerò**!	At dawn I will **win**!

Donizetti Arias

"Una furtiva lagrima" ("A furtive tear")
from *L'Elisir d'Amore*

Performed by Nemorino (simple peasant)

Dramatic setting: The unhappy Nemorino has been unsuccessful at trying to attract Adina, a popular village girl and farm owner. After pretending to ignore her, he notices her sadness and realizes she cares for him. Her tear frees his heart of its disappointment. He delights in the discovery that she loves him. This bel canto (beautiful singing) aria, also known as a "romanza," is considered one of the loveliest arias ever written.

Vocal requirements: This is one of the most popular tenor songs in the Italian repertory. It requires a strong lyric tenor voice that conveys great beauty and charm. It should sound smooth and tender but not heroic to convey Nemorino's simple and innocent character. It requires pianissimos (very soft notes), diminuendos (a vocal transition from loud to soft), and a crescendo of glorious and dramatic high notes. A solo bassoon first introduces the exquisite melody.

What to listen for: The tempo (speed) is on the slow side as Nemorino wonders about the cause of Adina's sadness. His voice is affectionate and very simple. "Those festive girls" refers to his recent popularity due to his rich inheritance. The phrase "she seemed to be envious" is reflective and expressed as a diminuendo. The question of "why should I look any further?" is sung piano (softly) and almost in disbelief. He repeats the words "I can see it" as a revelation and a sign of happiness at his discovery.

Una **furtiva** lagrima	A **furtive** tear
negl'occhi suoi spuntò:	welled up in her eyes:
quelle **festose** giovani	those **festive** girls
invidiar sembrò:	she seemed to be **envious**:
che più cercando io vo?	why should I look any further?

In the second verse, his voice becomes more intense as he imagines himself holding Adina in his arms. It begins soft and becomes louder and more exalted with the line "To blend my sighs..." There is a sensuous enjoyment and pianissimo "...with her sighs!"

Un **solo istante** i **palpiti**	To feel for just **one instant**
del suo **bel cor** sentir!	the **pounding** of her **lovely heart!**
I miei **sospir** confondere	To blend my **sighs**
per poco a'suoi sospir!	for a little with her sighs!

There is a diminuendo with the words "one can die." The final lines become a vocal showcase for the tenor to express his joy in glorious high notes. After reaching a crescendo, he should return quickly to a light and tender lyric voice.

...ah! Cielo, si può, si può morir,	...ah! heavens, yes one can, yes one can die,
di più non chiedo, non chiedo,	for more I don't ask, I don't ask,
si può morir, ah sì morir d'**amor**.	**yes** one can die, yes die of **love**.

"Quel guardo il cavaliere ... so anch'io come si bruciano" ("That glance struck the cavalier ... I, too, know how to set a heart on fire") from *Don Pasquale*

Performed by Norina (young widow)

Dramatic setting: Norina is in her garden reading a romantic, knightly tale about a very seductive young woman who conquers a cavalier with her irresistible charm. She compares her own charming qualities to the woman in the book. These two short arias are sung back-to-back and serve as Norina's entrance in act one. They introduce her lively and delightful personality.

Vocal requirements: The part of Norina requires a lyric soprano who can convey a youthful, clever, and charming character. Her essential cheerful, affectionate, and charming qualities are reflected throughout the two arias. As she nears the end of the second aria, she will display some coloratura trills to accent her cheerful character. The song usually ends with a cadenza to demonstrate Norina's virtuosity or vocal skills. She should always sound spontaneous and legato.

What to listen for: In the first short aria, Norina is reading lines from a book. She sings in a very legato (smooth and flowing) style to depict the character of the woman in the knightly tale. She should sound very feminine, soft, and docile. After reading ten lines, she laughs in amusement.

"Quel **guardo** il **cavaliere**
in mezzo al cor trafisse,
piegò il ginocchio e disse:
son vostro cavaliere."

"That **glance** struck the **cavalier**
in the center of his heart;
he dropped to his knee and said:
I am your cavalier."

The second aria is an adorable and enchanting character study of Norina. In the first section, her voice must sound natural and spontaneous. The passage from the book has caused her to reflect on her own charming qualities, and her voice will need to change color to express her different moods. The second line below should suggest seduction, the third line conveys a cheerful feeling, the fourth line ends with a crecendo on "l'effetto," the fifth line suggests a faked sadness, and the last line should sound languid and suggest weakness.

...so anch'io come si bruciano
i cori a lento foco;
d'un **breve** sorrisetto
conosco anch'io l'**effetto**,
di menzognera lagrima,
d'un **subito languor**.

...I, too, know how to set a heart on fire
and burn slowly;
I, too, know the **effect**
of a **brief** smile,
of a deceptive tear,
of a **sudden languor**.

In the second section, Norina becomes more self-reflective. She counters each shortcoming with a positive attribute. For example, she expresses how pleased she is with herself by stating that she offsets her anger with laughter, and a crazy head with an excellent heart. Sopranos usually end the aria with a cadenza (a virtuoso display of vocal skill), but the cadenza should not become a showpiece that detracts from Norina's spontaneous and genuine character.

Se monto in **furore**, di rado sto al segno,
ma in riso lo sdegno fo presto a cangiar.
Ho testa **bizzarro**, ma cor **eccellente**...

If I get **furious**, I seldom stay that way,
but my distain soon changes to laughter.
I have a **bizarre** head, but an **excellent** heart...

Bellini Arias

"Casta Diva"
("Chaste Goddess")
from *Norma*

Performed by Norma (High Priestess)

Dramatic setting: Norma stands at an altar in a moonlit forest and addresses an assembly of Druid priests and warriors. She urges them to pray for peace instead of war with Rome. She raises a sacred branch toward the sky and sends a prayer to the goddess to bring peace with the Romans. A choir echoes her prayer as Norma sings above it. It is considered one of the most beautiful and demanding soprano arias ever composed.

Vocal requirements: This spinto (dramatic capacity) soprano song requires a great voice with a wide range. It requires a flowing vocal line with a beautiful quality in both lyric and dramatic expression. It contains florid (highly ornamented) coloratura passages, and it is an outstanding example of a cantilena (a flowing and sustained vocal line). Each time the melodic line is repeated the tension rises as it moves to a higher and more sublime level. The aria requires great stamina, force, and intensity. Norma is required to sing several high A notes and a high B note.

What to listen for: The beginning must suggest a radiant moonlight in a sustained pianissimo (very soft sound). A feeling of devotion is expressed in the word "Diva." Norma uses a beautiful lyric (melodic) voice to win the favor of the goddess. She begins her prayer by requesting the Goddess to turn her beautiful face "toward us." The prayer grows in intensity and becomes more dramatic with several high A notes. As she repeats her request, her voice rises to a crescendo (increasing in volume) to a climax on a high B note. The voice remains very bright, as it becomes a diminuendo (turns softer) to end the first verse.

Casta Diva, che inargenti queste **sacre antiche** piante, a noi volgi il bel sembiante senza nube e senza vel...	**Chaste goddess,** who bathes these **sacred, ancient** trees in silver, turn thy lovely face toward us, unclouded and unveiled...

In the second verse, the voice becomes more pure and spiritual. The voice is fuller as it asks for the same peace on earth as the peace in the sky. The prayer takes on a growing urgency. The singing grows in dramatic intensity with the high notes ascending to a full note A. The singing should continue to have a beautiful, smooth and continuous flow, and the vocal changes should not detract from the noble beauty or vocal dignity of the aria.

Tempra, oh Diva, tempra tu de'cori **ardenti,** tempra ancora, tempra ancora lo **zelo audace,** **spargi** in terra, ah, quella **pace** che **regnar** tu fai nel ciel...	**Temper, oh Goddess,** temper these **ardent** hearts, temper still, temper the bold **zeal** of the **audacious.** **Spread** that **peace** upon the earth which thou causes to **reign** in heaven...

"Ah! non credea mirarti" ("Ah, I didn't think I would see you") from *La Sonnambula*

Performed by Amina (innocent peasant girl)

Dramatic setting: Amina is very saddened because her fiancé has broken off their marriage. He has accused her of being unfaithful. Suddenly, she appears on a bridge (a dangerous wooden plank) above a water mill sleepwalking in a trance. As she laments her situation, the villagers and her former fiancé realize that she is innocent. At the conclusion of the song, her fiancé puts a ring on her finger and the opera ends with a village celebration.

Vocal requirements: This song is composed for a lyric soprano who is trained in the bel canto style (beautiful singing). She must be capable of conveying a true pathos for a sincere, heart broken, and innocent peasant girl. Amina's voice must maintain a sad poetic quality, and it should remain controlled and restrained to avoid ornamentation. For the duration of the aria, she must convey the sense that she is in a sleepwalk trance.

What to listen for: In a slow tempo and soft voice, Amina begins by looking at her hand and searching for her ring. She is saddened and appears to be unaware that the villagers and her former fiancé are listening to her. There are pauses between her reflective words as she laments her situation. Her fiancé expresses regret between her passages at unjustly abandoning her.

L'anello mio ... l'anello...	The ring ... my ring...
Ei me l'ha tolto ... ma non può	He removed from me ... but
rapirmi l'**immagin** sua...	he cannot steal his **image**...
sculta ella è qui ... nel petto.	it's **sculpted** here ... in my breast.

Amina must evoke a romantic pathos (pity and endearment) when she addresses the "dear flowers" she received from her fiancé. She comments poignantly on how quickly they have extinguished. As she sings these moving words, she is accompanied by orchestral themes (motifs) that appeared earlier in the opera. These themes serve as recollections of earlier events that helped to reveal her sincere and romantic character.

Ah! non credea mirarti	Ah! I didn't think I would see you,
sì **presto estinto**, o **fiore**,	dear **flowers**, **extinguished** so **quickly**.
passasti al par d'amore,	You **passed** as did our love,
che un giorno **solo** durò.	who only lived for **one** day.

There is a sense of hopelessness when Amina states that "all my tears can never revive his love to me." The passionate words to these lines must be sung legato throughout because she is revealing her innermost feelings on a subconscious level while in a deep trance. This aria is often referred to as a "mad scene." In this case, the word "mad" does not refer to anger or a state of insanity. Instead, it refers to a temporary flight from reality and reason. Amina awakens from her trance at the end of the aria when her fiancé realizes he misjudged her and replaces his ring on her finger.

Potria novel **vigore**	If only **my** weeping could
il pianto **mio** donarti...	restore your **vigor** again...
Ma **ravvivar** l'amore	But all my tears can never
il pianto mio non può.	**revive** his love to me.

Leoncavallo Arias

"Il Pròlogo: Si può?"
("The Prologue: May I?")
from *I Pagliacci*

Performed by Tonio (a clown)

Dramatic setting: Tonio, the Clown, is a performer in a company of traveling players. Before the show begins, he steps in front of the curtain and addresses the village audience. He reminds the audience that actors, under their makeup, experience the same emotions as other human beings. The roles that stage actors perform may represent their real life emotions. His prologue will express a variety of emotions, including love, hatred, sorrow and rage.

Vocal requirements: This song calls for a baritone with an Italian flavor. The voice should be large, poised, friendly, persuasive and well modulated. It must convince the audience that actors have very human emotions. Parts of the song are almost spoken, and parts are sung in powerful lyric (smooth sounding) phrases, an eloquent legato, including a beautiful cantilena (a sustained, flowing melodic line).

What to listen for: The opening lines are meant to capture the attention of the audience. The first "May I?" pretends to be timid, and the second is more firm and confident. "I am the Prologue" is said with pride and vigor. It is an unusual and effective way to capture the audience's attention.

Si può? Si può?	May I? May I?
Signore! Signori!	**Ladies! Gentlemen!**
Scusatemi	**Excuse me,**
se da sol mi **presento**:	if I **present** alone:
io sono il **Pròlogo**.	I am the **Prologue**.

165

In the next section, Tonio explains what the author of the play has in mind. The author's drama should be taken seriously because it is a "slice of life." The song's famous cantilena begins piano as the voice creates a feeling of sensuous beauty. The cantilena tells how the author "wrote with real tears" based on "A nest of memories."

Un **nido** di **memorie**	A **nest** of **memories**
in fondo a l'anima	in his innermost heart
cantava un giorno,	sang one day,
ed ei con vere lacrime scisse...	and he wrote with real tears...

Now Tonio must express a variety of emotions to match the instruments. For example, love (English horn), hatred (woodwinds), sorrow (horns), and rage (winds and strings). He must color his voice and vary the intensity to express this variety of moods.

Dunque, vedrete amar	Now, then, you will see how **human**
siccome s'amano gli esseri **umani**;	beings love when they love, and
vedrete de l'odio i tristi **frutti**.	you will see the sad **fruit** of hate.

With the words "E voi" (And you), Tonio begins an eloquent legato directed at the audience. He tells the audience that we performers are just like you because we are also made of flesh and bone. The final line of the prologue reaches a dramatic climax with the words "Let's go. Begin!"

"Qual fiamma avea nel guardo! ... Hui! Stridono lassù" ("What a fire he had in his glance! ... Hui! How wildly they shriek up there")
from *I Pagliacci*

Performed by Nedda (Canio's wife)

Dramatic setting: Nedda has grown tired of her gypsy life and acting role with a troupe of entertainers who travel from village to village. She has started a love affair with a well-to-do villager. She is fearful of her suspicious and jealous husband. She is alone when she expresses her desire to be free like the birds overhead. It sounds like two different but connected songs.

Vocal requirements: The song calls for a lyric soprano (highest female voice) with a light and youthful sound. She must be able to change moods from a tense fear of her jealous husband to a joyful expression of freedom. She must sing trills to imitate the sound of the birds. At the song's conclusion, her sense of triumph is voiced with great lyric (melodic) expression.

What to listen for: Nedda is alone as she ponders her husband's jealous threat. In the opening lines, the rather fast tempo reflects her fear that he might discover her secret thoughts. She sings rapidly and tensely as she comments on his brutal nature.

Qual **fiamma** avea nel **guardo**!	What a **fire** he had in his **glance**!
Gli occhi abbassai per tema	I lowered my eyes for fear
ch'ei leggesse il mio pensier **segreto**!	that he read my **secret** thought!
Oh! s'ei mi **sorprendesse**...	Oh! if he should **surprise** me...
brutale come egli è!	**brutal** as he is!

Nedda then dismisses her worries as her voice becomes more light and free. Her expression becomes more sensuous as she anticipates fulfilling her desires. A flight of overhead birds symbolizes her desire to be free. She imitates their voices with ascending trills on "Hui! Hui!" She expresses their flight with vitality and a lively rhythm. Nedda follows their flight with warmth and reaches a soaring climax on the word "vanno."

Hui! **Stridano** lassù. **Liberamente**	Hui! How wildly they **shriek** up there.
lanciati a vol come frecce, gli augel.	**Freely launched** like arrows on their flight.
Disfidano le nubi e'l sol cocente,	They **defy** the clouds and the
e vanno per le vie del ciel.	burning sun, and travel over the roads in the sky.

Her voice takes on a darker hue and becomes more passionate to suggest the birds must endure wind and rain. With the words, "Vanno laggiù," her triumphant voice expresses how the birds have weathered the storm. They have reinforced her desire to be free. She repeats several expressions of "e van" (they go!) and ends with a climax on the last one.

Vanno laggiù verso un paese **strano**	They go yonder to a **strange** land
che sognan forse e che cercano **in van**.	of which they dream and which they
Ma i boëmi del ciel	look for **in vain**. But the gypsies of
seguon l'arcano **poter**	the sky obey the mysterious **power**
che li sospinge ... e van!	which urges them on ... and they go!

"Recitar! ... Vesti la giubba" ("Perform! ... Put on the costume")
from *I Pagliacci*

Performed by Canio (clown and Nedda's husband)

Dramatic setting: Canio the clown is depressed, angry, and jealous because he has discovered that his wife has another lover. He is overcome with bitterness and sadness as he puts on his make-up for the evening performance. He must now pretend to laugh like a clown even though he is heartbroken and filled with pain and grief. This is probably the most famous tenor aria ever written on the subject of pain and sorrow. The beautiful melody, combined with Canio's sadness, has a strong emotional impact on the audience and receives prolonged applause.

Vocal requirements: This song requires a dramatic tenor capable of expressing a powerful sincerity, a deep sadness and helplessness, and an outburst of sarcasm and despair. Even though it requires an outpouring of emotion and high A's, Canio must still come across as eloquent without losing his dignity.

What to listen for: The opening word "Recitar!" expresses Canio's bitterness and disbelief. The opening lines are andante (easy pace) with a dynamic level of mezzo forte (somewhat loud). He feels humiliation and helplessness at learning his wife is unfaithful.

Recitar!	**Perform!**
Mento preso dal **delirio**	While I am racked by **delirium**,
non so più quel che dico	I no longer know what
e quel che faccio!	I say or what I do!

The sudden outburst of laughter is meant to disguise his pain and sorrow. He refers to himself, "You are Pagliaccio!" ("You are a clown!") in a very sensitive voice. The melody begins piano with the famous words "Vesti la giubba." The words have a sad sound to them. The following lines have a sarcastic and cynical sound. The most tragic expression begins when Tonio announces that his own weeping must switch to jokes.

Vesti la giubba	Put on the **costume**
e la **faccia** infarina.	and powder your **face**.

| La gente **paga** | The people **pay** |
| e rider vuole qua. | and want to laugh. |

His bitterness grows to a fever with a powerful "Ah! Ridi, Pagliaccio." The concluding lines express his torture. The words "Laugh at the pain" reflect a deep despair and "il cor!" (your heart) should be heartrending. It is customary for the tenor to express some sobbing after the final line. To maintain his artistic dignity, it helps to avoid a prolonged or an exaggerated outburst.

Ah! Ridi, **Pagliaccio,**	Ah! Laugh, **Clown,**
sul tuo **amore** infranto!	at your broken **love!**
Ridi del duol	Laugh at the pain
che t'avvelena il cor!	that poisons your heart!

Bizet Arias

"L'amour est un oiseau rebelle" ("Love is a rebellious bird" [or "Habanera"])
from *Carmen*

Performed by Carmen (seductive gypsy)

Dramatic setting: Carmen has just emerged from a cigarette factory with her fellow workers. All eyes in the village square are on the attractive Carmen as she reveals her idea of love as a rebellious bird that comes and goes. It is a game of offering love and then withdrawing it. By comparing love to "a rebellious bird," she is asserting her desire to maintain her freedom.

Vocal requirements: This famous aria requires a mezzo-soprano (female voice lower than a soprano) with a wavy flexibility and warm seductive voice. She must sing with elegance and warmth. The delivery must be rhythmical and legato (melodic, smooth and flowing). She must avoid sounding coarse, overly sensuous or too heavy in the voice.

What to listen for: This song is based on a Spanish dance rhythm and it introduces Carmen's seductive and playful personality. It serves as a warning that her love is temporary and unreliable. The French text rhymes and serves to complement the rhythm. The song is in two verses and both should be sung with elegance and warmth. The first four bars, beginning with "Love is a rebellious bird," are sung piano and without a breath.

L'**amour** est un oiseau **rebelle** que nul ne peut apprivoiser	**Love** is a **rebellious** bird that nobody can tame,

170

et c'est bien **en vain**	and it's **in vain**
qu'on l'appelle,	that one calls him
s'il lui convient de **refuser**.	if it suits him to **refuse**.

The refrain, "Love is a gypsy child" is sung piano (softly) and legato and with extreme rhythm. The chorus sings the final words of the refrain and first verse "be on guard for yourself!" The chorus serves to warn Carmen's admirers of her inconstant affection.

L'**amour** est **enfant** de bohème,	**Love** is a gypsy **child**,
il n'a jamais connu de loi.	it has never known any law.
Si tu ne m'aimes pas, je t'aime,	If you don't love me, I love you,
et si je t'aime,	and if I love you,
prends **garde** à toi!	be on **guard** for yourself!

The second verse presents love as an elusive bird that comes and goes away. The phrase "Love is far away..." is sung piano, and the following phrase "...there it is!" grows louder to a crescendo. The second verse ends by repeating the refrain from the first verse.

L'oiseau que tu croyais **surprendre**	The bird you thought to **surprise**
battit de l'aile et s'envola.	flapped his wing and flew away.
L'**amour** est loin, tu peux l'**attendre**,	**Love** is far away, you can **wait for** it,
tu ne l'attends plus, il est là.	you don't expect it anymore, there it is!

"Près des remparts de Séville"
("By the ramparts of Séville"
[or "Seguidilla"])
from *Carmen*

Performed by Carmen (seductive gypsy)

Dramatic setting: Carmen has just been arrested for injuring a factory worker, and she sings this song with her hands tied behind her back. She wants Don Jose to help her escape in return for her love. Although he has forbidden her to speak, she pretends to be thinking aloud and singing to herself as she tries to seduce him into freeing her.

Vocal requirements: As in the case of the "Habanera," this song must also be sung with a warm and seductive voice but in an elegant and rhythmical style. It calls for legato (smooth and melodic) passages that sway back-and-forth because the Seguidilla (Séguédille in French) is a Spanish dance with a lilting melody. Her "la-la-la" dance rhythm spins to a high B-flat.

What to listen for: This aria has a fast 1-2-3 rhythm throughout and a sparkling timbre (intense tone color). The style indication is pianissimo (very soft) and light. The song begins with a soft volume and very legato. The only strongly accented phrase is when Carmen says "I shall go dance the séguédille."

Près des **remparts** de Séville,	Near the **ramparts** of Séville,
chez mon ami Lillas Pastia,	at my friend Lillas Pastia's,
j'irai **danser** la Séguédille	I shall go **dance** the seguidilla
et boire du Manzanilla.	and drink Manzanilla.

Carmen announces that she will take her lover along to catch Jose's attention and arouse his jealousy. She refers to "My poor heart" as "free as the air" in a legato voice with a touch of humor. After stating that her lovers are not to her liking, she offers her heart for the asking.

Mon pauvre coeur, très **consolable**,	**My poor** heart, very **consolable**,
mon **coeur** est **libre** comme **l'air**!	my **heart** is **free** as **the air**!
J'ai des gallants à la **douzaine**,	I have suitors by the **dozen**,
mais ils ne sont pas à **mon** gré.	but they are not to **my** liking.

The three lines beginning with "Who wants my heart? It's his for the taking" are sung in a full, sensuous and lovely voice. The line, "I scarcely have time to wait," must be sung with intensity and urgency. She closes by repeating the title line as she anticipates success. As a reward for her freedom, she announces that the time is right for her new lover.

Qui veut mon âme? Elle est à prendre.	Who wants my heart? It's his for the taking.
Vous arrivez au bon **moment**.	**You come** at the right **moment**.
Je n'ai guère le **temps d'attendre**...	I scarcely have **time to wait**...

"Votre toast, je peux vous le rendre" ("Your toast, I can return it")
from *Carmen*

Performed by Escamillo (toreador or bullfighter)

Dramatic setting: A crowd of gypsies, smugglers, and soldiers has gathered at a tavern. Escamillo, a famous toreador, arrives and the crowd honors him with a drink and he returns their toast. His aria describes the courage and skill it takes to be a toreador. He is attracted to Carmen as he sings the famous "Toreador's Song."

Vocal requirements: Even though a dramatic baritone commonly sings his famous song, the French tradition calls for a lyric baritone. Although he is proud of his physical skills and courage, he sings with elegance and behaves like a polished gentleman. He must sing in a smooth lyric (melodic) voice.

What to listen for: After returning the crowd's toast, "Your toast, I can return it," Escamillo vividly describes the excitement of the arena and the uproar of the spectators.

Le **cirque** est plein du haut en **bas**.	The **arena** is full from top to **bottom**.
Les **spectateurs**, perdant la tête,	The **spectators**, losing their heads,
s'interpellent à grand **fracas**!	trade jeers in a large **uproar**!

Several short, descriptive, and articulate phrases follow sung mezzo forte to forte (medium loud to loud). The toreador must sound calm, composed and confident in spite of the commotion surrounding him. In a legato (smooth and flowing) voice, he reminds the toreador to be on guard. He ends the first stanza on a gracious and elegant diminuendo (voice becomes softer) with the reward of a beautiful woman.

Toréador, en **garde**, **toréador**,	Toreador, be on **guard, toreador,**
et songe bien en **combattant**	and remember while **fighting**
qu'un oeil noir te **regarde**	that a dark eye is **watching** you
et que l'**amour** t'attend.	and that **love** is awaiting you.

In the second stanza, Escamillo stresses the silence of the crowd, as the bull comes forward, in short, half-spoken phrases. The short phrases mimick the movements of the bull. He is preparing the crowd for the courage and artistry of the toreador as he attracts the attention of the bull. He must convey the danger and suspense of the moment.

Tout d'un coup on fait **silence**,	All of a sudden everybody is **silent**,
ah, que se passe-t-il?	ah, what is happening?
Plus de cris, c'est l'**instant**!	No longer shouting, this is the **moment**!

The description continues mezzo forte in breathless phrases. As in the first stanza, the second stanza ends on a diminuendo to express the toreador's skill, pride and courage. Escamillo joins the tavern crowd in a rousing chorus to celebrate his glory.

"La fleur que tu m'avais jetée" ("The flower that you threw me" [or "The Flower Song"])
from *Carmen*

Performed by Don Jose (military officer)

Dramatic setting: Don Jose and Carmen have just had an angry disagreement in which she questioned his devotion to her. He takes the flower from his vest that she tossed at him. He curbs his temper and sings the sensitive "Flower Song" that expresses how Carmen's flower sustained him in jail, his torment over having met her, and his total passion and submission to her.

Vocal requirements: This song calls for a passionate sounding lyric tenor. He must be able to express a variety of intense emotions—torment, resentment, wonderment, submission, devotion and passion—without upsetting the rich melodic flow of the music. There are several crescendos, including one that ends in an A-flat, and a pianissimo.

What to listen for: The beginning style is marked con amore (lovingly) and the dynamic is piano (soft). The melodic line is simple, warm and intense in feeling. The introductory lines describe his devotion to Carmen and how the perfume from her flower produced a sweet intoxication.

La fleur que tu m'avais jetée, dans **ma prison** m'était restée. Flétrie et sèche, cette fleur gardait toujours sa douce **odeur**.	**The flower** that you threw me, stayed with me in **my prison**. Withered and dried up, that flower always kept its sweet **smell**.

Don Jose expresses the remorse and torment he experienced in jail, in the following lines. He expresses his resentment and anger by telling her that he cursed her in prison. These lines of regret end on a crescendo (the voice rises to express a dramatic moment).

Je me prenais à te maudire, à te **détester**, à me dire: pourquoi faut-il que le **destin** l'ait mise là sur mon chemin?	I would catch myself cursing you, **detesting** you, saying to myself: why did **destiny** have to put her across my way?

In the second half of the song, his mood changes from bitterness to an outpouring of passion and desire for Carmen. The voice returns to piano and the tempo becomes faster. The faster tempo at the end of the aria makes it easier for him to express worship and submission when he tells her that he belongs to her. His final words, "...belonging to you!" are said with a humble intensity and signal that he is completely devoted to her. Although Carmen remains silent during this lovely and sensitive aria, her initial anger subsides as she listens to his passionate appeal.

Car tu n'avais eu qu'à **paraître**,
qu'à jeter un **regard** sur moi,
pour t'emparer de tout mon être.
O ma Carmen, et j'étais une chose à toi!

For you had only to **appear**,
to throw one **glance** at me,
to take possession of my whole being.
O my Carmen, I turned into a thing
belonging to you!

Gounod Arias

"Avant de quitter ces lieux" ("Before leaving this place" [or "Valentin's aria"]) from *Faust*

Performed by Valentin (soldier and Marguerite's brother)

Dramatic setting: Valentin has just joined the army and he sings this song at a village fair. He calls on the Lord to protect his sister from danger while he is away. He feels it's his duty to fight for his country. If he should die in battle, he pledges to protect Marguerite from on high. Valentin holds a medal given to him by his sister.

Vocal requirements: This popular song calls for a baritone who must express courage as a soldier, devotion to his sister, and faith in the Lord. He must express these emotions in a dignified and controlled voice while sustaining a long and melodious flow. His range of emotions will include sadness, love, devotion, faith, bravery and pride.

What to listen for: The song has three parts with part C repeating part A. In part A, Valentin solemnly calls on the Lord to protect his sister in a long and flowing melody. He begins with a touch of sadness about leaving his native soil followed by words of devotion leading to a crescendo (vocal increase in volume). He refers to "my sister so dearly loved" with love and intensity, and ends with a pledge to protect her.

Daigne de tout **danger** toujours, toujours la **protéger**,	**Deign** to **protect** her always, always from every **danger**,

176

cette soeur si chérie	my sister so dearly loved,
daigne de tout danger la protéger.	deign to protect her from danger.

Part B has a march rhythm as Valentin pledges to be brave and place his faith in the Lord. It is sung with pride and vigor with a ringing sound but not loud or in a hurried manner. The last bars are slower and more peaceful as the thought of death is lightened by his faith in the afterlife.

j'irai **combattre** pour mon pays.	I shall go to **fight** for my country.
Et si vers Lui Dieu me rappelle,	And if God calls me back to Him,
je veillerai sur toi **fidèle**,	I shall watch over you **faithfully**,
o Marguerite!	O Marguerite!

After repeating part A, part C ends on a slow and sensitive note as Valentin once again calls with feeling on the Lord of Heaven to "protégé (protect) Marguerite." There is a solemn and religious sound to his voice.

O Roi des cieux,	**O King** of Heaven,
jette les yeux,	cast a glance,
protège Marguerite,	**protect** Marguerite,
o Roi des cieux, o Roi!	O King of Heaven, O King!

"Salut demeure chaste et pure" ("Greetings, chaste and pure abode")
from *Faust*

Performed by Faust (after restoring his youth)

Dramatic setting: The devil has led Faust to Marguerite's garden. Faust can feel her divine presence, even though Marguerite is absent. He is inspired by the surroundings and views the garden as a shrine for worshiping and praising her. In this cavatina (short entrance aria) he exalts her purity, innocence, beauty, and divine creation.

Vocal requirements: The song calls for a lyric tenor with a pure legato voice. He must express his gratitude, admiration, and reverence for Marguerite. Faust must maintain an elevated and spiritual tone throughout the song. There are no harsh tones are exceedingly high notes. The climax calls for two pure A-flats and a very soft ending (pianissimo).

What to listen for: The aria begins slowly as Faust is inspired by the surroundings that nurtured Marguerite. "I feel love taking hold" is expressed as a crescendo. In a loud outburst of emotion, he declares "O Marguerite! Here I am at your feet." He contemplates her divine dwelling and spirit in a simple and pure legato (smooth and melodic) voice. The "innocente et divine" includes two A notes and a pianissimo.

O Marguerite, à tes pieds me voici.	O Marguerite! Here I am at your feet.
Salut! demeure **chaste et pure,**	**Greetings, chaste and pure** abode,
où se devine la **présence**	where one devines the **presence**
d'une âme **innocente et divine.**	of an **innocent and divine** soul.

"O Nature" is sung softly with a warm feeling of gratitude for nurturing this beautiful child. "Beneath your wing" is expressed as an affectionate phrase with a crescendo. Even when his voice grows stronger, Faust must maintain a warm, vital, and spiritual tone.

O **nature,**	O **nature,**
c'est là que tu la fis si **belle!**	it is here that you made her so **beautiful!**
C'est là que cette **enfant**	It is here this **child** slumbered
a dormi sous ton aile...	beneath your wing...

He continues to express his gratitude. He refers to her as a blossoming woman in a warm and loving tone. The words "haleine" (breath) and "ame" (soul) reflect Faust's spiritual thoughts. They culminate with an A-natural on "avec amour." After completing the passage below, Faust will repeat some lines including the title line. The song's climax should have a pure and spiritual tone.

Là que de ton haleine	Here with your breath
enveloppant son âme	that **enveloped**
tu fis avec **amour**	her soul with **love,**
épanouir la **femme**	you made blossom the **woman**
en cet **ange** des cieux!	within this heavenly **angel!**

"Ah! Je ris de me voir" ("Ah! I laugh at seeing myself" [or "The Jewel Song"]) from *Faust*

Performed by Marguerite (Valentin's sister)

Dramatic setting: To help Faust attract Marguerite, the devil has left a casket of precious jewels in her garden. When she adorns herself with the gems and looks into a mirror, she is surprised to see how beautiful she looks. Her discovery reflects her warm and appealing personality.

Vocal requirements: This song calls for a brilliant lyric soprano with a very joyful, nimble, and youthful sounding voice. Marguerite must convey surprise and innocence by singing in a light, clear, and legato voice. In a sparkling and flexible voice, she expresses trills (ornamental and highly skilled singing), crescendos and decrescendos.

What to listen for: When she discovers the casket, Marguerite begins with a slow and wondering voice. She begins to sing faster, with some hesitation, as she tries to unlock the casket. As she opens the casket, she sings six loud bars with excitement and animation beginning with the words "Oh my God! Such jewels!"

O Dieu! Que de bijoux!	**Oh God**! Such jewels!
Est-ce un rêve **charmant**	Is it a **charming** dream
qui m'éblouit—ou si je veille?	that dazzles me—or am I awake?
Mes yeux n'ont jamais vu de	My eyes have never seen such
richesse pareille!	**wealth**!

There are short silences in the following lines to express her breathless curiosity as she searches the casket and discovers a mirror. The aria begins when she sings the title "Ah! I laugh at seeing myself" in a cheerful voice followed by sustained legato (smooth) phrases.

Ah! Je ris de me voir	Ah! I laugh at seeing myself
si **belle** en ce **miroir**!	so **beautiful** in this **mirror**!
Est-ce toi, Marguerite? Est-ce toi?	Is that you, Marguerite? Is that you?

A crescendo followed by a decrescendo occurs when she compares herself to a king's daughter. She sings with a brilliant enthusiasm the words "Pretty as a lady..." Her voice becomes softer as she explores the remaining jewels and puts on a necklace and bracelet. Her full joy is expressed throughout the repeat of the first part with the title words "Ah, I laugh at seeing myself."

C'est la **fille** d'un roi	It's the **daughter** of a king
qu'on salue au **passage**!	to whom all bow as she **passes**!
Ah, s'il était ici! S'il me voyait ainsi,	Ah, if only he were here! If he saw
comme une **demoiselle**,	me like this! **Pretty** as a **lady** he would
Il me trouverait **belle**.	find me then!

"Vous qui faites l'endormie" ("You who pretend to be asleep" [or "The Devil's Serenade"])
from *Faust*

Performed by Méphistophélès (the devil)

Dramatic setting: Méphistophélès sings a "moral" serenade under Marguerite's window warning her not to surrender herself to a lover until she receives a wedding ring. It is a sarcastic song because Faust, with Méphistophélès encouragement, has already seduced Marguerite. The devil substitutes the name "Catherine" in place of Marguerite.

Vocal requirements: This song requires a deep sounding bass to portray the cunning devil. Although it is a sarcastic song, the French tradition calls for an elegant and sophisticated devil with a seductive and irresistible voice. He should not sound ugly or vulgar. His sarcastic laugh requires three successive pitches: high, middle, and low G's.

What to listen for: A strange and mocking guitar sound provides the introduction. In the first verse, the devil sings mezzo forte (half loud) below Marguerite's (Catherine's) window. The singing should be legato (smooth flowing notes) with long phrases.

Vous qui faites l'**endormie**	**You** who pretend to be **asleep**,
n'entendez-vous pas,	do you not hear,
O Catherine ma mie...	O Catherine my love...

The line, "It is thus that your suitor call you," should sound pressing but elegant. The word "heart" is sung with a mixture of pathos and irony. The devil is so amused that he bursts into laughter. The phrase, "with your ring on your finger," should sound serious and as a warning. Méphistophélès is singing a song of sarcastic humor.

Ainsi ton gallant t'appelle,	It is thus that your suitor calls you,
et ton **coeur** l'en croit!	and your **heart** hears him!
Ah! ah! ah! ah!	Ah! ah! ah! ah!
N'ouvre ta **porte**, ma **belle**,	Only open your **door**, my **beauty**,
que la bague au doigt!	with your ring on your finger!

In the second verse, his voice becomes more persuasive and more legato while the orchestra provides a staccato (brief pauses between notes) accompaniment. There is a touching diminuendo (moving to a softer voice) with the words "...so sweet a kiss?" After the laughter, the devil provides the intimate advice "Don't grant a kiss." At the end of the song, the devil should laugh on several pitches starting with four high G's, followed by middle G's, and finally low G's or a very soft chuckle. This requires three humorous and successive transitions.

Catherine que j'**adore**,	Catherine whom I **adore**,
pourquoi **refuser**	why **refuse**
à l'amant qui vous **implore**	the lover who **beseeches** you
un si doux baiser?	so sweet a kiss?

"Je veux vivre"
("I want to live" [or
"Juliet's Waltz"])
from *Roméo et Juliette*

Performed by Juliette (Lord Capulet's daughter)

Dramatic setting: Juliette has just fallen in love after an exchange of glances and sweet words with Roméo at her family party. The waltz is Juliette's joyous outburst to her nurse. In Juliette's words, the waltz is meant to "let my soul enjoy its spring." She is a Capulet and is not aware that Roméo belongs to a rival family—the Montagues.

Vocal requirements: The song requires a lyric soprano with outstanding vocalization. Juliette must express a variety of qualities, such as charm, poise, happiness, youth, fear and melancholy. Her legato (smooth and melodic) passages must lead to crescendos and diminuendos. She will also be required to express high notes (B flat) and trills.

What to listen for: Juliette experiences several emotional transitions. First, the waltz begins with a joyous outburst of vitality at having discovered love. The piano (soft) opening, "Ah! I want to live in the dream that transports me..." resembles an intense sigh of well being, youth and health.

Ah! Je veux vivre...	I want to live...
Douce **flamme**	Sweet **flame**,
je te garde dans mon âme	I keep you in my soul
comme un **trésor**.	like a **treasure**.

After referring to "The drunkenness of youth," Juliette's thoughts turn to sadness and a sense of tragedy that love may kill happiness. These lines are very legato and with a darker sound. These lines require a sharp mood change from the joyful opening lines.

Cette ivresse de jeunesse...	The drunkenness of youth...
Puis vient **l'heure**	Then comes **the hour**
où l'on pleure,	when one weeps,
le coeur cède à l'**amour**	the heart yields to **love**
et le bonheur fuit sans **retour**.	and happiness escapes without **return**.

When her melancholy ends, the words "I want to live" call for a very tender diminuendo (softening of the voice). The cheerful waltz returns in crescendo waves, brilliant and warm, ending on a high B-flat. Like the "sweet flame" in her soul, she asks for more of a carefree youth symbolized by the rose. These lines call for a strong legato with deep yearning and tenderness. The concluding lines should sound brilliant and velvet. The trills should be very light and the high C conveys Juliette's happy exaltation.

Je veux vivre...	I want to live...
Loin de l'hiver **morose**	Far from the **sullen** winter,
laisse-moi sommeiller	let me linger and rest
et **respirer** la **rose**	and **breathe** the **rose**
avant de l'effeuiller.	before stripping it of its leaves.

"Ah! Lève-toi, soleil"
("Ah! Rise fair sun!"
[or "Roméo's Cavatina"])
from *Roméo et Juliette*

Performed by Roméo (member of the Montague family)

Dramatic setting: Roméo has just fallen in love with Juliette after attending her family's party as an uninvited guest. Later that night he leaves his friends and scales her orchard wall. After she lights a lamp in her room, he sings this song of adoration under her balcony. She is charmed but warns him that they belong to rival families.

Vocal requirements: The song calls for a lyric tenor capable of creating a prayer and poetic-like legato. The voice should sound youthful, suspenseful, passionate, and inspired to a poetic level. Roméo's adoration should be expressed with great intensity. The voice must encompass crescendos, decrescendos, diminuendos, and B-flats.

What to listen for: In the opening recitative, "L'amour, l'amour" are expressed with great intensity. There is suspense in Roméo's voice as Juliette lights the lamp in her room. He refers to her beauty "in the darkness of night" with adoration and a lovely decrescendo (voice decreases in volume).

Mais quelle soudaine **clarté**	But what sudden **brightness**
resplendit à cette fenêtre?	**shines** at that window?
C'est là que dans la **nuit**	That is where in the darkness of **night**
rayonne sa **beauté**.	**radiates** her **beauty**.

As the prayer grows more urgent, a crescendo (voice rises in volume) grows and reaches its climax with a B-flat on the word "parais" (appear). The dynamic turns to piano (softly) on the words, "pure, enchanting star." The voice blends with the lovely orchestral accompaniment on words like "caress" and "reve!" (dream).

Ah! Lève-toi, parais,	Ah! Rise, appear,
astre pur et **charmant**.	**pure**, **charming star**.
Elle rêve! Elle dénoue	She is dreaming! She unwinds
une boucle de cheveux	a lock of her hair
qui vient **caresser** sa joue.	which comes to **caress** her cheek.

The words "a repondu" (has responded) call for a diminuendo (voice becomes softer). The next crescendo occurs with the words "Ah, Rise..." The prayer should be intense but not loud. Roméo should end his wooing as an almost religious worship. To accomplish this desire, he reaches a B-flat in a beautiful pianissimo to reflect a deeply felt plea. Contrary to the composer's intention, many tenors prefer a loud B-flat to appeal to the audience.

Ah! Je n'ai rien entendu!	Ah! I have heard nothing!
Mais ses yeux parlent pour elle,	But her eyes speak for her
et **mon coeur** a **répondu**!	and **my heart** has **responded**!
Ah! Lève-toi, soleil...	Ah! Rise (fair) sun...

Massenet Arias

"Adieu, notre petite table"
("Farewell, our little table")
from *Manon*

Performed by Manon (courtesan and Des Grieux's lover)

Dramatic setting: Manon is alone in a modest apartment in Paris. She desires to have more wealth than her lover can provide. She sincerely loves Des Grieux, but she has started an affair with a man of wealth. The song expresses her emotional conflict between love and ambition. The table symbolizes the object that brought Des Grieux and Manon together. She finds it easier to bid farewell to the table than to her absent lover.

Vocal requirements: The song calls for a lyric soprano who can sincerely convey her changing moods spaced by brief silences. It should be sung with a steady tempo (speed), mostly piano (softly), and with a sustained tone. She must express the beauty and simplicity of the song by expressing the vowels precisely.

What to listen for: Manon expresses her changing moods before she reaches the title line. She tries to justify her decision to leave Des Grieux. As the orchestra plays a theme of wealth and power, Manon sings with more force and reaches crescendos (dramatic increases in volume) on the high notes. The words "queen" and "beauty" are sung with majesty, brilliance, and quality of tone.

J'entends cette **voix** qui m'entraîne contre **ma volonté**: "Manon, Manon! tu seras reine, reine par la **beauté**!	I hear this **voice** that carries me away against **my will**: "Manon, Manon! you will be queen, queen because of your **beauty**!"

Manon now realizes that she is giving up love and happiness in exchange for a life of luxury. Her emotions grow deeper but she continues to sing in a steady tempo and softly with tears in her eyes. She sees the little table as a symbol of the love she shared with Des Grieux. Manon expresses the appropriate inflections in a sustained tone.

Adieu, notre **petite table**,	**Farewell**, our **little table**,
qui nous **réunit** si souvent.	which **united** us so often!
Adieu, notre petite table,	Farewell, farewell, our little table,
si **grande** pour nous cependant.	so **big**, however, for the two of us!

Her voice becomes more intense as she remembers drinking from the same glass. The phrase "we tried to find the other's lips" is animated and broken into several parts. The words "Ah, poor friend" sound almost tragic. Her final vibrant farewell to the little table begins as a sob and fades away. It should convey the finality of her decision.

Un même verre était le nôtre,	We shared the same glass, the two of us,
chacun de nous quand il buvait	and when each one of us drank,
y cherchait les lèvres de l'autre...	we tried to find the other's lips.
Ah, **pauvre** ami, comme il m'aimait!	Ah, **poor** friend, how he loved me!

"En fermant les yeux" or "Le Rêve" ("Closing my eyes" or "The dream")
from *Manon*

Performed by Des Grieux (a cavalier of nobility)

Dramatic setting: Des Grieux is in a joyful mood because he has just written a letter to his father asking permission to marry Manon. When he returns to their apartment, he notices the tears in her eyes as he sings a soft and dream-like aria about their future together. He doesn't know that Manon has decided to leave him for a rich patron.

Vocal requirements: This is a demanding song because the tenor must suddenly change from a joyful and dramatic mood to an affectionate and subdued mood. He must sing a sustained piano (soft) line with sweetness, sensitivity, and intensity of feeling. The aria calls for a free, soft and warm voice.

It will require affectionate pianissimos (very soft) and tender diminuendos (becoming softer to create a calm mood).

What to listen for: In the prelude to the aria's title line, Des Grieux sings in a full voice "At last, Manon, we are together alone!" Her tears soften his voice in an expression of sweetness and sensitivity. He speaks about how happiness is fleeting and expresses a lovely diminuendo with the words "it might fly away."

...mais le bonheur est **passager**	...but happiness is **fleeting**,
et le ciel l'a fait si **léger**	and heaven has made it so **light**
qu'on a toujours peur	that one is always afraid
qu'il s'envole.	it might fly away.

He then asks her to listen to his dream with the words "closing my eyes." He sings with the conviction that happiness is within their reach. The dynamic (volume) is very quiet as his voice is soft and sustained.

En fermant les yeux je vois là-bas	Closing my eyes, I see far away
une **humble retraite**,	a **humble retreat**,
une **maisonnette** toute blanche	a white **little cottage**
au fond des bois!	lost in the woods!

After comparing his dream to paradise, he sings in a sad and darkened tone that it will be sad and lonely without Manon. "Manon" is sung pianissimo and very affectionately. In the final lines, he makes his plea in a round warm voice with a tender diminuendo ending with the words "Come! There will be our life, if you want to, O Manon!"

C'est le **paradis**! Oh non!	It's **paradise**! Oh no!
Tout est là triste et **morose**,	Everything there is sad and **sullen**,
car il y manque une chose...	because one thing is missing...
il y faut encor Manon!	it still needs Manon!

"Je marche sur tous les chemins" ("I walk on all roads") and Gavotte
from *Manon*

Performed by Manon (courtesan and woman of leisure)

Dramatic setting: It was a custom for people of leisure to be seen walking on a fashionable avenue in 18th century Paris. The youthful Manon is splendidly dressed as she stands next to her carriage on a fashionable avenue. Her song expresses her joy at attracting attention. A Gavotte refers to a French courtly dance rhythm.

Vocal requirements: The song calls for a soprano who can constantly change intentions and inflections to convey gaiety, youthfulness, self-confidence, sentimentality, and innocent pride in her beauty. She employs coloratura (decorative and rapid trills) and staccato (brief pauses between) notes. They lead to a high note to express laughter.

What to listen for: Manon's voice begins light and bright with some coyness and good humor. She describes her own beauty and happiness in a naïve and spontaneous manner without sounding boastful. She proudly stresses the words "marche" (walk) and "bien" (to do well). Her voice rises with pride as she refers to "beauty" and "queen."

Je **marche** sur tous les chemins	I **walk** on all roads
aussi bien qu'une **souveraine**;	as well as does a **sovereign**;
on s'**incline**, on baise ma main,	people **bow** and kiss my hand,
car par la **beauté** je suis reine!	for because of my **beauty** I am queen!

The second verse is often referred to as the *Gavotte*. It is more serious than the first verse. She advises young people to respond to the call of love before it is too late. Her voice is simple, melodious, and with a certain youthful authority.

Obéissons quand leurs **voix** appelent	Let's **obey** when their **voices** beckon us,
aux **tendres amours** toujours,	to **tender loves**, always; as long
tant que vous êtes **belle**, usez sans	as you are still **beautiful**, use up all your
les **compter** vos jours, tous vos jours.	days without **counting** them!

Manon becomes more sentimental and intimate and warns that the most faithful heart can forget love with her voice lingering on "amour." The concluding four lines repeat the final lines in the first verse and warn to "take full advantage of youth." The ending is light and fast with a brief sound of laughter.

Profitons bien de la jeunesse,	Let's take full advantage of youth,
des jours qu'amène le **printemps**,	of the days that **springtime** brings;
aimons, chantons, rions sans **cesse**,	let's love, laugh and sing without **stopping**,
nous n'aurons pas toujours vingt ans!	while we're still only twenty!

"Ah! fuyez, douce image"
("Ah! flee, sweet memory")
from *Manon*

Performed by Des Grieux (a cavalier of nobility)

Dramatic setting: Although Manon still loves Des Grieux, she has left him to live a life of pleasure and wealth with an older man. Des Grieux has entered a seminary to pursue a religious life. In a state of meditation, he declares that he can find peace by renouncing worldly desires, but he is still haunted by memories of Manon.

Vocal requirements: This song calls for a tenor who can convince the listener that he is struggling to achieve a state of serenity by overcoming his anxieties. In an effort to express his conflicting emotions, his voice will fluctuate between a warm legato (smooth and melodic flow) to an agitated crescendo, and from diminuendos and pianissimos to high A- and B-flats.

What to listen for: Des Grieux's opening words "I am alone! Alone at last!" suggest that he is struggling with inner conflicts. He acknowledges that the "moment suprême" has arrived with a forte on "suprême." The following three lines express a serene legato as he comments on how faith has given him a "sacred peace."

Je suis seul! Seul enfin!	I am alone! Alone at last!
C'est le **moment suprême!**	This is the **supreme moment!**
Il n'est plus rien que j'aime que le	There is no longer anything that I love but
repos sacré que m'apporte la foi!	the **sacred peace** that faith affords me!

His first charming vision of Manon "Ah! flee sweet memory..." is expressed in a warm legato voice. He will reach a crescendo and A-flat on "chère" (dear). His voice then grows more intense to reveal his suffering and how his heart has bled. He repeats the word "fuyez" (flee) several times and softly on the last "fuyez!"

Ah! fuyez, douce **image**,	**Ah!** flee sweet **memory** to dear,
à mon âme trop chère!	to my heart; **respect** the peace and
Respectez un repos **cruellement** gagné...	quiet **cruelly** earned...
Ah! fuyez! fuyez! loin de moi!...	Ah flee, flee far from me!...

The sound of the chapel organ helps to support Des Grieux's struggle to free himself from Manon's image. As he prays to the Lord in a hopeful voice, the obsession returns and his voice turns darker as he refers to the passing shadow. In the final lines, he again requests that the sweet image flee "...far from me, far from me." As he walks away, the aria fades away on a diminuendo (the voice diminishes).

Mon Dieu, de votre **flame purifiez** mon âme et **dissipez** à sa lueur l'ombre qui passe encor dans le fond de mon coeur.	Heavenly Father! **Purify** my soul and with your **fire**! And by its light **dispel** with your fire, the shadow that still lurks in the depths of my heart.

Offenbach Arias

"Les oiseaux dans la charmille" ("The birds in the arbor")
from *Les Contes d'Hoffmann*

Performed by Olympia (a mechanical doll)

Dramatic setting: The scene is a large ballroom with an assortment of strange inventions. Olympia seems very real to her party guests even though she has to be wound up several times, by her inventor, to complete this song. In this charming and amusing song, Olympia tells how everything about her speaks to her of love. When Olympia is wound up and performing well, the audience responses with loud and prolonged applause.

Vocal requirements: This very demanding song calls for a very skilled coloratura (decorative lines with rapid trills) with a crystal-clear, cheerful, and happy sound. She must be able to suddenly alternate from legato to staccato and from soft (piano) to loud (forte). She must climb to B- and E-flats, and descend from diminuendo (growing softer) to pianissimo (very soft). The trills express her vitality and cheerfulness.

What to listen for: The aria has two stanzas, a moderate tempo (speed), and a near constant legato with short interruptions (staccato). Her mechanical nature comes from repeating phrases and by runs that suggest turning and stopping wheels. The opening and title phrase is legato with short pauses, and "d'amour" is sung in a loud and brilliant voice.

Les oiseaux dans la charmille,	The birds in the arbor,
dans les cieux **l'astre** du jour,	**the star** of day in the heavens,

tout parle à la **jeune fille**
d'amour.

everything speaks to the **young girl**
of love.

The last two lines in each stanza are similar and begin with a trill on "Ah!" It signals a demonstration of the doll's mechanical success. The singer must be prepared to switch gears abruptly from legato to staccato (smooth to broken) and piano to forte (soft to loud). The trills demonstrate the technical achievements of her two inventors.

Ah! voilà la **chanson gentille**,
la chanson d'Olympia.

Ah! that is the **nice song**,
the song of Olympia.

The second stanza is written the same as the first stanza. After the inventor rewinds Olympia, she repeats her program with a new vitality. As in the first stanza, she must go from a bouncy and elegant staccato to an indifferent legato and from loud to soft. There is a feeling of anxiety as the staccato begins to stagger (time to rewind) and then stall on the high B-flats. In the final bars, her full voiced trills (adjacent notes sung with different tones) suggest a job well done. And enthusiastic applause is her reward.

Tout ce qui chante et **résonne**,
et soupire **tour** à tour,
émeut son **coeur** qui **frissonne**
d'amour. Ah! tout parle d'**amour**.

Everything that sings and **resounds**,
and in sighs in **turn**,
she excites his **fluttering heart**,
with love. Ah! Everything speaks of **love**.

"Scintille, diamant" ("Sparkle, diamond")
from *Les Contes d'Hoffmann*

Performed by Dappertutto (evil magician)

Dramatic setting: Dappertutto holds his diamond overhead and calls on its power to place a spell on the courtesan, Giulietta. Once she is under his spell, she will steal Hoffmann's reflection (soul) with a mirror. The diamond is Dappertutto's instrument for controlling lives and exercising his evil power.

Vocal requirements: This song calls for an outstanding baritone capable of combining elegance, sarcasm, and evil intentions. He must convey a strong will that cannot be resisted. His voice should have a velvet and beautiful tone that can sustain a long melodic passage. At the end, it must rise from a pianissimo to a G-sharp crescendo.

What to listen for: The opening recitative starts piano and requires poise and authority. The whole recitative is presented as one piece and expresses Dappertutto's strong will, irresistible power, and evil character. "On my word" is sung forte and reveals Dappertutto's evil nature. The rest of the recitative is sung with great and irresistible force.

Foi de **diable** et de **capitaine!**	On my word as **devil** and **captain!**
Tu feras comme lui.	You will do like him.
Je veux que Giulietta t'**ensorcelle**...	I want Giulietta to **enchant** you...

With the words, "Sparkle, diamond," the voice becomes magical and beautiful. Dappertutto must sound seductive as he sets his trap to capture Hoffmann's soul. He refers to "or woman" with a cheerful voice and becomes more intense with the words, "one leaves its life here..." The words, "loses her soul" must be powerful.

L'alouette ou la **femme**,	The lark or **woman**,
à cet appas vainqueur	both go to this triumphant bait
vont de l'aile ou du **coeur**:	by wings or by **heart**:
l'une y laisse la vie,	one leaves its life here,
et l'autre y perd son âme!	and the other loses her soul!

The magician speaks pianissimo (very softly) to his jewel, "Ah! Scintille, diamant," as the orchestra expresses the diamond's glitter. After a crescendo on the first "entice her," he sings, "Beau diamant" in a soft and caressing tone. The last "entice her" begins piano and slowly grows into a G-sharp crescendo at full strength.

Ah! Scintille, **diamant**,	Ah! Sparkle, **diamond**, you the
miroir où se prend l'alouette,	**mirror** by which the lark is caught,
scintille, diamant,	sparkle, diamond,
attire-la, attire-la.	**entice her**, entice her.
Beau diamant, scintille,	**Beautiful** diamond, sparkle,
attire-la!	entice her!

"O Dieu, de quelle ivresse" ("Oh God, with what ecstasy") from *Les Contes d'Hoffmann*

Performed by Hoffmann (a poet)

Dramatic setting: Hoffmann is outside Giulietta's residence on a moonlit night in Venice. He is enchanted by Giulietta, a lovely courtesan, and sings this passionate and beautiful song of love. He doesn't know that she is under the spell of an evil magician about to steal his soul. This is Hoffmann's second tale of an ill-fated love affair.

Vocal requirements: This song requires a lyric-spinto tenor of outstanding intensity. He must display great ease in handling a high tenor range and an outstanding legato. He must convey breathless enchantment and all-consuming passion. The song requires crescendos and diminuendos (growing louder and softer), and a high B-flat at the close.

What to listen for: The title line begins softly as Hoffmann speaks of Giulietta's overwhelming enchantment. The first three lines begin very light, in the upper registers, allowing him to sustain the notes. His voice begins to expand on the E-flat of "Ivresse" (rapture). The voice is more sustained with an enchanted lightness when he compares her voice to a "divine concert."

O Dieu, de quelle ivresse	O God, with what ecstasy do you
embrases-tu mon âme,	set my soul on fire,
comme un **concert divin**	your **voice** has **penetrated**
ta **voix** m'a **pénétré**!	me like a **divine concert**!

There is a crescendo of intensity with the words "my whole being is consumed." There is a long value on "flamme" (flame) as the voice builds toward a crescendo. The line "like radiant stars" increases in intensity with the feeling of growing passion. The legato must be maintained as the vocal line emphasizes the sensuous text.

D'un feu doux et brûlant	My whole being is **devoured**
mon être est **dévoré**;	by a sweet burning fire;
tes regards dans les miens	your eyes have poured forth
ont épanché leur **flamme**	their **flame** into mine
comme des **astres radieux**.	like **radiant stars**.

Hoffmann sings a diminuendo of sensuous delight when he refers to her "balmy breath" passing "over my lips..." The very soft legato takes on greater warmth. The final line "my beloved, I am your own!" ends on a high B-flat as Hoffmann unleashes his passion.

Et je sens, o ma bien-aimée,	And oh my beloved, I feel
passer ton haleine **embaumée**	your **balmy** breath **pass**
sur mes lèvres et sur mes yeux!	over my lips and my eyes!

"Elle a fui, la tourterelle!" ("She has fled, the turtle dove!")
from *Les Contes d'Hoffmann*

Performed by Antonia (singer and Hoffmann's fiancée)

Dramatic setting: Antonia is a sensitive young woman with singing ability, but she has been warned not to sing because she is weak from consumption (tuberculosis). She is engaged to Hoffmann, but they have been separated for some time. She sings a song, out of loneliness, to remind her of her absent lover, as she plays her clavichord.

Vocal requirements: This song calls for a lyric soprano with a clear and sensitive voice. Although not vocally demanding, the song requires Antonia to reveal her innermost emotions. She must convey to the listener a sweet sadness, anxious longing, intense faithfulness, and sincere devotion. She will end her song with signs of her frail condition.

What to listen for: The opening words of the recitative are soft and rather slow to express Antonia's sadness at being separated from her lover. To help her escape the memory of her dead mother, Antonia's father moved her to a distant house. The turtledove is a symbol of a girl separated from her lover. The words "I hear him, I see him" are expressed with sadness and difficulty.

Elle a **fui, la tourterelle!**	She has **fled, the turtle dove!**
Ah, **souvenir** trop doux!	Ah, too sweet a **memory!**
Image trop **cruelle!**	Too **bitter** an **image!**
Hélas, à mes genoux	Alas, I hear him, I see him
je l'entends, je le vois!	at my knees!

After expressing her faithfulness in the first verse, the second verse is a passionate call for a response. Her voice becomes more intense with the words "My beloved, my voice calls you..." There is an ascending pitch with the words "yes, my heart is yours alone!" Her voice changes to sweet sadness when she refers to the turtledove.

Mon bien-aimé, **ma voix** t'appelle,	My beloved, **my voice** calls you,
oui, tout **mon coeur** est à toi!	yes, **my heart** is yours alone!
Elle a fui, la tourterelle,	She has fled, the turtle dove,
elle a fui loin de toi.	she has fled far from you.

Antonia's voice become very intense with the words "My beloved," followed by a diminuendo on "my voice entreats you..." The tempo increases and broadens to a crescendo in the next line "...ah, your heart comes to me!" The final words are sung very softly and her voice fades on "toi" (you). This is a sign of exhaustion and her frailty.

Mon bien-aimé, ma **voix** t'**implore**,	My beloved, my **voice entreats** you,
Ah, que ton coeur vienne à moi!	ah, your heart comes to me!
Elle a fui, la tourterelle,	She has fled, the turtle dove,
elle a fui, loin de toi.	she has fled far from you.

Beethoven Arias

"Abscheulicher! ... Komm, Hoffnung" ("Monster! ... Come, hope")
from *Fidelio*

Performed by Fidelio (wife of the prisoner Florestan)

Dramatic setting: Fidelio's husband, Florestan, has been jailed as a political prisoner. She has disguised herself as a young man and has become an assistant to the jail keeper. She has just overheard the evil prison governor's plan to murder her husband. The beginning of the aria expresses her anger with the word "Abscheulicher!" (Monster!)

Vocal requirements: This aria calls for an outstanding dramatic soprano capable of first expressing outrage and anger and then changing to devotion and undying faith. It requires a voice with a broad range and scope and the capacity to change speeds from a moving adagio (slow) to a brisk allegro (lively). The aria requires great vocal agility, power and range.

What to listen for: The first section is a recitative that begins with a brief and agitated string introduction. Fidelio is alone when she denounces the evil jail governor. After expressing her outrage, her voice changes to mercy with a softer and slower accompaniment. She finds serenity in the glowing memories of a shining rainbow.

Doch toben auch wie Meereswogen	Even though like ocean waves
dir in der **Seele** Zorn und Wut,	anger and hatred storm in your **soul**,
so leuchtet mir ein Farbenbogen	in me shines a rainbow
der hell auf **dunklen** Wolken ruht.	resting bright on **dark** clouds.

The adagio section consists of a beautiful cantilena that reveals Fidelio's warm heart. The breathing must be timed to give eloquence and a natural sound to the phrasing. Each short phrase should increase in intensity. The voice becomes stronger and more urgent with the words "Oh come..." A hymn-like song of three horns signals her determination, nobility, and heroic character. The melody expresses her courage, devotion, and faith in her mission.

Komm, Hoffnung, lass den **letzten Stern**	**Come, hope,** do not let fade the **last star**
der Müden nicht erbleichen,	of the weary!
o komm, erhell'**mein Ziel**...	Oh come, light up **my goal**...

The allegro con brio section is driven by Fidelio's strong determination to locate and free her husband. The tempo is unrelenting and the dynamic changes follow her sentiments. Her fervent wish to "force my way to the place" is a sustained piano. She reaches a fast ending on a triumphal high note as she expresses her determination to be strong.

O du, für den ich alles trug,	**Oh you**, for whom I have borne it all,
könnt'ich zur Stelle dringen,	if only I could force my way to the place
wo Bosheit dich in Fesseln schlug	where spitefulness put you in chains
und **süssen** Trost dir **bringen!**	and **bring** you **sweet** relief!

A brief interlude of horns and bassoons sets the mood for her decisive and renewed dedication. Her voice must remain strong and determined without losing her nobility to the end of the aria. The words reflect Beethoven's faith in devotion to overcome injustice.

"In des Lebens Frühlingstagen" ("In the springtime of my life")
from *Fidelio*

Performed by Florestan (prisoner and Fidelio's husband)

Dramatic setting: Florestan is chained to a wall in a dark prison. In the opening recitative, he cries out his agony on a high note, "God, What darkness here! Oh gruesome silence!" In the aria that follows, Florestan expresses his faith in God and vision of freedom for speaking the truth and opposing evil and oppression. As the aria closes, he has the vision of an angel approaching before he collapses from physical weakness.

Vocal requirements: This song calls for a spinto tenor with strong heroic and dramatic qualities capable of expressing deep despair followed by high passages of hopefulness and a vision of freedom and righteousness. It requires a tenor with strong tone color and phrasing who is capable of expressing deep pathos for a character who has suffered great injustice but who has an unrelenting faith in goodness and truth.

What to listen for: The orchestral introduction sets the somber mood with the sound of kettledrums. In the first section, Florestan confirms his faith in God and his content in having spoken the truth. He justifies his miserable situation by his belief in God's will. In a sad but not angry voice, he explains how he was willing to endure his suffering because he fulfilled his responsibility by speaking the truth.

In des **Lebens** Frühlingstagen	In the springtime of my **life**,
ist das Glück von mir **gefloh'n.**	happiness has **flown away**.
Wahrheit wagt' ich kühn zu sagen,	I dared to boldly speak the truth,
und die Ketten sind mein Lohn.	and chains are my reward.

Beethoven paints a grim picture of horror in a minor key that could have come out of Dante's hell. The mood softens as Florestan sings an adagio cantabile (slowly sung) air that has been compared, to "the last flicker of life's flame before its extinction."

Willig duld' ich alle Schmerzen,	**Willingly** I endured all pain,
ende schmählich meine Bahn;	and **end** my life in misery;
süßer Trost in **meinem Herzen:**	**sweet** consolation of **my heart:**
meine Pflicht hab' ich getan!	I have done my duty!

An oboe accompanies his vision of freedom in the form of an approaching angel. In the final section, his voice becomes more agitated as he sings a very high and sustained passage. His voice creates a feeling of desperation and then fades with exhaustion as he collapses from physical weakness. A lonely oboe surrounds his voice as he sings this difficult passage.

Ich seh' wie **ein Engel** im **rosigen** Duft	**I see an angel** with a **rosy** scent
sich tröstend zur Seite mir stellet. Ein	providing comfort at my side in this place.
Engel. Leonoren, der Gattin so gleich,	An angel, the same as my wife, Leonore,
der führt mich zur **Freiheit** in's	who leads me to **freedom** in the
himmlische Reich!	**heavenly** Kingdom!

Wagner Arias

"Die Frist ist um"
("The time is up")
from *Der Fliegende Holländer*

Performed by Dutchman (a cursed sea captain)

Dramatic setting: The Dutchman's extended song describes how he was condemned by the devil to sail for all eternity. The only way to escape the curse is to find a woman who's completely devoted to him. He is only allowed to land once every seven years. The Dutchman sings about his fate after coming ashore, as he stands on a rocky cliff above his ship.

Vocal requirements: This song requires a dramatic baritone with a ringing spinto (a lyric voice capable of reaching a dramatic level). He must have good resonance (vocal richness) in the lower range and a broad range of dynamic levels (degrees of volume). He must convey a somber and sinister tone.

What to listen for: The first section expresses the Dutchman's endless wanderings. He sounds tired, cold, and passionless as he refers to the "proud ocean" and his "torment everlasting!" The orchestral accompaniment suggests a turbulent and stormy sea. There is a somber resentment and resignation as he accepts his fate.

Ha, stolzer **Ozean**! In kurzer Frist	Ha, proud **Ocean**! In a short time
sollst du mich wieder tragen!	you will carry me again!
Dein Trotz ist beugsam,	Your defiance is pliable,
doch ewig **meine** Qual!	but **my** torment everlasting!

In the second section, the Dutchman is resigned to never find death. He expresses excitement as he describes how he hoped to die when he fought a pirate. His voice rises from piano to forte (growing from soft to loud) as he relates how he was denied a grave even in the ocean's deepest abyss. Death would allow him to escape the curse he is under.

Wie oft in Meeres tiefsten Schlund	How often in the ocean's deepest abyss
stürzt'ich voll Sehnsucht mich hinab.	did I plunge most longingly.
Da, wo der Schiffe furchtbar **Grab,**	There, in the dreaded **tomb** of ships,
trieb **mein Schiff** ich zum Klippengrund.	I drove **mine ship** on the rocks.

The final section calls for great vocal energy as the Dutchman calls on the end of the world to receive him. His voice should not reach its climax until the concluding lines. This section begins with the words, "One only hope shall now remain..." because the Dutchman sees one possibility for redemption. His voice rises to forte when he declares the earth "must perish nonetheless!" When the world collapses, he will enter a state of "nothingness."

Nur eine **Hoffnung** soll mir bleiben,	One only **hope** shall now remain for me,
nur eine **unerschüttert** steh'n:	one alone stands **unshakable**:
so **lang'** der **Erde** Keim' auch treiben,	as **long** as the **earth's** seeds may grow,
so **muss** sie doch zu Grunde geh'n!	it **must** perish nevertheless!

"Johohoe! Traft ihr das Schiff im Meere?" ("Johohoe! Have you met the ship at sea?" [or "Senta's Ballad"])
from *Der Fliegende Holländer*

Performed by Senta (sea captain's daughter)

Dramatic setting: Senta, her nurse, and several friends are spinning cloth. A portrait of the Flying Dutchman hangs on the wall of her father's house. The portrait has long fascinated the romantic Senta. She sings the legend of how the Dutchman goes ashore every seven years in search of a faithful wife.

Vocal requirements: The song requires a lirico-spinto (the vocal ability to move from melodic to dramatic) voice with a comfortable top range. The voice must sound young and capable of deep feeling and intense sensitivity. The deep desire to redeem the Dutchman covers the lower and middle part of the voice. The voice becomes brilliant as she calls on the Lord's angel to show her the way.

What to listen for: In the first verse, the voice must convey a distant ship and then imitate the sound of the wind. Vivid colors should be created in the mind of the listener. The voice softens with the mention of the pale man (Dutchman). After a reference to "find a woman," the following phrase calls for a long lyrical (smooth and melodic) expression.

Doch kann dem **bleichen Manne**	But for the **pale man**
Erlösung einstens noch werden,	salvation still may come one day,
fänd'er ein Weib, das bis in **den Tod**	should he find a woman who **until death**
getreu ihm auf **Erden**.	would be faithful here on **earth**.

The second verse repeats the pattern of the first. In a firm voice, we learn that the Dutchman swore that he would search for all eternity. With a touch of horror in the voice, we learn that Satan has condemned him to crisscross the ocean without rest. The voice becomes softer and more intense as Senta prays for his salvation.

Doch, dass der arme **Mann** noch	But, so that the poor **man**
Erlösung fände auf Erden,	may still be redeemed on earth,
zeigt **Gottes Engel** an	the **Lord's angel** shows
wie sein Heil ihm einst könne werden.	how one day his salvation may
	come about.

The third verse expresses a deeper involvement as Senta sees herself as the Dutchman's salvation. The voice becomes more brilliant and ecstatic and ends on a triumphant note. Senta has exposed her desire to redeem the Dutchman, by singing the ballad.

Auf in **See**, ohne **Rast**, ohne Ruh.'	Out to the **sea**, without **rest**, without peace.
Ich sei's die dich durch ihre Treu erlöse!	I be the one who by her faith will redeem you!
Mög' Gottes Engel mich dir zeigen!	May the Lord's angel reveal me to you!
Durch **mich sollst** du das Heil erreichen!	Through **me shall** you obtain salvation!

"Einsam in trüben Tagen"
("Alone in dark days"
[or "Elsa's Dream"])
from *Lohengrin*

Performed by Elsa (Gottfried's sister)

Dramatic setting: Elsa's brother, the young Gottfried, is the legitimate heir to the late duke of Brabant. Gottfried has disappeared mysteriously on a forest journey with Elsa, and she has been accused of murdering him. She appears radiant and pure before the king and his hostile court and sings about a knight who rescued her in a dream.

Vocal requirements: This song requires a lyrico-spinto (the ability to move from melodic to dramatic expression) soprano with a bright and luminous sound. Her voice must remain pure, clear, and uplifting in front of a hostile audience. The knight in her dream has placed her under a magic spell. She must express sorrow, adoration, faith, and dedication as she faces her accusers.

What to listen for: The first part has a slow speed (tempo). Elsa gives a brief and simple description of the grief she experienced at her brother's disappearance. Her reference to "Lord" and "my heart's deepest sorrows" should arouse sympathy in the listener. Prayer helped her to bear the burden of losing her brother and being accused of murder.

Einsam in trüben Tagen	Alone in dark days
hab ich zu **Gott** gefleht,	did I implore the **Lord**,
des **Herzens** tiefstes Klagen	my **heart's** deepest sorrows
ergoss **ich im** Gebet...	**I** poured out **in** prayer...

The next part relates to Elsa's dream. Her voice softens to suggest the approaching "sweet sleep." A beautiful orchestral theme is heard before she describes her enchanted dream. A radiant pianissimo (very soft sound) introduces her shining vision of a knight. The word "lichter" (light) should ring brightly. Her voice rises and becomes more animated as she identifies the knight who has come to her defense.

...ich **sank** in **süssen Schlaf.**	...I **sank** into **sweet sleep.**
In **lichter** Waffen Scheine	In brilliant **light** armor
ein Ritter nahte da,	a knight approached,
so tugendlicher Reine...	so virtuous and pure...

In the final part, Elsa announces her pledge to the knight in a full and glorious voice. She ends on a note of exaltation by offering him a crown to wear in her father's land and herself in marriage. This more spinto part requires Elsa to express herself in a more dramatic voice.

Hört, was dem Gottgesandten	**Hear** what the envoy of God
ich biete für Gawähr:	I offer as a pledge:
in meines Vaters Landen	**in my father's countries**
die **Krone** trage er...	he shall wear the **crown**...

"In fernem Land" ("In a distant land")
from *Lohengrin*

Performed by Lohengrin (knight of the Holy Grail)

Dramatic setting: Lohengrin is the knight who came to Elsa's defense. He betroths himself to Elsa on condition that she should never ask his name, rank, or birthplace, due to a vow he took when he became a knight of the Holy Grail. If she does so, he must leave her. When she breaks his condition, he reveals his background in this song and departs in a swan drawn boat.

Vocal requirements: The song calls for a vigorous and flexible tenor voice. The phrases require many inflections as he reveals his miraculous tale with deep conviction. He must maintain a steady mezzo-forte (medium-loud) narration while suggesting a noble and holy mission. He must also be able to sing ringing high notes with sincerity.

What to listen for: The opening bars have a spiritual and luminous quality that captures Lohengrin's character. He begins with a pianissimo (very soft sound) narration to suggest a distant and reverent land. The tone becomes more lyrical (smooth and melodic) with the name of his fortress "Montsalvat." His voice becomes lighter and pianissimo as he refers to "a lighter temple."

In fernem **Land**,	In a distant **land**,
unnahbar euren Schritten,	unapproachable to your steps,
liegt **eine Burg**,	there lies **a fortress**,
die Montsalvat genannt.	named Montsalvat.
Ein **lichter Tempel**...	A **shining temple**...

He sings with serene beauty as he describes the vessel within the temple. Lohengrin's voice rises to a crescendo (vocal increase in volume) as he mentions the yearly coming of a dove and the bird's renewal power. The word "Grail" is sung with a glowing and glorious high note.

Alljährlich naht vom **Himmel** eine Taube, um **neu** zu **stärken** seine Wunderkraft. Es heisst der **Gral**...	Once a year from **heaven** a dove approaches to give **new strength** to its miraculous power. It is called the **Grail**...

He goes on to describe how the sacred power of the Grail accompanies the chosen knight even when he travels to distant lands. His message becomes more earthlike as he states the law of the grail. He warns that if he is recognized, then he must depart. The warning begins on a loud crescendo and ends with a diminuendo (to a softer tone). In the final lines of his aria, Lohengrin reveals his identity with solemnity and grandeur.

Des Ritters drum sollt Zweifel ihr **nicht** hegen, erkennt ihr **ihn,** dann **muss** er von euch ziehn.	Therefore do **not** harbor doubts about the knight, if you recognize **him,** then he **must** depart from you.

"Morgenlich leuchtend im rosigen Schein" ("Shining in the rosy morning glow")
from *Die Meistersinger von Nürnberg*

Performed by Walter (a knight and mastersinger contestant)

Dramatic setting: The city of Nuremberg is holding its midsummer festival of poetry and music. Walter sings this song in a contest conducted by the Mastersingers' Guild. If he wins the contest, he becomes a Mastersinger and wins the right to marry the goldsmith's daughter, Eva. He must perform the song in front of the city's population.

Vocal requirements: The song calls for a lyrico-spinto (both melodic and dramatic) tenor with the flexibility to sing long melodic lines. He must demonstrate power and brilliance with growing intensity and lyricism from verse-to-verse. The tenor should demonstrate a particular beauty in the high medium and higher part of his range.

What to listen for: The first verse begins softly with a moderate speed (tempo). The voice has a warm and glowing sound. It builds into a loud crescendo (vocal climax) with the word "Wonnen" (delights). It is a passionate vision of an enchanted garden, a tree hanging with fruit, and a beautiful woman (Eva) in paradise.

Morgenlish leuchtend im **rosigen Schein,**	**Shining** in the **rosy morning** glow,
von Blüt' und Duft geschwellt die Luft,	the air heavy with blossoms and fragrances,
voll aller Wonnen nie ersonnen,	full with unimagined delights,
ein Garten lud mich ein,	**a garden** invited me,
dort **unter** einem **Wunderbaum,**	there **under** a **wondrous tree**
von **Früchten reich behangen**...	with **richly hanging fruit**...

There is a short chorus before the second verse. This verse has a similar pattern to the first. Walter sings as an inspired poet and his voice is firmer and slightly faster. His voice brightens and shines with the words "Quelle" and "Welle." He will go on to tell how he observed a sublime woman, "the Muse of the Parnassus," beneath a laurel tree.

Abendlich dämmernd umschloss mich die **Nacht.**	At **evening's** dusk **night** wrapped around me.
Auf steilem **Pfad** war **ich** genaht	On a steep **path I** had come near
zu einer Quelle reiner Welle...	a spring of clear water...

Again, a short chorus precedes the final verse. This verse combines the elements of love and poetry (Paradise and Parnassus), and ends on a triumphal note of having won Eva and the prize. There is a series of crescendos and decrescendos (vocal increases and decreases in volume). The final reference to "Parnassus and Paradise!" represents the fulfillment of his effort. Parnassus refers to a sacred mountain in Greek times.

...ward kühn von mir gefreit;	...boldly was she wooed by me;
am lichten **Tag** der **Sonnen**	on a sparkling **sunny day**
durch **Sanges** Sieg gewonnen,	won through the triumph of **song,**
Parnass und Paradies!	**Parnassus and Paradise!**

"Dich, teure Halle"
("You, dear hall")
from *Tannhäuser*

Performed by Elisabeth (niece of Thuringia's ruler)

Dramatic setting: Elisabeth fell in love with the knight Tannhäuser after he distinguished himself in a music festival. After a long absence, he has returned to the court to take part in another contest. Elisabeth is radiant with joy as she sings her aria in the empty Hall of the Minstrels.

Vocal requirements: The song calls for a lyrico-spinto (ability to move from melodic to dramatic) soprano of power, intensity, and brilliance. Her voice must convey purity, enthusiasm, and warmth. Although she has a royal sound to her voice, she must also express the charm, beauty, and joy of a young woman in love. She will be required to reach a B-flat to express her happiness.

What to listen for: The basic tempo is allegro (lively) because Elisabeth is addressing the empty hall like a living person. The words, "You, dear hall" are full of affection. After this joyful outburst, the mood changes to a sweet emotion and piano legato (a soft, smooth sound) as she recalls Tannhäuser's songs.

Dich, **teure Halle**, grüss **ich** wieder,	You, **dear hall**, **I** greet you again,
froh grüss ich dich, geliebter **Raum**!	joyfully I greet you, beloved **room**!
In dir **erwachen** seine Lieder	In you **awaken** his songs
und wechen mich aus düstrem **Traum**.	**and** rouse me from darkest **dreams**.

Her voice saddens as she recalls how empty the hall was after Tannhäuser's departure. She expresses her compassion for the hall with the words, "joy departed!"

Da er aus dir geschieden,	After he left you,
wie öd' erschienst du **mir**!	how empty you seemed to **me**!
Aus mir entfloh der **Frieden**,	**Peace** fled from you,
die Freude zog aus dir!	and joy departed!

Suddenly, the joyful sound of the orchestra signals a spirit of hope and celebration. Elisabeth's vibrant voice rises above the orchestra. She shares her resilient emotions with the hall with the thought that Tannhäuser will bring "new life to you and me." There is a triumphant feeling that he is no longer far away.

Wie jetzt **mein Busen** hoch sich hebet,	Now, as **my bosom** swells high,
so scheinst du jetzt mir stolz und hehr;	so you now seem proud and noble to me;
der mich und dich so neu belebet,	the one who gives new life to you and me,
nicht **länger** weilt er **ferne** mehr!	no **longer** does he stay so **far** away!

The four lines above are repeated with more vocal power and exaltation. The final two lines are "hail to you!" repeated twice. Her voice rises to a crescendo (volume peak) and soars to a high note as she releases the happiness inside her.

Weber Arias

"Durch die Wälder, durch die Auen" ("Through woods and through fields")
from *Der Freischütz*

Performed by Max (assistant forester)

Dramatic setting: Max is depressed because he has lost his shooting skills. He wants to win a shooting contest to become the new head ranger and marry the retiring head ranger's daughter. Max doesn't know that another ranger has cast a spell upon his ability to shoot straight. He reflects on his situation in front of a tavern.

Vocal requirements: the song requires a vigorous tenor (highest natural male voice) capable of switching from dramatic outburst to a legato (melodic and flowing) passage and back to a dramatic climax. The singer must respond to these sharp contrasts in vocal color and emotion, such as anger, love and despair, because Max is under the control of an evil force.

What to listen for: In the opening lines, Max's voice is loud and explosive as he asks questions that express his bewilderment. The orchestra then introduces a more sentimental sound, and Max begins to recall happier times with the words "Through woods and through fields..." The melody's moderate tempo (speed) expresses his joyful memories as a skilled hunter. The opera's title refers to someone with straight shooting skills.

Durch die **Wälder**, durch die Auen	Through **woods** and through fields
zog ich **leichten** Sinn's dahin;	I roamed with a **light** mind;
alles, was ich konnt'erschauen,	whatever I could behold
war des sichren Rohrs Gewinn.	**was the sure** barrel's prize.

The voice becomes softer and more lyrical (melodic) as he recalls Agathe's loving gaze. Some sinister notes and Max's unanswered questions interrupt these tender thoughts. After the evil spirit in the background disappears, he pictures Agathe at her window listening for his return. This warm portrait of faithful affection is sung with firmness and charm.

Jetzt ist wohl ihr Fenster **offen**	Now her window must be **open**
und sie horcht auf **meinen** Tritt,	and she harkens for **my** steps,
lässt nicht ab vom treuen **Hoffen**:	does not stop her faithful **hoping**:
Max **bringt gute** Zeichen mit.	Max **brings good** omens with him.

But then Max's anxiety returns and he expresses a deep sadness and despair that grabs him. The words convey anguish and a sense of rebellion. The short orchestral interludes give the singer time to prepare for a climatic question of "is there no living God?"

Doch mich **umgarnen** finstre Mächte,	But I am **ensnared** by obscure powers, I am
mich fasst Verzweiflung, foltert Spott.	seized by despair, and tormented by mockery.
O dringt kein Strahl durch diese **Nächte**,	Oh, does no ray penetrate this **darkness**,
herrscht **blind** das Schicksal,	does Fate reign **blindly**,
lebt kein **Gott**?	is there no living **God**?

"Leise, leise, fromme Weise"
("Softly, softly, pious melody")
from *Der Freischütz*

Performed by Agathe (head forester's daughter)

Dramatic setting: It is the eve of Agathe's wedding to Max, and she is alone in her father's house. She is worried because a hermit warned her that her life is in danger. Agathe steps out on the moonlit balcony and raises her hands in prayer for heavenly protection. She reflects on how sorrow accompanies love. She anxiously awaits Max's return.

Vocal requirements: The song requires a lirico-spinto (capacity for melodic and dramatic expression) soprano capable of expressing prayer-like devotion and crystal clear tones in the first part. The singer must capture Agathe's deep sincerity, sensitivity, and confidence that good will overcome evil. In the second part, she becomes more animated and enthusiastic as she anticipates Max's return.

What to listen for: The introduction is very slow and soft because Agathe's voice is filled with love for Max. With the words, "Softly, softly, pious melody," she sends a legato (smooth and melodic) prayer. The tender and bright tones reflect the beautiful night overhead. Her voice becomes darker and more urgent as she senses a storm in the distance. The prayer becomes louder and more intense as she calls on the Lord for protection.

Leise, leise, fromme Weise,	Softly, softly, pious melody,
schwing'dich auf zum **Sternenkreise**.	rise up to the **starry sky**.
Lied, erschalle, feiernd walle	Song, ring out, let in celebration
mein Gebet zur **Himmelshalle**.	my prayer flow up to the **heavenly vault**.

After concluding her prayer, she listens to the sounds of the forest, including a nightingale and cricket. The sound of horns suggests that someone is approaching. She expresses her agitated anticipation with the words, "It sounds like steps..." And her enthusiasm grows when she refers to keeping watch in the night.

Dort klingt's wie Schritte,	It sounds like steps over there,
dort aus der Tannen Mitte	there among the pine trees
kommt was hervor. Er ist's! Er ist's!	something steps forward. It is he! It is he!
Die **Flagge** der **Liebe mag wehn!**	The **flag** of **love may wave!**

Agathe still expresses some misgivings in the question, "Could I dare hope this?" The voice becomes more confident with a touch of affection when referring "to my dear love again." The song ends with the sound of vocal enjoyment as Agathe thanks heaven.

Konnt'ich das zu **hoffen** wagen?	Could I dare **hope** this?
Ja, es wandte sich das Glück	Yes, Fortune has turned around
zu dem teuren Freund zurück.	to my dear love again.
Will sich's **morgen** treu bewähren?	Will it prove faithful **tomorrow**?

"Und ob die Wolke sie verhülle" ("And though hidden by a cloud")
from *Der Freischütz*

Performed by Agathe (head forester's daughter)

Dramatic setting: Agathe is alone in her father's house and dressed in her bridal gown. She has been praying before her own altar and expressing her confidence in the Lord. She has faith that her fiancé, Max, will win the final shooting contest. If he is victorious, they will get married and he will become the new head forester.

Vocal requirements: This song calls for a lyric-spinto (capacity for melodic and dramatic expression) soprano. The lyric dimension is required to express a pure and melodious legato (smooth and flowing). The spinto dimension provides a dramatic element that conveys Agathe's active vitality. The more lively and dynamic side to her voice will suggest her attempt to communicate with Max while he is in the forest.

What to listen for: The song has three parts with the third part repeating the first. At the opening, a cello solo introduces Agathe's melody. Her voice must rise above the background of dark strings. Her reference to "Himmelszelt" should produce a radiant sound. A somewhat louder legato stresses her belief in a supreme power. The words "dort" (there) and "Welt" (world) are used to sustain the firmness of her beliefs. She must maintain the dynamic level reached on the high notes along with a constant legato.

Und ob die Wolke sie verhülle,	And though hidden by a cloud,
die **Sonne** bleibt am Himmelszelt,	the **sun** remains on the firmament,
es waltet dort ein heil'ger **Wille**,	there reigns a sacred **will**,
nicht **blindem** Zufall dient die **Welt**.	the **world** does not serve **blind** chance.

The second part affirms Agathe's belief that "Father will take good care..." of her. This part has a more personal, warmer and faster (speed) tempo. Her feelings have become more positive, radiant, and obedient to the Lord. Her reference to "letzter Morgen" and "sein Vaterwort" rise to a crescendo (rising to a vocal climax). The voice is serene, flowing and expresses great simplicity.

Für mich wird auch der **Vater** sorgen,	Of me, too, **Father** will take good care in
dem **kindlich Herz** und Sinn vertraut,	whom my **heart** and mind puts **childlike** trust;
und wär'dies auch **mein letzter Morgen**,	though this be **my last morning**,
rief mich sein **Vaterwort** als **Braut.**	though his **fatherly word** call me, the **bride**, away.

The return of part one should sound even more spiritual than the first time with the voice even more crystal clear and radiant. The last two lines are similar to the final lines in the first part. This return should capture both the lyric and the dramatic character of Agathe as she longs for Max's return and the Lord's protection.

Sein Auge, ewig rein und **klar,**	His eye, eternally pure and **clear,**
nimmt meiner auch mit **Liebe** wahr.	bestows me, too, his **loving** care.

Mozart Arias

"Dies Bildnis ist bezaubernd schön" ("This portrait is ravishingly beautiful")
from *Die Zauberflöte*

Performed by Tamino (a noble prince)

Dramatic setting: Prince Tamino falls unconscious while being pursued by a dragon. The Three Ladies, who serve the Queen of the Night, kill the serpent. A little later, they return and give him a portrait of the Queen's beautiful daughter. He instantly falls in love at first sight before meeting her evil and revengeful mother. He sings the famous aria, "This portrait is ravishingly beautiful."

Vocal requirements: The song calls for a lyric (smooth and melodic) tenor who can express deep sincerity and conviction. The voice should convey a noble respect, deep warmth, purity of admiration, and a poetic atmosphere. The tenor voice must be very flexible, melodious, and inflective as Tamino contemplates the beautiful portrait.

What to listen for: This is a very demanding song because it requires a variety of inflections. It has a very slow speed (tempo). For example, in the opening line, Tamino expresses a series of long and ringing vowels. The word "Götterbild" (divine picture) is lyrical and full of admiration. His reference to "Herz" (heart) is very enduring.

Dies Bildnis ist bezaubernd schön,	This portrait is ravishingly beautiful,
wie noch kein Auge je gesehn!	such as no eyes have ever seen!
Ich fühl'es, ich fühl'es,	**I feel** how this divine picture
wie dies Götterbild	is filling **my heart**
mein Herz mit **neuer** Regung füllt.	with **new** emotion.

The line "I cannot name..." is full of wonder. The next line "I feel it burn..." is full of passion. After answering his own question, he repeats the word "Liebe" (love) several times from piano to forte. He expresses a desire to "find her!" in an intense crescendo (growing climax).

Dies Etwas kann ich zwar nicht **nennen**,	This "something" I cannot **name**;
doch fühl'ich's hier wie **Feuer brennen**.	but I feel it **burn like fire**.
Soll die Empfindung **Liebe** sein?	Can this sensation be **love**?
Ja, ja, die Liebe ist's allein.	Yes, yes! It can only be love.
O wenn ich sie nur **finden** könnte!	Oh, if only I could **find** her!

In the final three lines, Tamino begins softly and then changes to a crescendo and forte as he imagines pressing her to "this burning heart." In the final line, he declares, "she would then be mine..." The last line is repeated five times with the final repeat being the most forceful and glorious. The five repeats reveal contrasting moods. By alternating piano and forte (soft and loud), the repeated line produces a more poetic and enduring love.

Ich würde sie voll Enzücken	Filled with delight I would
an diesen heissen Busen drücken,	place her against this burning heart,
und ewig wäre sie dann **mein**!	and she would then be **mine** forever!

"O zittre nicht, mein lieber Sohn!" ("Oh tremble not, my dear son!")
from *Die Zauberflöte*

Performed by Queen of the Night

Dramatic setting: Tamino is still contemplating the portrait when the Three Ladies reappear. They tell him that the Queen of the Night has chosen him to free her daughter. The Queen makes a dramatic entrance, often descending from the starry sky, and tells Tamino how her daughter was kidnapped. If he rescues her, he may have her as his bride.

Vocal requirements: This song is very demanding and calls for a soprano with strong lyrical and coloratura (rapid trills with great agility) skills. She must create a feeling of power and majesty. Although the Queen is evil, she must sound kind, cordial, and trustworthy. She must convey a variety of vocal accomplishments, including high notes, runs (rapid vocal passages), clarity and intensity. The queen must possess a high tessitura (a character's major vocal range).

What to listen for: In the short recitative (imitation of natural speech before the song), the orchestra creates a sense of majesty. In her opening lines, the Queen praises Tamino's goodness and wisdom. She then tries to win his sympathy by expressing her deep sadness over losing her daughter. There is a growing intensity as she goes from soft to moderately loud when referring to her lost happiness. Having won his sympathy, she refers to the villain with great resentment.

O zittre **nicht**, mein lieber **Sohn!**
Du bist unschuldig, weise, fromm...
Zum Leiden bin ich auserkoren,
denn **meine Tochter** fehlet mir.
Durch sie ging all **mein** Glück verloren,
ein Bösewicht entfloh mit ihr.

Oh tremble **not**, my dear **son!**
You are innocent, reasonable, good...
I am destined to grieve,
for I am longing for **my daughter.**
With her all **my** happiness was gone,
a villain escaped with her.

The Queen shifts the attention from herself to her daughter's frightening abduction. Her voice changes to a tragic and frightening tone to describe her panic-stricken daughter. The Queen was helpless to respond to her daughter's cry for help.

Noch seh'ich ihr Zittern
mit bangem Erschüttern,
ihr **ängstliches** Beben,
ihr schüchternes Streben!

I still see her trembling
with fearful emotion,
her **anguished** quivering,
her timid resistance!

In the final section, the Queen will employ a dazzling display of high coloratura and B-flats. She will use her vocal brilliance to overwhelm Tamino. She relies on a sustained legato (smooth and flowing) and allegro (lively and brisk) tempo. Her voice grows loud when she refers to "my daughter's savior!" She ends the song with a series of lively and remarkable runs on a high note.

Du, du wirst sie zu **befreien** gehen,
du wirst der **Tochter** Retter sein!
Und werd'ich dich als Sieger sehen,
so sei sie dann auf ewig dein!

You, you will go and set her **free;**
you will be my **daughter's** savior!
And if I see you victorious,
then will she be yours forever!

"Ach, ich fühl's es ist verschwunden" ("Ah, I feel that all is vanished") from *Die Zauberflöte)*

Performed by Pamina (Queen's daughter)

Dramatic setting: Tamino and Pamina must undergo rites of initiation to prove worthy of each other and to enter the Temple of Light. Pamina is happy to be reunited with Tamino, but she does not know that he has been ordered not to speak. She thinks his silence is a sign that he no longer loves her. Pamina's song expresses her deep grief.

Vocal requirements: This song requires a lyric soprano capable of expressing an intense grief. Each phrase should convey a simple beauty, purity of sound, and vibrant vowels. The voice must flow evenly and sustain a long range without breaks. The mood of hopelessness must prevail because she concludes by speaking of peace in death.

What to listen for: The tempo is a very slow andante. The opening bars express hopelessness with total conviction. Pamina expresses a tragic regret with the words "all is vanished." The next line reads "love's happiness." The word "love's" should convey warmth and a pleasant sound.

Ach, **ich fühl's**,	Alas, **I feel** that
es ist verschwunden,	all is vanished,
ewig hin mein ganzes Glück,	finished is **love**'s happiness,
ewig hin der **Liebe** Glück.	my total bliss.

The mood of hopelessness gains vocal strength with the next two lines when she states that he will never come "back again into my heart." The final words of this line end with a decrescendo (decrease in volume) of depression and despair.

Nimmer kommt ihr, Wonnestunden,	**Never** will you **come**, hours of enchantment,
meinem Herzen mehr zurück.	back again into **my heart**.

Pamina continues to speak to the silent Tamino trying to make him react to her sorrow. After several pleas, she expresses her yearning for peace in death.

Even when pleading for his attention, the sound of her love remains in her voice. The feeling of hopelessness and grief return with the line "If you do not feel love's longing," The voice turns very dark with a quiet sigh of despair in her final words "...then my peace must be in death."

Sieh, Tamino, **diese Tränen**	**See**, Tamino, see **these tears**
fließen, Trauter, dir **allein**.	**flow**, beloved, for you **alone**.
Fühlst du nicht der Liebe Sehnen,	If you do not feel love's longing,
so wird Ruhe im Tode sein.	then my peace must be in death.

"Voi, che sapete"
("You, who know")
from *Le Nozze di Figaro*

Performed by Cherubino (boy attendant)

Dramatic setting: The young Cherubino tends to fall in love with every woman. He adores the Countess Almaviva and has written a song about his affection. He sings the song to the Countess while Susanna, the chambermaid, accompanies him on the guitar. Cherubino is dressed in an elegant outfit, including a three-cornered hat with plumes.

Vocal requirements: In Mozart's time, it was common for a soprano or mezzo-soprano to sing the part of a young male. Cherubino should have a youthful and sincere sounding voice, and convey an elegant and simple rhythm. He must present his troubles and desires in a stately manner that will win the ladies' sympathy.

What to listen for: The first part has a sincere and formal sound without a sign of passion. Cherubino is presenting his new feelings of unrest and confusion before the Countess. The line beginning with "What I feel..." and ending with "...I don't understand it" should sound very candid to arouse the curiosity of the ladies. Cherubino is sincerely mystified by his new feelings.

Voi, che sapete che cosa è **amor**,	**You**, who know what **love** is,
Donne, vedete, s'io l'ho nel cor.	ladies, look if I have it in my heart.
Quello ch'io provo, vi ridirò,	What I feel, I tell you,
è per me **nuovo**, capir nol so.	is **new** to me, I don't understand it.

He begins to explain his emotions in detail in a lyric voice "I feel an emotion..." The word "desire" is intense, "delight" lighter, and "torment" more earnest and dark. The words "...my soul is burning" are expressed ardently. The contrasts between these words should not be harsh but, rather, have a delicate and tasteful sound. Cherubino is an attendant and must maintain a certain dignity and restraint.

Sento un affetto pien di **desir,**	I feel an emotion full of **desire,** which
ch'ora è **diletto,** ch'ora è martir.	now is a **delight,** and then is a torment.
Gelo, e poi sento l'alma avvampar,	I am freezing, and then I feel my soul is burning,
e **in un momento torno** a gelar.	and **in an instant I return** to freezing.

The phrase "I don't find peace neither night nor day" suggests a serious unrest, but the following phrase suddenly expresses deep enjoyment. As the song ends, Cherubino will have expressed his troubles in a graceful fashion. The Countess will realize that she is the object of his unrest.

Sospiro e gemo senza voler,	I sigh and moan without wanting to,
palpito e **tremo** senza saper,	I quiver and **tremble** without knowing it,
non trovo **pace notte** nè di,	I don't find **peace** neither **night** nor day,
ma pur mi piace **languir** così.	and yet I enjoy **languishing** like this.

"Dove sono i bei momenti" ("Where are the beautiful moments") from *Le Nozze di Figaro*

Performed by Countess Almaviva

Dramatic setting: Countess Almaviva's husband has been flirting with the chambermaid Susanna. To win back his affection, she has agreed to Figaro's scheme to trick her husband. Susanna will arrange a date with the Count, and the Countess will disguise herself as Susanna. Prior to the scheme, the Countess reflects sadly on her husband's indifference.

Vocal requirements: The song calls for a spinto soprano capable of expressing her inner thoughts. She must convey the tender and hopeful heart of a woman who seeks to regain her husband's affection. The song balances her current sorrows with memories of happier times. She must maintain a beautiful vocal line and express her words with great clarity.

What to listen for: In the opening recitative, the Countess reflects on the plan to regain her husband with both amusement and misgivings. She enjoys the thought of exchanging clothes with Susanna to deceive her husband. The following words "Oh, heavens!" lead to a crescendo (vocal increase in volume) of dismay. Her humiliation leads her to denounce her husband's misconduct.

Cangiando i miei vestiti con quelli	Exhanging my clothes with Susanna's
di Susanna, e i suoi co'miei:	and hers with mine:
al favor della **notte**. Oh, cielo!	under cover of **night**. Oh, heavens!
A quale umil stato **fatale**	To what a **fatal**, humiliating state
io son **ridotta** da un consorte **crudel**.	I have been **reduced** by a **cruel** spouse.

The aria is sung piano with clarity and tonal beauty. The opening lines are a longing for the "beautiful moments" of the past. This is followed by regret and accusation. The voice grows more intense with the words "those deceitful lips..." But each accusation is tempered by fond memories and because the Countess has a friendly and virtuous nature.

Dove sono i bei **momenti** di	Where are the beautiful **moments** of
dolcezza e di **piacer**? Dove andaro i	tenderness and **pleasure**? Where did the
giuramenti di quel **labbro** menzogner?	promises of those deceitful **lips** go?

In the final lines, the Countess expresses her hope that she can recapture her husband's heart through her "longing and loving..." faithfulness. She makes her commitment known in a charming legato (melodic and flowing) voice. She then expresses a note of sorrow about his "...ungrateful heart!"

Ah, se almen la mia **costanza**,	Ah, if at least my **constance**,
nel **languire** amando ognor,	**longing** and loving as ever,
mi portasse una speranza	would bring me some hope
di cangiar l'**ingrato** cor!	to change that **ungrateful** heart!

"O wie ängstlich"
("O how fearfully")
from "Die Entführung aus dem Serail"

Performed by Belmonte (a Spanish nobleman)

Dramatic setting: Belmonte's beloved Constanze is being held captive after being abducted by pirates. His servant has located Constanze, and he tells his master that he will rescue her. The hope of being reunited inspires him to sing this aria. (Note: Mozart had his approaching marriage to Constanze in mind when he composed this aria.)

Vocal requirements: This song requires a light lyric tenor (a melodic and high voice) with a sweet and flexible voice. He must express his romantic and lyrical thoughts for a woman who is being held captive. The song expresses his love, faith, and noble thoughts. He must maintain a warm legato (smooth and melodic) sound even when his impatience rises to a crescendo (voice increases to a high dramatic level).

What to listen for: The first two lines are pianissimo (very soft sound) and express adoration. The name "Constanze" is repeated twice in a tender and rising pianissimo. The voice remains warm and legato with the phrases broken into short spans to suggest an anxious heart. There is a feeling of impatience in the fourth line ending with a crescendo with the word "Herz!" (heart!).

Constanze, Constanze!	Constanze, Constanze!
dich wieder zu sehen, dich!	to see you again, you!
O wie **ängstlich**, o wie feurig	Oh how **fearfully**, oh how ardently
klopft **mein** liebevolles **Herz!**	beats **my** love filled **heart!**

When he refers to his "...hesitating and shaking," the voice and accompaniment change from forte to piano (loud to soft). Each repeat of his "chest is heaving..." becomes faster and stronger. After questioning whether he heard her whisper, he slowly expresses his apprehension and continues with a mixture of hope and fear.

Schon zittr'ich und wanke,	Already I am trembling and faltering,
schon zag'ich und **schwanke,**	already I am hesitating and **shaking,**
es hebt sich die **schwellende** Brust.	my chest is heaving and **swelling.**
Ist das ihr **Lispeln?**	Is that her **whisper?**
Es wird mir so bange!	I am so afraid!

After asking "...war es ein Traum?" (was it a dream?) with intense feeling, he repeats the phrases beginning with the third line in the first stanza "O how fearfully..." Again, he has the heavenly expectation of being reunited with his beloved Constanze.

Es glüht mir die Wange.	My cheek is burning.
Täuscht mich die **Liebe,**	Does **love** deceive me,
War es **ein Traum?**	was it **a dream?**

PART III

Literary and Rhyming Exercises

Match the Aria
to Its Literary Source

*A*lthough operatic composers and their librettists give their own inter-
pretation to source material, there are situations, characters, and passages in the literary texts that have obviously inspired songs from each of these
operas.

After introducing a popular work that served as an inspiration for a
famous opera, the exercises that follow challenge the reader to match passages
from the original text to excerpts from the song they inspired.

The two most famous novels attached to these six operas are Goethe's
Faust and Prévost's *Manon Lescaut*. *Faust* is still revered as the greatest piece
of German literature, and *Manon Lescaut* was the most popular French novel
for over two hundred years. Several of the passages from each of these novels
are connected to songs composed by Gounod and Massenet.

Il Barbiere di Siviglia

Pierre-Augustin Caron de Beaumarchais appears to have had much in
common with the central character in both of his plays, *Il Barbiere di Siviglia*
and *Le Nozze di Figaro*. Just as Figaro claims to be a man of many crafts and
skills, Beaumarchais (1732–1799) was an artisan (watchmaker to the king),
musician, writer, diplomat, financier, and merchant to name a few of his titles.
He also had an aptitude for music. He was employed by Louis XV to teach
his daughters how to play the harp. It's not surprising that Figaro, in addition
to his many other accomplishments, accompanies himself on the guitar in his

famous "Largo al factotum." Beaumarchais, like the character Figaro, was also fun loving and carefree as a young man. Figaro helps to set the character of the play and define the audience's impression of Rosina and Almaviva. However, Beaumarchais appears to have experienced far more vicissitudes in his lifetime than the high-spirited Figaro. Beaumarchais experienced honor and dishonor, wealth and poverty, success and failure, the patronage of royalty and the constraint of prison.

Beaumarchais originally composed *Il Barbiere di Siviglia* as a comic opera but, after being rejected by the Opéra Comique in Paris, he rewrote it as a play. Even in the play version, four of the main characters—Figaro, Rosina, Count Almaviva, and Dr. Bartolo—are given an opportunity to express their feelings in song. Beaumarchais' four-act play, like Rossini's three act opera, was initially jeered by the audience and panned by the critics. After being revised, both the play (1775) and later the opera (1816) became triumphal successes. In Beaumarchais' famous sequel, *Le Nozze di Figaro*, Figaro is still witty and humorous, but his master, the Count, has become his rival. Figaro reflects his author's growing discontent with the privileges of social class. And Rosina becomes a heroine of sympathy as she tries to win her freedom from the protective and class conscious Dr. Bartolo. The plays by Beaumarchais and the operas they inspired by Rossini and Mozart end on a joyous note.

Fortunately, Rossini was more successful than Beaumarchais at adapting *Il Barbiere di Siviglia* for the operatic stage. As one might expect, Rossini's opera takes many liberties with Beaumarchais' play. Unfortunately, it's difficult to connect some of Rossini's most famous songs to scenes in the play, such as Figaro's "Largo al factotum" and Rosina's "Una voce poco fa." Rather than singing about his success and importance as a handyman, Figaro sings a short song about the virtues of wine and leisure. Instead of expressing her strong determination to free herself from her guardian, Rosina sings a sentimental song about springtime, flowers, lambs, and lovers' hearts. Four songs in the opera appear to be connected to the play: the Count sings a serenade below Rosina's balcony; Figaro reflects on the gold he will receive for assisting the Count; Don Basilio provides a clear and rather detailed description on how to engage in slander (calumny); and a trio of characters convince Don Basilio that he is sick and should go to bed.

Matching Beaumarchais' Passages to Rossini's Songs

Directions: After reading a passage in the left column, read the words to each song in the right column, and choose one that best relates to the passage.

Add the song number you chose for the passage and select the song title from the four choices listed. Finally, write the name of the character who performs the song. After you've matched the four passages to their songs, check your work with the answer key.

Song Titles: "Slander is a little breeze" • **"Well, good-night to you, dear sir"**
"At the idea of all this metal" • **"Lo, in the smiling sky"**

Passage A matched with Song # _____
Since you so wish, my name I will reveal
although unknown I would adore.
Once known what can I hope for more?
But still—my mistress' wish I must obey.
Wealth too, alas, I cannot proffer
my love for you is all I have to offer.
(pages 51, 52)

Song 1 title: _____
Character: _____
...a breeze which softly, subtly, lightly and sweetly, commences to whisper. From the mouth it emerges, the noise grows crescendo, gathers force little by little, runs its course from place to place, seems like the thunder of the tempest..

Passage B matched with Song # _____
Look! I'm going in there—and with one stroke of my wand I'll lull vigilance to sleep, awake the transports of love ... and overcome every obstacle that confronts us. As for you, My Lord, come to my house with plenty of gold...
(page 53)

Song 2 title: _____
Character: _____
...the dawn is breaking, and you are not awake, and you are still asleep?
Arise, my sweetest love, oh, come, my idolized one, soften the pain of the dart which pierces me. Oh joy!
Do I now see that dearest vision...

Passage C matched with Song # _____
Someone picks it up and—piano piano—insinuates it into your ear. It takes wing, extending its flight in ever-widening circles, swooping and swirling ... and breaks forth at last like a thunder clap to become ... a public Crescendo....
(pages 61, 62)

Song 3 title: _____
Character: _____
...go away from here. Well, good night, with all my heart, then we shall talk tomorrow. Well, good night, away from here. Well, good night, dear sir, peace and slumber and good health.
Quickly go away from here.

Passage D matched with Song # _____
Go straight to bed, my dear Basilio. You are not well. You are frightening us to death. Go to bed. Why ever did you
  come out?
They say it's infectious. Go to bed!
Well then, gentlemen, I think I had
  better retire.
I don't think I am quite myself.
(page 89)

Song 4 title: _____
Character: _____
I'm ready. You cannot imagine what a prodigious devotion the sweet thought of gold makes me feel towards Lindoro. At the idea of that metal marvelous, omnipotent, my mind like a volcano commences to erupt, yes.

La Bohème

Puccini's inspiration for his most famous and popular opera was Henri Murger's *The Bohemians of the Latin Quarter* (1851). It was one of the most popular and influential novels of the nineteenth century. It captures the difficult life of the artists or Bohemians in Paris as they struggled for food and shelter. The novel is largely based on Murger's own experiences and close friends, Marcel, Schaunard and Colline, known in the novel as "The Brotherhood." The episodes in the novel are drawn from these real-life characters, with Rodolphe representing the author. Mademoiselle Mimì and Musette have prominent roles as their coquettish lovers. Life was very difficult for women who usually had low paying jobs, such as seamstresses, and had to depend on men for support.

Puccini and his librettists had to take liberties with the novel to craft the events and lyrics for *La Bohème*. There are character descriptions and events that suggest that they probably influenced some of the songs composed by Puccini. For example, there is an episode when Rodolphe hears "timid taps on his door." A charming girl named "Louise" enters and complains that her shoe hurts her (It sounds like Musetta's trick to get rid of her elderly escort so that she can leave with Marcello.) Rodolphe and Louise laugh when the candle is blown out while Rodolphe unlaces her shoe. Mademoiselle Mimì is introduced later in the novel and appears to have the right size shoes.

There are several passages where Marcel and Rodolphe reminisce and regret parting with their sweethearts, Mimì and Musette. There are descriptions of Musette that describe her as coquettish and fond of luxuries, including elegant clothes to draw attention. Although there's no passage that describes her singing a waltz, there is a reference saying she likes to entertain at suppers, even though she doesn't always sing in tune. Colline has a "black overcoat" with pockets filled with books. However, there is no mention of him selling his "venerable coat" to purchase medicine for Mimì. Finally, there are references to Rodolphe and Marcel separating temporarily from Mimì and Musette, taking on new lovers, and then returning to their old sweethearts. And Rodolphe is present and heartbroken when Mimì passes away.

While there are no examples of musical lyrics from the literary source that relate directly to the songs in the opera, Puccini and his librettists clearly drew inspiration from the characters and some of the situations in Murger's novel. And his use of the term "bohemians" made its entry into the English language and is derived from the French "bohème."

Matching Murger's Passages to Puccini's Songs

Directions: After reading a passage in the left column, read the words to each song in the right column, and choose one that best relates to the passage. Add the song number you chose for the passage and select the song title from the four choices listed. Finally, write the name of the character who performs the song. After you've matched the four passages to their songs, check your work with the answer key.

Song Titles: "When I walk alone" • "From the place I left"
"Oh Mimì, you're not coming back" • "What a cold little hand!"

Passage A matched with Song # _____
She was a pretty girl of twenty, who shortly after her arrival in Paris, began to live as pretty girls are apt to live... She was the delight of Latin Quarter suppers, for if she did not always sing in tune, her voice was quite fresh... (page 88)

Song 1 title: _____
Character: _____
Let me warm it for you.
What's the use of searching?
It can't be found in the dark.
But fortunately it is a moonlit night...

Passage B matched with Song # _____
"Oh, little Mimì, joy of my home, is it true that you are gone—that I have sent you away, and that I shall never see you again? My God!" (page 211)

Song 2 title: _____
Character: _____
...people stop to look at my beauty they search for in me, looked for from head to toe. And then I savor the subtle longing that shows in their eyes.

Passage C matched with Song # _____
Yet these hands, which were so fragile, so small, so soft to the touch of his lips, those childlike hands into whose keeping Rodolphe had given his heart, with its renewed blossom... (page 201)

Song 3 title: _____
Character: _____
...happily at your call of love. Mimì returns alone to a lonely nest. She returns again to make false flowers. Gather up the few things I left behind.

Passage D matched with Song # _____
Mlle. Mimì arrived next day to fetch away her things. Rodolphe was in and alone. It needed all of his powers of self-control to keep him from casting his arms about her neck. (page 213)

Song 4 title: _____
Character: _____
anymore! Oh beautiful days...
The brush draws two dark eyes and a provocative mouth, and Musetta's face emerges from it...

Carmen

In Prosper Mérimée's short story of *Carmen*, both Carmen and Don José are depicted as hardened and unappealing characters. Don José is willing to overlook Carmen's devious and cunning personality because of his infatuation for her physical attributes. In the beginning of the novel, José relates the story of *Carmen* to a stranger he has just met. In addition to slaying Carmen, we learn that he is guilty of other murders, and it is just a matter of time before he is captured and headed to the gallows.

Mérimée (1803–1870) portrays José as weak-willed, submissive, and easily corrupted. Whenever Carmen gets annoyed with his jealous complaints, she reminds him that he's a mere "simpleton." Surprisingly, this label doesn't seem to upset him or cool his passion for her. When he eventually learns that Carmen is already married to a nasty one-eyed gypsy, José decides to eliminate his competitor by cutting his throat. As a reflection of their callous personalities, neither José or Carmen show any sign of remorse over this incident.

Georges Bizet and his librettists, Henri Meilhac and Ludovic Halévy, were wise to add a few attractive characters to the operatic version of *Carmen*; otherwise, the opera would probably have been far less appealing to the audience. For example, Micaëla, the sweet and innocent country girl, and Escamillo, the proud and bold toreador, are not present in Mérimée's novel. Instead of a famous and dashing toreador, Carmen has a brief flirtation with a simple picador. This brief affair ends abruptly when the horse flattens the picador with the bull resting on top. There is no indication that Mérimée meant for the reader to find this pileup amusing; after all, *Carmen* is a somber story of two indifferent characters with little sense of compassion or a sense of humor. By altering Merimee's story of Carmen, Bizet and his librettists were able to compose, according to most critics, one of the greatest and most perfect operas.

Although Bizet and his librettists have altered some of the settings, there appear to be some textual situations in Mérimée's novel that inspired some of Bizet's most famous songs: including "Love is a rebellious bird"; "The sistrums"; "I am going to dance in your honor"; "The flower song"; "In vain"; "Carmen, there is still time." The settings vary between the novel and the opera for several of these songs. In the novel, José reminisces about the flower he treasures while he is alone in prison rather than with Carmen at a tavern. Instead of using cards to reveal her approaching death, Carmen discovers her fate from pieces of molten lead in a bowl of water. In the novel's final scene,

José stalks and stabs Carmen to death along a lonely gorge instead of outside a boisterous bull fighting arena.

Matching Mérimée's Passages to Bizet's Songs

Directions: After reading a passage in the left column, read the words to each song in the right column, and choose one that best relates to the passage. Add the song number you chose for the passage and select the song title from the four choices listed. Finally, write the name of the character who performs the song. After you've matched the four passages to their songs, check your work with the answer key.

Song Titles: "Carmen, there is still time" • "Love is a rebellious bird" "The flower you threw me" • "I am going to dance in your honor"

Passage A matched with Song # _____
I returned to my task; but, acting as women and cats usually do, refusing to come when they are called, but coming when they are not called, she stopped in front of me... And taking the acacia flower, she flicked it at me...
(page 21)

Song 1 title: _____
Character: _____
...stayed with me in my prison. Withered and dried up, that flower always kept its sweet smell; and for hours on end, with my eyes closed, I became drunk with its smell and in the night I used to see you!

Passage B matched with Song # _____
I used to look out into the street through the prison bars, and among all the women who went past I never saw a single one who could hold a candle to that devil in female form.... And then, despite myself, I used to smell the acacia flower...
(page 26)

Song 2 title: _____
Character: _____
...that no one can tame, and it's in vain that one calls him if it suits him to refuse. Nothing moves him, neither threat nor plea, one man speaks freely, the other keeps mum...

Passage C matched with Song # _____
I told her I would like to see her dance; but where were we to find any castanets? At once she took the old woman's plate, broke it in pieces, and began to dance... Evening came, and I heard the drums sounding the retreat...
(pages 30, 31)

Song 3 title: _____
Character: _____
...oh my Carmen, let me save you, you whom I adore; ah! Let me save you and save myself with you!

Passage D matched with Song # _____
I fell at her feet, I took her hands, I moistened them with my tears. I re-minded her of all the moments of hap-

Song 4 title: _____
Character: _____
...and you will see, my lord, how I am able to accompany my dance myself! Sit

piness we had spent together. I offered
to remain a brigand to please her. I
offered to do anything for her...
(page 52)

down there, Don José, I'll begin!
"Taratata, my God! It's the retreat!
Taratata, I'am going to be late!"

Les Contes d'Hoffmann

E.T.A. Hoffmann (1776–1822) was a German writer of fantastic and mysterious tales, including the *Nutcracker and the King of Mice*. Several of his Gothic tales served as an inspiration for Offenbach's opera. In Act I, the tale of Olympia, the mechanical doll, is based on E.T.A. Hoffmann's *The Sandman*. Coppelius, the sandman, is a creepy character who peddles live eyes and magic glasses. Nathanael (Hoffmann in the opera) buys a pair of "weather glasses" which give Olympia a more lifelike expression. Nathanael tells his skeptical friend that he is impressed by Olympia's limited speech pattern of "Ah! Ah! Ah!" The love struck Nathanael states "It is true, she speaks but few words; but the few words she does speak are genuine hieroglyphs of the inner world of Love..." (p. 208). He is convinced that her one-syllable sighs are proof that he has met a divine woman who really understands him. He describes Olympia is an "exemplary listener" by her ability to sit quietly and listen with "great reverence" as he shares his writings. The story captures E.T.A. Hoffmann's vivid imagination, inventiveness, and sense of humor. There are references in *The Sandman* that appear to have inspired several of Offenbach's songs in Act I. For example, Hoffmann's friend compares Olympia to a "singing machine." Coppelius does peddle his live eyes and magic glasses. In an effort to win Olympia's affection, Hoffmann expresses his passion for the mechanical doll in the aria, "With the sweet pledge of our love."

Act II of Offenbach's opera is derived from E.T.A. Hoffmann's *A New Year's Eve Adventure*. This gothic tale takes place in Florence instead of moonlit Venice; thus, there is no gliding gondola and romantic barcarolle. The evil magician, Dappertutto, does depend on the beautiful Giuletta to help him steal reflections; but instead of resorting to a sparkling diamond to hypnotize her, he sells her magic potions. Dappertutto is described as a "tall, thin, dried out looking man" and Giuletta's companion, Schlemil, is reduced to a "spindle-shanked cretin." (Incidentally, many of E.T.A. Hoffmann's characters have eccentric personalities, malevolent motives, and grotesque physical features—not especially suitable for bedtime stories.) There are several brief textual passages that could have inspired Hoffmann to declare his love for Giuletta, "Oh God, with what ecstasy."

E.T.A. Hoffmann's short story of *Rath Krespel* is the basis for Act III of the opera. Krespel is an eccentric violinmaker and the father of the ailing Antonia. She is diagnosed as having "an organic failure of the chest." This condition is also responsible for her wonderful vocal power and timbre. There is no reference to her lost turtledove as she sadly reflects on her fiancé's absence. However, there is a setting in *Rath Krespel* for the famous duet between Antonia and Hoffmann, "It is a song of love." Antonia sings joyfully while her fiancé plays the piano. Finally, there is no reference to Antonia's death after singing in response to a call from her mother's portrait. Instead, her father dreams that he hears his daughter singing an "ear-splitting fortissimo" to her fiancé's piano accompaniment. He rushes to her room and finds her on the sofa, "... her hands devoutly folded, and looking as if asleep and dreaming of the joys and raptures of heaven" (p. 235).

Matching Hoffmann's Passages to Offenbach's Songs

Directions: After reading a passage in the left column, read the words to each song in the right column, and choose one that best relates to the passage. Add the song number you chose for the passage and select the song title from the four choices listed. Finally, write the name of the character who performs the song. After you've matched the four passages to their songs, check your work with the answer key.

Song Titles: "A doll with enamel eyes" • **"It is a song of love"**
"With the sweet pledge of our love" • **"Oh God, with what ecstasy"**

Passage A matched with Song # ____
The tones of her voice conveyed a secret ardor, which inflamed them all. He lost consciousness, but felt himself being lifted and carried away. When he awoke later, as if from a deep enchantment, he lay at Giuletta's feet. (pages 118, 121)

Song 1 title: _____
Character: _____
...you belong to me, our hearts are for ever united! Ah, tell me, do you understand this eternal joy of our silent hearts? To be alive with only one soul, and with the same wings, we soar to the heavens!

Passage B matched with Song # ____
She sat with her eyes fixed unchangeably upon his, sighing repeatedly, "Ah! Ah! Ah!" Upon this he would answer, "Oh, you glorious heavenly lady! You ray from the promised paradise of love! Oh! What a profound soul you have!" (page 206)

Song 2 title: _____
Character: _____
...artfully fluttered a fan close to a little copper cockerel. Both would sing marvelously together in unison, they would dance and chat, and seemed to be alive. Ah, the little cockerel, shiny and lively, with a forbidding look...

Passage C matched with Song # ____
She is strangely measured in her movements, they all seem as if they were
dependent upon some wound-up clock-
work. Her playing and singing have the
disagreeably perfect, but insensitive
timing of a singing machine...
(page 208)

Song 3 title: _____
Character: _____
...that is floating away, sad or delirious,
that is floating away, sad or delirious...
My heart has told me I was missed!
My soul is filled with happiness!
Tomorrow you will be my wife.

Passage D matched with Song # ____
Antonia, blushing with joy and happiness, sang on and on—all her most
beautiful songs, her (fiancé) playing
the piano as only enthusiasm that is
intoxicated with delight can play.
(page 232)

Song 4 title: _____
Character: _____
...do you set my soul on fire? Your voice
has penetrated me like a heavenly concert,
my whole being is consumed by a sweet
burning fire. Your eyes have poured forth
their flame into mine like radiant stars...

Faust

Johann Wolfgang von Goethe lived from 1749 to 1832. Goethe's *Faust* is
generally recognized as the greatest German novel. Gounod's *Faust* is based
on Book One of Goethe's two books. In spite of what some critics claim, the
opera is quite faithful to Book I. For example, it is noteworthy that both the
book and the opera are written in rhyme, and many of the songs can be linked
to passages in Goethe's drama. (Of course, Gounod's librettists, Jules Barbier
and Michel Carre, deserve the credit for composing rhyming lines to complement Gounod's music and Goethe's text.) In addition to avoiding an overly
long opera, the highly literate Gounod was aware that Book I of Goethe's masterpiece is considered far superior, in a literary sense, to Book II.

To develop a greater appreciation for two masterpieces, composed in different genres, it's interesting to compare some similarities and differences
between the novel and the opera. Walter Kaufmann's rhyming translation
(1961) of Goethe's *Faust* is recognized by scholars as an outstanding English
translation of the original German text. Kaufmann states, "No translation of
a world-historic poem equals the original" (p. 46). He adds that the translator
"can and should try to be faithful to the poet's meaning and form. Meter
should be preserved as far as possible" (p. 47). It is a difficult task to translate
lyric and rhyming poetry in one language to another language. To make the
task even more challenging, Kaufmann points out that Goethe uses different
rhyme schemes and meters to vary the mood and portray characters.

Valentine and Siebel are two of the major characters in Gounod's *Faust*, and each one sings a famous aria. However, in Goethe's *Faust*, Valentine only appears on a few pages, and not until after Marguerite has been seduced and deserted by Faust. He does praise his sister's virtues, but he does not call on the Lord to protect her and makes no mention of marching off to battle. Siebel is a very minor character in Goethe's book, and there is no mention of Siebel leaving flowers to express his adoration in Marguerite's garden. When Siebel becomes Marguerite's suitor, Faust now has a competitor and Méphistophélès uses his devilish ingenuity to remove the competition by causing the flowers to wilt.

If we examine the four songs on the following page, each of them conveys very similar thoughts to passages in Goethe's text. For example, when Faust requests "youth and pleasures," the devil responds by presenting a lovely image of a young lady. As in the case of Goethe's text, Faust celebrates Marguerite's garden dwelling as a shrine in his cavatina. In the book and the opera, Marguerite discovers a case of jewels, adorns herself before a mirror, and compares herself to a queen. Perhaps, the closest comparison between the book and the opera occurs when Méphistophélès sings his sarcastic serenade.

Finally, both the book and the opera mention how Faust and Méphistophélès attempt to rescue Marguerite from prison as dawn is breaking and the "horses are quavering." She decides to face her judgment and is granted salvation. In book two of Goethe's novel, Faust also receives salvation and the devil fails to capture his soul.

Matching Goethe's Passages to Gounod's Songs

Directions: After reading a passage in the left column, read the words to each song in the right column, and choose one that best relates to the passage. Add the song number you chose for the passage and select the song title from the four choices listed. Finally, write the name of the character who performs the song. After you've matched the four passages to their songs, check your work with the answer key.

Song Titles: "Pleasures for me" • "Beware, beware"
"Greetings, chaste and pure abode" • "Ah! I can't help laughing"

Passage A matched with Song # _____	**Song 1 title:** _____
If you prefer, I shall stay	**Character:** _____
With you, and I shall not depart,	Ah, I see beauty
Upon condition that I may	that is smiling back at me.
Amuse you with samples of my art.	Is it true?

What tender spirits now will sing,
The lovely pictures that they bring...
(page 167)

Marguerite, is it you?
No, no! What can this mean?
You are more like a queen.

Passage B matched with Song # ____
Sweet light of dusk, guest from above
That fills this shrine, be welcome you!
Seize now my heart, sweet agony of love
That languishes and feeds on hope's
clear dew!
(page 263)

Song 2 title: _____
Character: _____
The morning is breaking, the sky is aglow!
Hear the horses stamping below!
Come, it's I! Come away!
Come, come, let us fly!
Night is gone and the day is nigh!

Passage C matched with Song # ____
What is that? God in heaven! There—
I never saw such fine array!
Why a lord's lady could wear
These on the highest holiday.
Who owns all this? It is so fine.
If those earrings were only mine!
(page 271)

Song 3 title: _____
Character: _____
I am here! Why should it surprise you?
My sword at my side, a feather in my hat
Or is it my clothes that displease you?
When I've come from far away,
Just to be with you today,
All you have to say is "Go away!"

Passage D matched with Song # ____
What good to flee?
They lie in wait for me.
To have to go begging is misery,
And to have a bad conscience, too.
It is misery to stray far and forsaken,
And, anyhow, I would be taken.
(page 417)

Song 4 title: _____
Character: _____
The shrine of an angel from heaven!
What hidden treasures in this
humble place!
What happy dreams, what wealth of
joy and grace!

Manon

Abbé Prévost's famous French novel, *Manon Lescaut*, was the inspiration for Massenet's *Manon* and Puccini's *Manon Lescaut*. Prèvost's (1697–1763) novel is written as a personal narrative. It is the story of a pleasure-loving young courtesan and her love for a young theologian, Des Grieux, who sacrifices his monastic training to support her. In spite of the fact that she leaves him for an older man and a luxurious lifestyle, she returns to her young lover and they turn to gambling and thievery to support her indulgences. Des Grieux soon learns that "...however attached to me she might be when things went well, it was no use counting on her in hard times. She was too fond of wealth and pleasure to give them up for me" (p. 38). In a letter to her distraught lover, she states "I swear that you are the idol of my heart, my dear Chevalier, and there is nobody else in the world I love as I love you. But don't you see, my poor darling, that loyalty is a silly virtue in the pass we are in?" (p. 49). On a more eloquent level, Des Grieux explains why he is willing to sacrifice his religious vows for more earthly desires. He states, "The human heart does not need prolonged study to feel that of all pleasures those of love are sweetest, and it very soon perceives that a promise of greater joys elsewhere is a fraud, and a fraud which predisposes it to mistrust the most solemn assurances. Let the preachers who seek to lead me back to virtue say by all means that virtue is necessary and indispensable, but they must not hide the fact that it is austere and painful" (p. 67).

In order to compose a popular opera, composers and librettists take liberties and add scenes that are not in the novel. As a result, some of the most popular songs have no literary reference. For example, in the first act of Massenet's opera, Manon tells her cousin Lescaut about the excitement of her journey, "I am still completely dizzy." Lescaut then warns her against talking to strangers, "Look me straight in the eyes!" There are no textual references in Prévost's novel to support these opening songs. In fact, Manon's cousin is not introduced until later in the story. Just before leaving her young lover, there is no suggestion in the novel that Manon felt inclined to bid a sweet and melancholic farewell to a piece of furniture, such as "Farewell, our little table." Two other popular songs in the opera, "I walk on all roads" and "Obey when their voices beckon us," occur after Manon arrives in a coach along a fashionable avenue in Paris. Although the novel briefly mentions the fact that Manon's elderly patron has provided her with a coach, there is no reference to her addressing a crowd of admirers to display her beauty and then offering advice to youth on not letting love pass them by.

There does appear to be some connection between five passages from the novel and five songs from the opera. For example, Manon does appear to be reluctant to abandon her pleasure seeking for life in a convent. After arriving in Paris, Des Grieux does write his father describing Manon's charm and beauty. He later tries to rid himself of any visions of love by entering a seminary. In an effort to dissuade him from his religious vows, she reminds him of her charm and promises to be faithful. As she is about to die, Manon admits that her frivolous behavior was responsible for destroying their relationship.

Matching Prévost's Passages to Massenet's Songs

Directions: After reading a passage in the left column, read the words to each song in the right column, and choose one that best relates to the passage. Add the song number you chose for the passage and select the song title from the four choices listed. Finally, write the name of the character who performs the song. After you've matched the four passages to their songs, check your work with the answer key.

**Song Titles: "Is this no longer my hand..." • "I'm writing to my father"
"Come now, Manon, no more day-dreaming" • "I hate and curse myself"**

Passage A matched with Song # ____
I gathered that she was being sent to the convent against her will, and I see now that it was probably to check her pleasure-loving tendencies that had already shown themselves in her, and that were to bring so much suffering...
(page 13)

Passage B matched with Song # ____
In this frame of mind I decided to seek a reconciliation with my father. Manon was so enchanting that it seemed to me she could not fail to please him, if only I could find a way of telling him about her many qualities...
(page 18)

Passage C matched with Song # ____
She expressed her penitence in such pathetic terms, and swore to be true with so many oaths and protestations, that she touched my heart and stirred me to the depths of my being. She had come to the seminary with a mind to die...
(pages 33, 34)

Passage D matched with Song # ____
I have hurt you in ways you could never have forgiven but for your unfailing goodness. I have been frivolous and fickle, and even while loving you pas-sionately, as I have always done, I have never been anything but graceless...
(page 144)

Song 1 title: _____
Character: _____
...that yours is pressing?
Is this no longer my voice?
Am I no longer myself?
Have I no longer my name?
Ah! Look at me, look at me!

Song 2 title: _____
Character: _____
Where does your spirit go in your dreams?
Leave these fleeting desires
at the door of your convent!
Come now, Manon! Come now!
No more desires, no more idle fancies!

Song 3 title: _____
Character: _____
...and I tremble with fear that this letter, into which I have put all my heart may make him angry ... everything about her is seductive, her beauty, her youth, her grace. No voice has a sweeter sound...

Song 4 title: _____
Character: _____
...when I think about the sweetness of our love, which I destroyed, and I will not pay enough with all my blood for even half the pain I have caused you!

Answer Key to Matching Exercises

Matching Beaumarchais' Passages to Rossini's Songs. The four passages were selected from John Wood's French to English translation (1964) of Beaumarchais' play.

Passage A, Song 2: "Lo, in the smiling sky" (Count Almaviva); Passage B, Song 4: "At the idea of this metal" (Figaro); Passage C, Song 1: "Slander is a little breeze" (Don Basilio); Passage D, Song 3: "Well, good-night to you, dear sir" (Trio: Count Almaviva, Rosina, Figaro).

Matching Murger's Passages to Puccini's Songs. Four passages were selected from Murger's translation (1901) of *The Bohemians of the Latin Quarter.*

Passage A, Song 2: "When I walk alone" (Musetta); Passage B, Song 4: "Oh Mimì, you're not coming back!" (Rodolfo); Passage C, Song 1: "What a cold little hand!" (Rodolfo); Passage D, Song 3: "From the place I left" (Mimì).

Matching Mérimée's Passages to Bizet's Songs. Five passages were selected from Jotcham's French to English translation (1989) of Mérimée's *Carmen and Other Stories.*

Passage A, Song 2: "Love is a rebellious bird" (Carmen); Passage B, Song 1: "The flower that you threw me" (Don José); Passage C, Song 4: "I am going to dance in your honor" (Carmen); Passage D, Song 3: "Carmen, there is still time" (Don José).

Matching Hoffmann's Passages to Offenbach's Songs. Four passages were selected from Bleiler's edition of *The Best Tales of Hoffmann* (1967).

Passage A, Song 4: "Oh God, with what ecstasy" (Hoffmann); Passage B, Song 1: "With this sweet pledge of out love" (Hoffmann); Passage C, Song 2: "A doll with enamel eyes" (Nicklausse); Passage D, Song 3: "It is a love song" (Hoffmann).

Matching Goethe's Passages to Gounod's Songs. Four passages were selected from Kaufmann's German to English translation (1961) of Goethe's *Faust.*

Passage A, Song 3: "Pleasures for me" (Méphistophélès); Passage B, Song 4: "Greetings, chaste and pure" (Faust); Passage C, Song 1: "Ah! I can't help laughing" (Marguerite); Passage D, Song 2: "Beware, beware" (Méphistophélès).

Matching Prévost's Passages to Massenet's Songs. Four passages were selected from Tancock's French to English translation (1949) of Prévost's *Manon Lescaut.*

    Passage A, Song 2: "Come now, Manon, no more day dreaming" (Manon); Passage B, Song 3: "I am writing to my father" (Des Grieux); Passage C, Song 1: "Is this no longer my hand?" (Manon); Passage D, Song 4: "I hate and curse myself" (Manon).

Complete the
Rhyming Passage

*I*t was very common in the 18th and 19th centuries for librettists to rhyme large portions of the libretto. Most of the original source material of all fourteen operas in Part I was written in rhyme. The following exercises provide condensed rhyming translations for a set of four songs from each of the fourteen operas. The reader is asked to complete the translator's rhyme and select the correct title of the song. Those who are familiar with the opera are challenged to name the character who performs the song and sequence the four songs as they occurred in the opera.

The task of translating a rhyming libretto into another language using rhyme is challenging. Creating a rhyming translation, in an effort to match the original text, usually requires the translator to take liberties with the original text. The result is that the meaning of the original text is often seriously distorted. Many translators avoid using rhyme because they prefer to write more literal translations. For many early librettists, rhyme served several useful purposes. They found that rhyme schemes and meters helped to capture moods and portray characters. Singers found it easier to learn their lines in rhyme, and the rhyme also added rhythm and flow to the words. Finally, the audiences appreciated the melodic cadence of the rhyming lyrics, especially if the opera was presented in their native language.

It's not surprising that Goethe's rhyming novel *"Faust"* served as an inspiration to Gounod and his two librettists. It's a masterful example of rhyming text. Consider this clever exchange when Faust first approaches Marguerite:
"Fair lady, may I be so free / to offer my arm and company?"
"I'm neither a lady nor am I fair, / and can go home without your care."

Aida

Much of the original Italian libretto by Antonio Ghislanzoni to *Aida* is written in rhyme. The English rhyming translation of the songs below is by Walter Ducloux for G. Schirmer, Inc., 1963. Some passages have been condensed and key rhyming words are boldfaced.

Directions: (1) Complete the rhymes by filling in the blanks. (2) Select the correct song title from the choices below. (3) Name the character and number the songs in sequence, from one to four, based on when they occur in the opera. After you complete the blanks below, check the answer key.

Song Titles: "Oh, my homeland" • "To die! so pure, so lovely!"
"The fortunes of war" • "Her father ... But you, king"

1. Song title: _____
Character: _____
Sequence: _____

If to love king and country can be treason,
we are guilty and ready to **die!**
Mighty King the gods have **defended,**
may your hand be in mercy _____!
On this day it is we who suffer, but
tomorrow may see your people _____.
(Lines two and six rhyme and
lines three and four rhyme.)

2. Song title: _____
Character: _____
Sequence: _____

Land of my fathers, you, my home,
I'll see you **nevermore.**
Memories of childhood,
recall my native _____!
You I shall see no **more,**
never, no, no, not _____.
(Lines two and four rhyme and
lines five and six rhyme.)

3. Song title: _____
Character: _____
Sequence: _____

To die, so pure and **lovely!**
To die, because you love me!
Blooming in radiant _____,
love was born amid the stars above **you.**
Now you must die,
for it was my crime to love _____.
(Lines one and three rhyme and
lines four and six rhyme.)

4. Song title: _____
Character: _____
Sequence: _____

At the joyous feast of welcome
I command you to stay near **me,**
you, my servant, on your _____,
I, a princess proud and **free.**
Follow me and I will show you
what it means to compete with _____.
(Lines two and three rhyme and
lines four and six rhyme.)

Il Barbiere di Siviglia

Much of the original Italian libretto by Cesare Sterbini to *The Barber of Seville* is written in rhyme. The English rhyming translation of the songs below is by Ruth and Thomas Martin for G. Schirmer, Inc., 1984. Some passages have been condensed and key rhyming words are boldfaced.

Directions: (1) Complete the rhymes by filling in the blanks. (2) Select the correct song title from the choices below. (3) Name the character and number the songs in sequence, from one to four, based on when they occur in the opera. After you complete the blanks below, check the answer key.

**Song Titles: "A voice just now" • "Slander is a little breeze"
"For a doctor of my standing" • "Make way for the handyman"**

1. Song title: _____
Character: _____
Sequence: _____
Though my guardian will **object,**
that's no more than I _____.
I'll rely on my wit and **ruse,**
to do exactly as I _____.
But if you cross my will,
a thousand tricks I will **play**
until I have my _____.
(Lines one and two, lines three and
four, and lines six and seven rhyme.)

2. Song title: _____
Character: _____
Sequence: _____
Neither begging, crying, **sighing,**
nor entreating, cheating, _____,
will deter me or will sway me.
I will lock the doors and windows
ev'ry minute, day and **night.**
I'll never let you out of _____.
(Lines one and two, lines five and
six rhyme.)

3. Song title: _____
Character: _____
Sequence: _____
First a murmur, slowly **seeping,**
then a whisper, lowly _____.
What began as **innuendo**
soon is swelling in _____.
Gossip turning into **scandal,**
stopping nowhere, hard to _____.

(Lines one and two, lines three and
four, and lines five and six rhyme.)

4. Song title: _____
Character: _____
Sequence: _____
In any circle I feel at **home.**
I am the king of lather and _____.
Figaro, yes; Figaro, **no;**
Figaro, fast; Figaro _____;
Figaro, come; Figaro, ____!
I am the king of razor and **blade,**
I am the king of my _____.
(Lines one and two, lines three, four and
five, and lines six and seven rhyme.)

La Bohème

Much of the original Italian libretto by G. Giacosa and L. Illica to *La Bohème* is written in rhyme. The English rhyming translation of the songs below is by Ruth and Thomas Martin for G. Schirmer, Inc., 1954. Some passages have been condensed and key rhyming words are boldfaced.

Directions: (1) Complete the rhymes by filling in the blanks. (2) Select the correct song title from the choices below. (3) Name the character and number the songs in sequence, from one to four, based on when they occur in the opera. After you complete the blanks below, check the answer key.

Song Titles: "When I walk alone" • "They call me Mimì"
"What a cold little hand!" • "Listen, my venerable coat"

1. Song title: _____
Character: _____
Sequence: _____
Very soon the light will be **stronger,**
so stay a little _____.
Ev'ry poetic **measure**
holds a fabulous _____.
In dreams and flights of fantasy
and castles in the **air,**
I am indeed a _____.
(Lines one and two, lines three and four, and lines six and seven rhyme.)

2. Song title: _____
Character: _____
Sequence: _____
That intense **desire,**
which is burning in their **glances,**
I proudly show my ravishing _____,
with enchanting appeal.
Fervent longing invites _____.
Your passion still must burn for **me,**
why do you not return to _____?
(Lines one and three, lines two and five, and lines six and seven rhyme.)

3. Song title: _____
Character: _____
Sequence: _____
You journey to higher, better **regions,**
take my grateful _____.
Neither to wealth nor temporal power
have you ever **yielded.**
Hidden deep in your **pockets,**
cozily there have _____
philosophers and _____.
(Lines one and two, lines four and six, and lines five and seven rhyme.)

4. Song title: _____
Character: _____
Sequence: _____
I dearly love those flowers,
they delight and chant **me.**
When the snow is **thawing,**
spring's first caress belongs to _____.
Then I watch them _____.
I'm afraid my life is not too **exciting,**
and have interrupted your _____.
(Lines two and four, lines three and five, and lines six and seven rhyme.)

L'Elisir d'Amore

Much of the original Italian libretto by Felice Romani to *The Elixir of Love* is written in rhyme. The English rhyming translation of the songs below is by Ruth and Thomas Martin for G. Schirmer, Inc., 1960. Some passages have been condensed and key rhyming words are boldfaced.

Directions: (1) Complete the rhymes by filling in the blanks. (2) Select the correct song title from the choices below. (3) Name the character and number the songs in sequence, from one to four, based on when they occur in the opera. After you complete the blanks below, check the answer key.

Song Titles: "Listen, listen country folk" • "Ask the flattering breeze"
"A furtive tear" • "How lovely she is, how dear she is!"

1. Song title: _____
Character: _____
Sequence: _____

Who can hold a wayward **breeze**?
I'm at liberty to go as I _____.
Ask the swiftly rolling river
why it rushes on **unknowing**,
with a force forever _____,
till it dies in the endless **sea**.
That's its fate, and meant to ____.
(Lines one and two, lines four and five,
and lines six and seven rhyme.)

2. Song title: _____
Character: _____
Sequence: _____

Love is not blind but **wise**.
I saw two glowing tears appear
like twin stars in your _____.
If I could hear your heart **reply**
in answer to my own,
if I could hear your loving _____,
then I would gladly _____.
(Lines one and three, and lines four,
six and seven rhyme.)

3. Song title: _____
Character: _____
Sequence: _____

For ev'ry ill, for all who **ail**
I sell the proper cure.
My panaceas never _____.
For cases which are **cronic**,
there's nothing like this _____.
Don't think it over **twice**.
I'll make a special _____.
(Lines one and three, lines four and five,
and lines six and seven rhyme.)

4. Song title: _____
Character: _____
Sequence: _____

That I wilt beneath her **eye**,
for all I do is dream and _____.
But I'll always love her **vainly**
for she shows me very _____
it's no use for me to try.
Who'll advise me where to **start**?
Who will help me win her _____?
(Lines one and two, lines three and four,
lines six and seven rhyme.)

Norma

Much of the original Italian libretto by F. Romani to *Norma* is written in rhyme. The English rhyming translation of the songs below is by the author of this handbook. Some passages have been condensed and key rhyming words are boldfaced.

Directions: (1) Complete the rhymes by filling in the blanks. (2) Select the correct song title from the choices below. (3) Name the character and number the songs in sequence, from one to four, based on when they occur in the opera. After you complete the blanks below, check the answer key.

Song Titles: "Oh, what memories!" • "The heart you betrayed"
"At the altar of Venus" • "Chaste goddess"

1. Song title: _____
Character: _____
Sequence: _____
The heart you selfishly **betrayed**
was the loving heart you _____.
Cruel Roman, now you are with **me**.
You tried in vain to _____,
and now your eternal fate is with _____.
It's the final hour to leave this **earth**;
together, united in life and _____.
(Lines one and two, lines three, four, and
five, and lines six and seven rhyme.)

2. Song title: _____
Character: _____
Sequence: _____
In Rome, we visited the altar of **Venus**.
Dressed with flowers in her hair, her
attire made it difficult to conceal **us**.
I heard the hymns in a state of **rapture**,
and my senses she managed to _____.
Then a shadow descended between ___,
and we were veiled in _____.
(Lines one and seven, lines three and
six, and lines four and five rhyme.)

3. Song title: _____
Character: _____
Sequence: _____
Goddess who bathes these trees in **silver**,
turn thy face toward us without _____.
Goddess to whom I worship and **appeal**,
temper our people and their bold _____.
Send down your peace upon the **earth**,
and in heaven, the place of your _____.
(Lines one and two, lines three and four,
and lines five and six rhyme.)

4. Song title: _____
Character: _____
Sequence: _____
In my memories, I was **enraptured**!
By observing his face, I was _____.
I too felt my defenses **reduced**,
as if my thoughts had been _____.
Alone, in the temple, I waited **secretly**,
and each day the flame grew _____.
(Lines one and two, lines three and
four, and lines five and six rhyme.)

I Pagliacci

Much of the original Italian libretto by Leoncavallo to I Pagliacci is written in rhyme. The English rhyming translation of the songs below is by the
author of this handbook. Some passages have been condensed and key rhyming
words are boldfaced.

Directions: (1) Complete the rhymes by filling in the blanks. (2) Select
the correct song title from the choices below. (3) Name the character and number the songs in sequence, from one to four, based on when they occur in the
opera. After you complete the blanks below, check the answer key.

Song Titles: "Put on the costume" • "Hui! How wildly they shriek up there"
"Not to play such a game" • "Prologue: May I! May I!"

1. Song title: _____
Character: _____
Sequence: _____

2. Song title: _____
Character: _____
Sequence: _____

Birds in flight, how gracefully they **fly**!
Upward they seek the blue _____.
Onward they pass and follow the **light**,
they continue to fly at great _____.
In thunder and lightning they stay in
  flight.
They continue until they reach their
  _____.
(Lines one and two, and lines three and four, and lines five and six rhyme.)

3. Song title: _____
Character: _____
Sequence: _____
Racked with grief, I must perform the
  play,
not knowing what to do or what to _____.
Put on the costume, the powder and **paint**,
for they are merely a disguise,
for my anger, tears, and _____.
People laugh and that's why they ____.
(Lines one, two, and six, and lines three
and five rhyme.)

The stage is one thing and life **another**.
I better not find my wife with a _____.
As sure as I am clearly **warning**,
the story will have a different _____.
As you would suddenly **see**,
it's better not to play games with ____.
(Lines one and two, lines three and four, lines five and six rhyme.)

4. Song title: _____
Character: _____
Sequence: _____
Will you please allow me?
Our author sends me to address **you**,
but not, as you expect, to amuse _____.
Rather to paint you a slice of **life**
from events that may not sound _____.
Deep within his heart as he **sighed**,
he recalled and recorded as he _____.
(Lines two and three, lines four and
five, and lines six and seven rhyme.)

Answer Key to Complete the Italian Rhyming Passages

Aida

1. Title: "Her father ... But you, king"
Character: Amonastro
Sequence: Second
Rhyming lines:
Lines 2 (die), 6 (cry)
Lines 3 (defended), 4 (extended)

2. Title: "Oh, my homeland"
Character: Aida
Sequence: third
Rhyming lines:
Lines 2 (nevermore), 6 (evermore)
Lines 4 (shore), 5 (more)

3. Title: "To die! so pure, so lovely!"
Character: Radamès
Sequence: fourth
Rhyming lines:
Lines 1 (lovely), 3 (beauty)
Lines 4 (you), 6 (you)

4. Title: "The fortunes of war"
Character: Amneris
Sequence: first
Rhyming lines:
Lines 2 (me), 3 (knee)
Lines 4 (free), 6 (me)

Il Barbiere di Siviglia

1. Title: "A voice just now"
Character: Rosina
Sequence: second
Rhyming lines:
Lines 1 (object), 2 (expect)
Lines 3 (ruse), 4 (choose)
Lines 6 (play), 7 (way)

2. Title: "A doctor of my standing"
Character: Doctor Bartolo
Sequence: fourth
Rhyming lines:
Lines 1 (sighing), 2 (lying)
Lines 5 (night), 6 (sight)

3. Title: "Slander is a little breeze"
Character: Don Basilio
Sequence: third
Rhyming lines:
Lines 1 (seeping), 2 (creeping)
Lines 3 (innuendo), 4 (crescendo)
Lines 5 (scandal), 6 (handle)

4. Title: "Make way for the handyman"
Character: Figaro
Sequence: first
Rhyming lines:
Lines 1 (home), 2 (foam)
Lines 3 (no), 4 (slow), 5 (go)
Lines 6 (blade), 7 (trade)

La Bohème

1. Title: "What a cold little hand!"
Character: Rodolfo
Sequence: first
Rhyming lines:
Lines 1 (stronger), 2 (longer)
Lines 3 (measure), 4 (treasure)
Lines 6 (air), 7 (millionaire)

2. Title: "When I walk alone"
Character: Musetta
Sequence: third
Rhyming lines:
Lines 1 (desire), 3 (attire)
Lines 2 (glances), 5 (romances)
Lines 6 (me), 7 (me)

3. Title: "They call me Mimì"
Character: Mimì
Sequence: second
Rhyming lines:
Lines 2 (me), 4 (me)
Lines 3 (thawing), 5 (unfolding)
Lines 6 (exciting), 7 (writing)

4. Title: "Listen, my venerable coat"
Character: Colline
Sequence: fourth
Rhyming lines:
Lines 1 (regions), 2 (allegiance)
Lines 4 (yielded), 6 (rested)
Lines 5 (pockets), 7 (poets)

L'Elisir d'Amore

1. Title: "Ask the flattering breeze"
Character: Adina, Nemorino
Sequence: second
Rhyming lines:
Lines 1 (breeze), 2 (please)
Lines 4 (unknowing), (growing)
Lines 6 (sea), 7 (be)

2. Title: "A furtive tear"
Character: Nemorino
Sequence: fourth
Rhyming lines:
Lines 1 (wise), 3 (eyes)
Lines 4 (reply), 6 (sigh), 7 (die)

3. Title: "Listen, listen country folk"

Character: Dulcamara
Sequence: third

4. Title: "How lovely she is, how dear she is!"
Character: Nemorino
Sequence: first

Rhyming lines:
Lines 1 (ail), 3 (fail)
Lines 4 (cronic), 5 (tonic)
Lines 6 (twice), 7 (price)

Rhyming lines:
Lines 1 (eye), 2 (sigh)
Lines 3 (vainly), 4 (plainly)
Lines 6 (start), 7 (heart)

Norma

1. Title: "The heart you betrayed"
Character: Norma
Sequence: fourth
Rhyming lines:
Lines 1 (betrayed), 2 (destroyed)
Lines 3 (me), 4 (flee), 5 (me)
Lines 6 (earth), 7 (death)

2. Title: "At the altar of Venus"
Character: Pollione
Sequence: first
Rhyming lines:
Lines 1 (Venus), 7 (darkness)
Lines 3 (us), 6 (us)
Lines 4 (rapture), 5 (capture)

3. Title: "Chaste Goddess"
Character: Norma
Sequence: second
Rhyming lines:
Lines 1 (silver), 2 (cover)
Lines 3 (appeal), 4 (zeal)
Lines 5 (earth), 6 (birth)

4. Title: "Oh, what memories!"
Characters: Norma, Adalgisa
Sequence: third
Rhyming lines:
Lines 1 (enraptured), 2 (captured)
Lines 3 (reduced), 4 (seduced)
Lines 5 (secretly), 6 (increasingly)

I Pagliacci

1. Title: "Hui! How wildly they shriek up there"
Character: Nedda
Sequence: third
Rhyming lines:
Lines 1 (fly), 2 (sky)
Lines 3 (light), 4 (height)
Lines 5 (flight), 6 (site)

2. Title: "Not to play such a game"
Character: Canio
Sequence: second
Rhyming lines:
Lines 1 (another), 2 (lover)
Lines 3 (warning), 4 (closing)
Lines 5 (see), 6 (me)

3. Title: "Put on the costume"
Character: Canio
Sequence: fourth
Rhyming lines:
Lines 1 (play), 2 (say), 6 (pay)
Lines 3 (paint), 5 (pain)

4. Title: "Prologue: May I? May I?"
Character: Tonio
Sequence: first
Rhyming lines:
Lines 2 (you), 3 (you)
Lines 4 (life), 5 (nice)
Lines 6 (sighed), 7 (cried)

Carmen

Much of the original French libretto by H. Meilhac and L. Halévy to *Carmen* is written in rhyme. The English rhyming translation of the songs below is by Ruth and Thomas Martin for G. Schirmer, Inc., 1973. Some passages have been condensed and key rhyming words are boldfaced.

Directions: (1) Complete the rhymes by filling in the blanks. (2) Select the correct song title from the choices below. (3) Name the character and number the songs in sequence, from one to four, based on when they occur in the opera. After you complete the blanks below, check the answer key.

Song Titles: "Nothing frightens me" • "Love is a rebellious bird"
"I return your toast!" • "The Flower that you threw me"

1. Song title: _____
Character: _____
Sequence: _____

In prison there, I kept your flower,
though its bloom was swiftly **gone**,
its haunting fragrance lingered _____.
In the darkness, as I lay **dreaming**,
its perfume consoling, _____,
recalled your image night and **day**,
and my despair would fade _____.
(Lines two and three, lines four and five, and lines six and seven rhyme.)

2. Song title: _____
Character: _____
Sequence: _____

And in return I drink to you **tonight!**
We live to share a common joy,
the thrill of the _____.
Excitement fills the **atmosphere**.
Wild with impatience,
they raise a thunderous _____.
(Lines one and three, and lines four and six rhyme.)

3. Song title: _____
Character: _____
Sequence: _____

I thought I could master my **terror**.
I was so sure I would be brave and **strong**.
But now, too late, I see my _____!
Deep in my heart I know I was _____.
I'm alone and afraid, but I will not
despair!
God in His kindness all-abounding will make me strong and hear my _____.
(Lines one and three, lines two and four, and lines five and seven rhyme.)

4. Song title: _____
Character: _____
Sequence: _____

Love has so many forms and **shapes**,
each day it wears a new **disguise**.
Think you've caught it and it _____.
to catch you later by _____.
Wait for love and you wait **forever**,
don't wait at all, it comes to you.
Try to grasp it, it's far too _____.
(Lines one and three, lines two and four, and lines five and seven rhyme.)

Les Contes d'Hoffmann

Much of the original French libretto by Jules Barbier and Michel Carre to *The Tales of Hoffmann* is written in rhyme. The English rhyming translation of the songs below is by Ruth and Thomas Martin for G. Schirmer, Inc., 1973. Some passages have been condensed and key rhyming words are boldfaced.

Directions: (1) Complete the rhymes by filling in the blanks. (2) Select the correct song title from the choices below. (3) Name the character and number the songs in sequence, from one to four, based on when they occur in the opera. After you complete the blanks below, check the answer key.

Song Titles: **"A doll with enamel eyes"** • **"Night and day, I go out of my way"**
"Beautiful night, oh night of love" • **"Once upon a time at the court of Eisenach"**

1. Song title: _____
Character: _____
Sequence: _____
Starry heavens high **above**,
smile on us, oh night of _____.
Time is fleet and bears **away**
the passions that possess us.
Enjoy while you **may**
before the dawn of _____,
speeds the moment _____.
(Lines one and two, lines three and six, and lines five and seven rhyme.)

2. Song title: _____
Character: _____
Sequence: _____
There was a doll with enamel **eyes**,
so true to life in form and _____.
Just exactly like a pretty **woman**,
she even learned a song to **sing**,
that was the most amusing _____,
and when she danced the waltz,
you'd think that she was _____.
(Lines one and two, lines three and seven, and lines four and five rhyme.)

3. Song title: _____
Character: _____
Sequence: _____
There lived a dwarf named **Kleinzack**!
He had a mighty hump on his _____.
His hair stood up like hay on a **stack**.
His feet were big and flat like a _____.
His head was so heavy, it went crick **crack**!
That was the dwarf called _____.
(Lines one and two, lines three and four, and lines five and six rhyme)

4. Song title: _____
Character: _____
Sequence: _____
All night and day, till I almost **drop**,
I work and work without a _____.
I don't complain about a **thing**,
but now and then I like to _____.
If I sometimes miss a **beat**,
do not blame it on my _____.
Lines one and two, lines three and four, and lines five and six rhyme.)

Faust

Much of the original French libretto by Jules Barbier and Michel Carré to *Faust* is written in rhyme. The English rhyming translation of the songs below is by George Mead for G. Schirmer, Inc., 1966. Some passages have been condensed and key rhyming words are boldfaced.

Directions: (1) Complete the rhymes by filling in the blanks. (2) Select the correct song title from the choices below. (3) Name the character and number the songs in sequence, from one to four, based on when they occur in the opera. After you complete the blanks below, check the answer key.

Song Titles: "Before I leave these parts" • "Greetings, chaste and pure abode"
"Ah! I laugh at seeing myself" • "You who pretend to be asleep"

1. Song title: _____
Character: _____
Sequence: _____

Ah, I can **see**
beauty smiling back at _____.
Is it really **true**?
Marguerite, is it really _____?
What can this **mean**?
You're as fair as a _____!
(Lines one and two, lines three and
four, and lines five and six rhyme.)

2. Song title: _____
Character: _____
Sequence: _____

As I leave my sister **here**,
oh, Lord, be Thou ever _____!
Let me be the bravest in the **fight**,
in the strength of God and the _____.
What if at last death may call **me**,
I may know that she is safe with _____!
(Lines one and two, lines three and
four, and lines five and six rhyme.)

3. Song title: _____
Character: _____
Sequence: _____

To you I bring my heart's **devotion**.
Here creation bloomed in full _____.
What hidden treasures in this humble
  place!
What happy dreams, what joy and ____!
The sun sent brightness to shine in her
  eyes,
sent sunrays down from the _____.
(Lines one and two, lines three and
four, and lines five and six rhyme.)

4. Song title: _____
Character: _____
Sequence: _____

So a lover sings **politely**,
so he comes to greet you _____.
Don't you smile at him too **brightly**,
bar your doors and windows _____.
Thus a lover comes a **wooing**,
lady, watch what you are _____!

(Lines one and two, lines three and
four, and lines five and six rhyme.)

Manon

Much of the original French libretto by Henri Meilhac and Philippe Gille
to *Manon* is written in rhyme. The English rhyming translation of the songs
below is by George and Phyllis Mead for G. Schirmer, Inc., 1963. Some passages
have been condensed and key rhyming words are boldfaced.

Directions: (1) Complete the rhymes by filling in the blanks. (2) Select
the correct song title from the choices below. (3) Name the character and number the songs in sequence, from one to four, based on when they occur in the
opera. After you complete the blanks below, check the answer key.

Song Titles: "I am still completely dizzy" • "Ah! Sweet memory flee"
"I walk on all roads" • "Obey when their voices beckon us"

1. Song title: _____
Character: _____
Sequence: _____

Let there be no sorrowing and **sighing,**
youth is a joyous time to **sing.**
While your golden hours are _____,
oh, come and taste the joy of _____.
The lover may forget his love some **day.**
So why delay and then discover
that your youth has flown _____.
(Lines one and three, lines two and four,
and lines five and seven rhyme.)

2. Song title: _____
Character: _____
Sequence: _____

I've seen so much that amazes me,
all is so fair, all is so **new,**
pardon the foolish things I ____!
Everything was smiling and **glowing,**
and I forgot where I was _____.
To the convent where I am to **stay,**
where I must go this very _____.
(Lines two and three, lines four and
five, and lines six and seven rhyme.)

3. Song title: _____
Character: _____
Sequence: _____

I go my triumphant **way**
with no other rivals remaining,
all the world adores me _____.
When my horses prance down the **street,**
the crowd finds it rather **alarming,**
the nobles all kneel at my _____.
I have beauty, and life is _____.
(Lines one and three, lines four and six,
and lines five and seven rhyme.)

4. Song title: _____
Character: _____
Sequence: _____

Let my soul be at **peace.**
Peace, oh, so dearly **won!**
I have sought some _____,
but seeking, and finding _____!
In dreams of love and **glory!**
Let the vows I have made
be the end of the _____.
(Lines one and three, lines two and
four, and lines five and seven rhyme.)

Answer Key to Complete the French Rhyming Passages

Carmen

1. Title: "The flower that you threw me"
Character: Don José
Sequence: third
Rhyming lines:
Lines 2 (gone), 3 (on)
Lines 4 (dreaming), 5 (redeeming)
Lines 6 (day), 7 (away)

2. Title: "I return your toast!"
Character: Escamillo
Sequence: second
Rhyming lines:
Lines 1 (tonight), 3 (fight)
Lines 4 (atmosphere), 6 (cheer)

3. Title: "Nothing frightens me"
Character: Micaëla
Sequence: fourth
Rhyming lines:

4. Title: "Love is a rebellious bird"
Character: Carmen
Sequence: first
Rhyming lines:

Lines 1 (terror), 3 (error)
Lines 2 (strong), 4 (wrong)
Lines 5 (despair), 7 (prayer)

Lines 1 (shapes), 3 (escapes)
Lines 2 (disguise), 4 (surprise)
Lines 5 (forever), 7 (clever)

Les Contes d'Hoffmann

1. Title: "Beautiful night, oh night of love"
Characters: Giulietta, Nicklausse
Sequence: third
Rhyming lines:
Lines 1 (above), 2 (love)
Lines 3 (away), 6 (day)
Lines 5 (may), 7 (away)

2. Title: "A doll with enamel eyes"
Character: Nicklausse
Sequence: second
Rhyming lines:
Lines 1 (eyes), 2 (size)
Lines 3 (woman), 7 (human)
Lines 4 (sing), 5 (thing)

3. Title: "Night and day"
Character: Franz
Sequence: fourth
Rhyming lines:
Lines 1 (drop), 2 (stop)
Lines 3 (thing), 4 (sing)
Lines 5 (beat), 6 (feet)

4. Title: "A dwarf named Kleinzack"
Character: Hoffmann
Sequence: first
Rhyming lines:
Lines 1 (Kleinzack), 2 (back)
Lines 3 (stack), 4 (duck)
Lines 5 (crack), 6 (Kleinzack)

Faust

1. Title: "Ah! I laugh at seeing mtself (Jewel Song)"
Character: Marguerite
Sequence: third
Rhyming lines:
Lines 1 (see), 2 (me)
Lines 3 (true), 4 (you)
Lines 5 (mean), 6 (queen)

2. Title: "Before I leave these parts"
Character: Valentin
Sequence: first
Rhyming lines:
Lines 1 (here), 2 (near)
Lines 3 (fight), 4 (right)
Lines 5 (me), 6 (thee)

3. Title: "Greetings, chaste and pure"
Character: Faust
Sequence: second
Rhyming lines:
Lines 1 (devotion), 2 (perfection)
Lines 3 (place), 4 (grace)
Lines 5 (eyes), 6 (skies)

4. Title: "You who pretend to be asleep"
Character: Mephistophélès
Sequence: fourth
Rhyming lines:
Lines 1 (politely), 2 (nightly)
Lines 3 (brightly), 4 (tightly)
Lines 5 (wooing), 6 (doing)

Manon

1. Title: "Obey when their voices beckon us"
Character: Manon
Sequence: third
Rhyming lines:
Lines 1 (sighing), 3 (flying)

2. Title: "I am still completely dizzy"
Character: Manon
Sequence: first
Rhyming lines:
Lines 2 (new), 3 (do)

Lines 2 (sing), 4 (spring)
Lines 5 (day), 7 (away)

Lines 4 (glowing), 5 (going)
Lines 6 (stay), 7 (day)

3. Title: "I walk on all roads"
Character: Manon
Sequence: second
Rhyming lines:
Lines 1 (way), 3 (today)
Lines 4 (street), 6 (feet)
Lines 5 (alarming), 7 (charming)

4. Title: "Ah! sweet memory flee"
Character: Des Grieux
Sequence: fourth
Rhyming lines:
Lines 1 (peace), 3 (release)
Lines 2 (won), 4 (none)
Lines 5 (glory), 7 (story)

Fidelio

Much of the original German libretto by Joseph Sonnleithner and Georg Friedrich Treitschke to *Fidelio* is written in rhyme. The English rhyming translation of the songs below is by Edward Dent for Oxford University Press (date unlisted). Some passages have been condensed and key rhyming words are boldfaced.

Directions: (1) Complete the rhymes by filling in the blanks. (2) Select the correct song title from the choices below. (3) Name the character and number the songs in sequence, from one to four, based on when they occur in the opera. After you complete the blanks below, check the answer key.

Song Titles: "In the springtime of my life" • "Oh! I wish I were united with you"
"I feel so wonderful" • "Monster! ... Come, Hope"

1. Song title: _____
Character: _____
Sequence: _____

In my heart, so softly **gleaming**,
speaks of love and grace _____.
Oh, Hope, let not thy last faint **star**,
in dark despair be blinded!
Fair light, point me the way _____.
I know not **fear**
my path lies _____.
(Lines one and two, lines three and five,
and lines six and seven rhyme.)

2. Song title: _____
Character: _____
Sequence: _____

Who is it, that figure so **bright**,
that radiant vision arising before **me**?
An angel in a garment of _____,
with a word of comfort to restore ____!
My Leonore, my angel, my **wife**,
whom God sends me to heavenly ____,
an angel in a garment of _____!
(Lines one, three, and seven, lines two
and four, lines five and six rhyme.)

3. Song title: _____
Character: _____
Sequence: _____

How blest will be the humble **cot**,
that I with him will be **sharing**!

4. Song title: _____
Character: _____
Sequence: _____

My heart had told me **so**,
before one word he **said**.

Contented we'll accept our _____,
and each other's burdens _____.
For nothing can ever divide us.
May hope sustain my trembling **heart**,
to church they soon will _____.
(Lines one and three, lines two and
four, and lines six and seven rhyme.)

He loves me, now I _____;
the path of joy I now may _____.
She loves the lad, I **know**;
till I from him shall never _____.

(Lines one and three, lines two and
four, and lines five and six rhyme.)

Der Fliegende Holländer

Much of the original German libretto by Richard Wagner to *The Flying Dutchman* is written in rhyme. The English rhyming translation of the songs below is by Stewart Robb for G. Schirmer, Inc., 1964. Some passages have been condensed and key rhyming words are boldfaced.

Directions: (1) Complete the rhymes by filling in the blanks. (2) Select the correct song title from the choices below. (3) Name the character and number the songs in sequence, from one to four, based on when they occur in the opera. After you complete the blanks below, check the answer key.

Song Titles:
"Have you met the ship at sea?" • **"My child, do welcome this stranger"**
"The time is up" • **"In storm and gale from distant lands"**

1. Song title: _____
Character: _____
Sequence: _____

Can he be redeemed from **damnation**,
if he finds a woman for _____.
Around the cape he once would **sail**;
In foolish pride he cursed and swore:
"Spite God or the devil I'll not _____."
In hope thereby to find a **wife**;
he woos one every seven years,
but finds none true in all his _____.
(Lines one and two, lines three and five,
and lines six and eight rhyme.)

2. Song title: _____
Character: _____
Sequence: _____

The term is up, and once again are ended.
How many times I've longed to die...
Shall roll, until the ocean dries **away**!
I hoped for death in a savage _____.
It still must one day have an **end**,
when all the dead are raised _____.
You planets, cease to whirl **about,**
endless oblivion, blot me _____!
(Lines three and four, lines five and six,
and lines seven and eight rhyme.)

3. Song title: _____
Character: _____
Sequence: _____

My sweetheart, if no southwind **blew**,
I'd never have come home to _____.
I have you in my **thoughts**;

4. Song title: _____
Character: _____
Sequence: _____

Seaman is he and asks to be our **guest**;
far off he's won treasure for his _____.
You see her now, is she not **fair**?

accept the gift that I've _____ .
I bring you a golden **chain**;
these trinkets you won't _____ .
(Lines one and two, lines three and
four, and lines five and six rhyme.)

Confess, is she not past _____?
He asks for a heart that's kindly **bred**.
In father's mind, tomorrow you'll _____.
(Lines one and two, lines three and four,
and lines five and six rhyme.)

Der Freischütz

Much of the original German libretto by Friedrich Kind to *The Free Shooter* is written in rhyme. The English rhyming translation below is by George and Phyllis Mead for G. Schirmer, Inc., 1971. Some passages have been condensed and key rhyming words are boldfaced.

Directions: (1) Complete the rhymes by filling in the blanks. (2) Select the correct song title from the choices below. (3) Name the character and number the songs in sequence, from one to four, based on when they occur in the opera. After you complete the blanks below, check the answer key.

Song Titles: "Softly, softly, pious melody" • "When a slim boy comes along" "Sad eyes" • "Through woods and through fields"

1. Song title: _____
Character: _____
Sequence: _____

Through the darkness in the **grove**
I can hear the mourning _____.
Hear the gentle breezes **sighing**
and the nightingale _____!
Am I free from care and **grieving,**
and is it all beyond _____?
Surely nothing can **arise**
to becloud my shinning _____.
(Lines one and two, three and four,
five and six, and seven and eight rhyme.)

2. Song title: _____
Character: _____
Sequence: _____

In the hopeless fear and chilling **dread,**
what evil looms above my _____?
I would roam in days gone **by,**
in the forest, field or _____.
There beside her open window
even now I know she **stands,**
never doubting I shall bring her
proof of victory in my _____.
(Lines one and two, lines three and four,
and lines six and eight rhyme.)

3. Song title: _____
Character: _____
Sequence: _____

When I find a man **attractive,**
bright of eye and strong and _____,
then I strike some charming **poses.**
Drawing back with modest **shame,**
then I blush like twenty _____,
hoping he will do the _____.

4. Song title: _____
Character: _____
Sequence: _____

A bride like you should not be **crying.**
It is your duty to be _____.
Soon will come your joyful **day.**
Show your beauty while you _____!
Wipe your tears and fears **away,**
now before your wedding _____!

That is when he meets his **doom!**
Very soon we're bride and _____.
(Lines one and two, three and five, lines   (Lines one and two, lines three and
four and six, and seven and eight rhyme.)   four, and lines five and six rhyme.)

Die Zauberflöte

Much of the original German libretto by Emanuel Schikaneder to *The Magic Flute* is written in rhyme. The English rhyming translation of the songs below is by the author of this handbook. Some passages have been condensed and key rhyming words are boldfaced.

Directions: (1) Complete the rhymes by filling in the blanks. (2) Select the correct song title from the choices below. (3) Name the character and number the songs in sequence, from one to four, based on when they occur in the opera. After you complete the blanks below, check the answer key.

Song Titles: "In those sacred halls" • "Oh tremble not, my dear son!"
"I am the birdcatcher" • "How powerful is your magic sound!"

1. Song title: _____   2. Song title: _____
Character: _____   Character: _____
Sequence: _____   Sequence: _____

How powerful is your magic **sound!**   Within these mighty and sacred **halls,**
Sweet flute, for when you **play**   seeking revenge has no place.
even wild beasts begin to _____.   And even if a man _____,
Yet Pamina has not been _____.   then, with a friend hand-in-**hand,**
Pamina! Pamina! Do you hear **me?**   he goes to a far better _____,
Where, oh where, shall I find _____.   and protected by sacred _____.
(Lines one and four, lines two and   (Lines one, three, and six, and
three, and lines five and six rhyme.)   lines four and five rhyme.)

3. Song title: _____   4. Song title: _____
Character: _____   Character: _____
Sequence: _____   Sequence: _____

You need not tremble my **dear,**   I'm known far and wide as a **birdcatcher,**
you are righteous and without _____.   and a carefree bird _____,
My daughter was abducted by a **villain.**   who whistles to attract his prey.
Her appeals for help were in _____,   I would rather trap girls for my **own**
which left my maternal heart broken.   and catch them throughout the **land.**
You can win her if you set her **free,**   I would cage them in my very _____,
and mend my heart by returning her   and to marry the best one is my _____.
  to ___.
(Lines one and two, lines three and four, (Lines one and two, lines four and six,
and lines six and seven rhyme.)   and lines five and seven rhyme.)

Answer Key to Complete the German Rhyming Passages

Fidelio

1. Title: "Monster! ... Come, Hope"
Character: Leonore
Sequence: third
Rhyming lines:
Lines 1 (gleaming), 2 (redeeming)
Lines 3 (star), 5 (afar)
Lines 6 (fear), 7 (here)

2. Title: "In the springtime of my life"
Character: Florestan
Sequence: fourth
Rhyming lines:
Lines 1 (bright), 3 (light), 7 (light)
Lines 2 (me), 4 (me)
Lines 5 (wife), 6 (life)

3. Title: "Oh! I wish I were united with you"
Character: Marzelline

Squence: first
Rhyming lines:
Lines 1 (cot), 3 (lot)
Lines 2 (sharing), 4 (bearing)
Lines 6 (heart), 7 (part)

4. Title: "I feel so wonderful"

Characters: Marzelline, Leonore, Rocco, Jaquino
Sequence: second
Rhyming lines:
Lines 1 (so), 3 (know)
Lines 2 (said), 4 (tread)
Lines 5 (know), 6 (go)

Der Fliegende Holländer

1. Title: "Have you met the ship at sea?"
Character: Senta
Sequence: third
Rhyming lines:
Lines 1 (damnation), 2 (salvation)
Lines 3 (sail), 5 (fail)
Lines 6 (wife), 8 (life)

2. Title: "The time is up"
Character: Dutchman
Sequence: second
Rhyming lines:
Lines 3 (away), 4 (fray)
Lines 5 (end), 6 (again)
Lines 7 (about), 8 (out)

3. Title: "In storm and gale from distant seas"
Character: Steersman
Sequence: first
Rhyming lines:
Lines 1 (blew), 2 (you)
Lines 3 (thoughts), 4 (brought)
Lines 5 (chain), 6 (distain)

4. Title: "My child, do welcome this stranger"
Character: Daland
Sequence: fourth
Rhyming lines:
Lines 1 (guest), 2 (chest)
Lines 3 (fair), 4 (compare)
Lines 5 (bred), 6 (wed)

Der Freischütz

1. Title: "Softly, softly, pious melody"

Character: Agathe

2. Title: "Through woods and through fields"

Character: Max

Sequence: third
Rhyming lines:
Lines 1 (grove), 2 (dove)
Lines 3 (sighing), 4 (replying)
Lines 5 (grieving), 6 (believing)
Lines 7 (arise), 8 (skies)

3. Title: "When a slim boy comes along"
Character: Ännchen
Sequence: second
Rhyming lines:
Lines 1 (attractive), 2 (active)
Lines 3 (poses), 5 (roses)
Lines 4 (shame), 6 (same)
Lines 7 (doom), 8 (groom)

Sequence: first
Rhyming lines:
Lines 1 (dread), 2 (head)
Lines 3 (by), 4 (sky)
Lines 6 (stands), 8 (hands)

4. Title: "Sad eyes, don't suit a bride"
Character: Ännchen
Sequence: fourth
Rhyming lines:
Lines 1 (crying), 2 (smiling)
Lines 3 (day), 4 (may)
Lines 5 (away), 6 (day)

Die Zauberflöte

1. Title: "How powerful is your
magic sound!"
Character: Tamino
Sequence: third
Rhyming lines:
Lines 1 (sound), 4 (found)
Lines 2 (play), 3 (sway)
Lines 5 (me), 6 (thee)

2. Title: "In those sacred halls"

Character: Sarastro
Sequence: fourth
Rhyming lines:
Lines 1 (halls), 3 (falls), 6 (walls)
Lines 4 (hand), 5 (land)

3. Title: "Oh tremble not, my dear son!"
Character: Queen of the Night
Sequence: second
Rhyming lines:
Lines 1 (dear), 2 (fear)
Lines 3 (villain), 4 (vain)
Lines 6 (free), 7 (me)

4. Title: "Yes, I am the bird catcher"
Character: Papageno
Sequence: first
Rhyming lines:
Lines 1 (catcher), 2 (collector)
Lines 4 (own), 6 (home)
Lines 5 (land), 7 (plan)

Glossary of
Operatic Terms

Aria (Ital., "air" or "atmosphere"). An extended and self-contained solo song with orchestral accompaniment. An opportunity to display a singer's vocal skills.

Arietta (Ital., "breeze"). A simple aria that is shorter and less elaborate than a fully developed aria. Usually lacks development or a middle section.

Arioso (Ital., "aria-like"). A short aria passage in the middle or at the end of a recitative. It combines the dramatic character of the recitative with the formal structure of the aria.

Barcarolle (Ital., "barcarola"). A Venetian boating song with a lilting swing, romantic lure, and rowing rhythm. The song glides along at an easy pace.

Baritone (Gr., "full sounding"). A moderately low-pitched male voice in the middle register between a tenor and bass. Common types include lyric, dramatic, and comic.

Bel canto (Ital., "fine singing"). A clear melodic line but decorated by frills, smoothness, and beauty of tone. Elegant vocal style applied to Italian classic legato singing.

Bravura (Ital., "bravery"). A musical passage requiring exceptional agility and technical skill; a florid style. Difficult runs and passagework to show vocal brilliance.

Cabaletta (Ital., "couplet"). The concluding section of an extended song. Usually in a fairly rapid tempo and with mounting excitement. A lively bravura conclusion.

Cadenza (Ital., "cadence"). An opportunity to show off one's vocal skills after the main aria is over. A virtuoso passage, interrupting the final cadence of an aria.

Canon. Two or more voices in counterpoint. Each singer repeats the same melody in succession and note for note. The first singer continues as the other singer(s) join(s) in.

Cantabile (Ital., "in a singing style"). Usually the first and slower part of a two-part aria or duet. It can also indicate an aria in slow or moderate tempo.

Cantilena (Ital., "sing-song"). Used to indicate a flowing vocal line, such as lyrical singing. A sustained, flowing melodic line.

Cavatina (Ital., "to produce a sound"). A short aria; often an expressive and romantic piece. Often used as an entrance aria of a principal character.

Coloratura (Lat., "coloring"). A virtuoso and decorative solo by means of rapid runs and trills. Elaborate ornamentation of melody. A high pitch with lightness and agility.

259

Counterpoint. A technique of combining musical lines. Two or more tunes sung at the same time. Usually one singer starts first and the second follows.

Crescendo (Ital., "gradual increase"). Indicates that the voice is increasing in volume, often at a very dramatic or emotional moment. Opposite of decrescendo.

Diminuendo (Ital., "diminishing"). Used to indicate the voice is getting softer; like decrescendo. Ability to move from loud to soft. Often to create a calmer mood.

Dynamics. The degree of volume called for in the performance. The markings include pianissimo (very soft), piano (soft), forte (loud), fortissimo (very loud).

Ensemble (Fr., "the same time"). Two or more soloists singing together. May express complementary or opposing thoughts and emotions.

Fermata (Ital., "literally a stop"). A prolonged musical note, chord or rest.

Florid passage. A musical passage that is highly ornamented, especially an elaborate version of a simpler melody or theme.

Intermezzo (Ital., "interlude"). Instrumental or sung music between two acts. Provides a break in the action and often sets the mood for the following act.

Intonation (from Lat., "intonare"). The ability of a singer to be in tune, as opposed to being sharp or flat.

Largo (Ital., "broad"). At a very slow tempo. Larghetto refers to slow but not as slow as largo. Often depicts a somber, serious or religious mood.

Legato (Ital., "tied"). A smooth and connected melodic phrase, with one note flowing or gliding into the next. The uninterrupted connection of successive notes.

Libretto (Ital., "little book"). The text of the opera printed for the benefit of the audience. Often containing literary value but without music.

Lyric. A vocal weight between light and heavy. Often associated with a smooth and melodic sound, such as legato singing.

Major/Minor scale. The major scales or keys tend to depict a bright and cheerful mood. Minor scales or keys often depict a more melancholy and tearful mood.

Mezzo-soprano. A female voice with a lower register than a soprano. Often used in more sultry and seductive roles, such as Carmen and Delilah.

Motif or **Motive.** A brief but distinctive musical idea. A short unit of music, which may contribute to a theme. Often identified with an idea, theme, or character.

Obbligato (Ital., "obligatory"). A necessary solo instrumental accompaniment. Often used to introduce an aria and set the mood or atmosphere.

Opera (Ital., "work"). A staged musical drama, for the most part sung, with instrumental accompaniment. Grand opera involves majestic sets and heroic themes.

Opera buffa (Ital., "comic opera"). A type of Italian comic opera with lighthearted situations. Distinguished by fast-moving musical textures and ensemble numbers.

Ornamental. A melodic embellishment added to vocal or instrumental music by the vocalist or composer. Often referred to as "decoration" or a "decorative phrase."

Patter song. A comic song with very quickly spoken words. Often used in buffa solos to add humorous expression (e.g., Rossini's *The Barber of Seville*).

Prelude. An instrumental piece used to introduce motifs, a mood or atmosphere for the act to follow. For example, *Carmen* has three famous preludes to acts II, III, and IV.

Prima donna (Ital., "first lady"). The leading female singer, usually with the most difficult role. Sometimes has a connotation of being temperamental.

Prompter. A musical assistant who sits in a sunken box at the footlights and cues the singer's memory by calling out the first word of a line.

Recitative (Ital., "reciting"). An imitation of natural speech between songs. Often a note for each syllable and accompanied instrumentally.

Register. Any of the different parts of the range of the human voice, such as a high range, medium range, low range.

Rhythm. The arrangement of notes in a piece of music in relation to time, such as a lively or brisk rhythm. Rhythm is influenced and reflected in the tempo.

Rondo. A type of aria consisting of two sections, one slow and one fast. Best known examples are by Mozart.

Singspiel (Ger., "song play"). Spoken German dialogue between songs in place of sung recitative (e.g., *The Magic Flute*, *Fidelio*, and *Der Frieschütz*).

Soprano (Ital., "above"). The highest female voice. Four common types include dramatic, lyric, spinto and coloratura.

Spinto (Ital., "pushed"). A lyric voice with the capacity to push into more dramatic roles. It may apply to sopranos and tenors.

Staccato (Ital., "to detach"). A brief pause between notes; a sharp way of singing a note. The opposite of legato.

Stanza. A set of vocal lines which together form a unit with a space after the last line and before the following stanza. The lines are often related and convey a theme.

Tempo (Ital., "time"). The speed at which the voice moves, as indicated by tempo marks such as adagio (slow), andante (easy pace), moderato, and allegro (lively or brisk).

Tenor (from Ital., "to hold"). The highest natural male voice. Four common types include dramatic or heroic, lyric, spinto and light tenor.

Tessitura (Ital., "texture"). That part of the vocal range most used for a composition or role. For example, the Queen of the Night requires a soprano with a high tessitura.

Timbre (or tone color). The quality of a sound characteristic of a particular voice. Determined by the number and intensity of the overtones present in the sound.

Trill (Ital., "shake"). Two adjacent notes, with different tones, sung alternately and rather quickly; ornamental singing. A highly skilled accomplishment.

Verismo (Ital., "realism"). Meaning true to life, realistic events and characters. Often involving strong emotions, violent passions and actions.

Verse. A short vocal piece or passage often poetic and melodic in content. The verse often contains a melody from the work.

Vivace (Ital., "lively"). A direction meaning that the melodic phrases should be sung in a lively and vivacious manner, especially comic situations.

Appendix A:
A Comparison of Unrhymed and Rhymed Translations

*I*t was very common in the eighteenth and nineteenth centuries for librettists to rhyme large portions of the libretto. However, this popular process has always presented an obstacle to translators who have the task of interpreting the original text into another language. Many translators prefer to translate rhymed text into unrhymed text in order to provide a more literal translation of the original text. The task of translating a rhyming text in one language into a rhyming text in another language usually requires the translator to take greater liberties in an effort to create rhyme, while trying not to seriously distort the meaning of the original text.

The three famous arias below compare the effort to provide an unrhymed and more literal translation with a rhymed and more poetic translation. The rhymed versions are based on *G. Schirmer's Librettos*. Some lines are missing in these condensed versions. To help compare the two versions, words with a similar meaning have been highlighted. (The in-depth description of each of the following songs can be found in Part II.)

Consider the following questions as you read the unrhymed and rhymed translations. Does the unrhymed translation appear to express the character's thoughts and emotions more effectively than the rhymed translation? If we assume that the unrhymed translation is closer in meaning to the original libretto, do you think the rhymed translation exaggerates or misrepresents the thoughts and feelings of the character? Finally, if the singer was given a choice, which translation do you think he or she would prefer?

"La donna è mobile" ("Woman is [women are] fickle")
from Verdi's *Rigoletto*

The Duke of Mantua is known to be a libertine whose list of seductions can rival Don Giovanni's. The irony of the song is that the Duke himself is probably more fickle and deceitful than any woman he is likely to seduce.

Unrhymed Translation

The woman is **fickle**,
like a feather in the wind
she changes speech
and thoughts.
A **lovable**,
graceful face,
in tears or in laughter
is always lying.
He is always **miserable**
who trusts in her,
who entrusts his
unwary heart to her!
Yet nobody feels
fully **happy**
who on that bosom
does not drink love.

Rhymed Translation

Women are frivolous,
women are **changeable**.
Now they adore you,
now they ignore you!
Women are **lovable**,
women are dangerous.
One day they kiss you,
then they dismiss you.
Smiling seductively,
they bring us **misery**,
yet we pursue them,
tenderly woo them.
Pleasure and **happiness**
lie at their mercy.
Though we may doubt them,
can't do without them!

"Il balen del suo sorriso" ("The radiance of her smile")
from Verdi's *Il Trovatore*

This lovely romanza is sung by the Count di Luna. Later, he learns that the woman he seeks has deceived him to save the man she loves—a troubadour.

In a fit of anger and jealousy, he burns his rival at the stake only to learn that his rival was his own brother. It's a terrible price to pay for the tempest inside him.

Unrhymed Translation

The **radiance** of her **smile**
wins over the rays of a **star**;
the glow of her beautiful face
inspires me with new courage.
Ah! may the **love** with which I burn
speak to her in my favor,
may the sunshine of one glance of hers
disperse the **tempest** in my **heart**!

Rhymed Translation

Her **bright smile** like lightning flashes,
sparkles like the **starlight**, brighter
than the sunshine.
And the glory of her eyes would make
dead ashes
rise in glowing splendor—glory
that must be mine.
All my **love** had frozen in my **heart**;
life itself was ready to depart.
Then her face with passion fired me,
and a **tempest** seized me, and with love
inspired me.

"D'amor sull'ali rosee"
("On love's rosy wings")
from Verdi's *Il Trovatore*

Leonora is a lady of nobility. She reflects on her love for a troubadour who has been confined to a dungeon in the Count di Luna's castle. She hopes that her thoughts will reach and comfort him on rosy wings. It's a very lovely song even though her airborne thoughts may never reach her lover.

Unrhymed Translation

On **love's** rosy **wings**
fly, mournful sigh,
comfort the wretched prisoner's
ailing mind...
Like a breeze of **hope**
linger in that **room**,
awaken him to the **memories**,
to the dreams of **love**!
But, ah, do not tell him of the pains,
the pains of my **heart**!

Rhymed Translation

Love's tender **wings** I pray may bear
prayers that my heart speaks bitterly.
Message of **hope** within my prayer—
oh, may God help to set him free.
If hope has left him utterly,
abandoned in his prison's gloom,
may love live again in his **memory**,
may true **love** to cheer his lonely **room**.
But if our ways should forever part,
he will not know the breaking of my
heart.

Appendix B: Vocal Profiles of 25 Exemplary Opera Singers

$\mathcal{T}$he following descriptions of 25 famous opera singers are meant to highlight their special vocal skills. This is a limited list of past and present famous singers. These singers were chosen for several reasons. First, even though many of them have passed away, their recordings are still very popular and readily available. Second, these singers are included on some of the most outstanding recordings of the operas and arias discussed in this handbook. Third, there are high quality recordings of each of these singers because most of them were recorded over the last half-century. Each entry is followed by a recommended recording.

Björling, Jussi (b. Stora Tuna, Sweden, 1911; d. Stockholm, 1960). Swedish tenor with a bright, sweet lyric sound. Acquired a brilliant timbre, gentle pianissimos, and considerable heroic thrust. Excelled in spinto roles of Verdi and Puccini. Noted for a perfect legato, elegant phrasing, and a regal sound. Died while still in excellent voice.
  The Very Best of Jussi Björling (2 discs, 43 songs). EMI Classics, 2003.

Caballé, Montserrat (b. Barcelona, 1933). A lyric soprano known for her creamy tone, superb breath control, and poised stage presence. Could produce glorious high notes and sustain and float high pianissimos that sounded effortless. Exceptional ability to spin out a long legato and make it vibrate with emotion. A master of bel canto roles.
  The Very Best of Montserrat Caballé (2 discs, 32 songs). EMI Classics, 2003.

Callas, Maria (b. New York, 1923; d. Paris, 1977). Powerful and wide ranging (up to high E-flat) voice. Wonderful flexibility, great dramatic power, unusual breadth of

phrasing, variety of color and spontaneity of feeling governed by intelligence and rigorous musicality. Great actress and ability to illuminate words.
100 Best Classics (3 discs). EMI Classics, 2007.

Corelli, Franco (b. Ancona, Italy, 1923; d. Milan, 2003). A spinto tenor known for stylish phrasing and intense expression. Capable of brilliant B-flats, ringing high C's to sudden soft singing. Noted for diminuendos on high notes. A clear, vibrant, urgent, passionate, virile and powerful voice. A very handsome and striking appearance.
The Very Best of Franco Corelli (2 discs, 32 songs). EMI Classics, 2003.

de los Angeles, Victoria (b. Barcelona, Spain, 1923; d. Barcelona, Spain, 2005). A radiant, flexible, creamy soprano with precise and evocative shading. Known for her perfect intonation, exquisite pianissimos, coloratura dexterity, sound lower register, and lyric roles. A fresh, youthful and bell-like tone. A warm and sympathetic singing actress.
The Very Best of Victoria de los Angeles (2 discs, 46 songs). EMI Classics, 2003.

di Stefano, Giuseppe (b. Sicily, Italy, 1921; d. near Milan, 2008). Early career noted for smooth and beautiful tone, with liquid pianissimos, and great intensity in lyric parts. Best in bel canto roles. Move to spinto and dramatic parts tended to spread his voice. Excellent intonation and clean legato. The definitive recording of *Tosca* with Callas and Gobbi.
Grandi Voci: Giuseppe di Stefano (16 songs). Decca Record Company, London, 1993.

Domingo, Placido (b. Madrid, 1941). Known for his tremendous range from a smooth lyric to dramatic tenor to a baritone weight. A warm tone with perfect intonation. Remarkable versatility with a wide repertory in several languages. A quick musical intelligence and memory.
The Best of Domingo (11 songs). Deutsche Grammophon, 1990.

Fleming, Renée (b. Indiana, Penn., 1959). A lustrous and warm voice with great beauty of tone and tonal coloration. Very clear projection and evenly integrated registers. Ability to melt a phrase or float a note. A radiant sound with creamy and lyrical elegance. A striking vocal and warm stage presence. Exquisite phrasing and technical excellence.
Renée Fleming (14 songs). Decca, London, 2000.

Freni, Mirella (b. Modena, Italy, 1935). A lyric soprano with a very clear and steady voice for lighter heroines, such as Mimì and Micaëla. Has an appealing and spontaneous presence. In her later career, she took on spinto and dramatic roles, such as Aïda and Desdemona.
The Very Best of Mirella Freni (2 discs, 28 songs). EMI Classics, 2003.

Gedda, Nicolai (b. Stockholm, Sweden, 1923). A sweet lyric tenor with a broad repertory, keen intelligence, stylistic elegance, and great versatility. Innate sense of style. Engaging actor and superior linguist. Outstanding enunciation in eight languages. Widely regarded by critics as the most underrated tenor of his time.
The Very Best of Nicolai Gedda (2 discs, 37 songs). EMI Classics, 2003.

Gheorghiu, Angela (b. Adjud, Romania, 1965). A lyric soprano voice known for its warm and radiant quality. Strong interpretative insight with the agility to move from lyric roles, such as Violetta and Juliet, to mezzo characters, such as Carmen. An outstanding and wide vocal colorist with a pure and classic legato line. Very attractive stage presence.

Angela Gheorghiu Diva (14 songs). EMI Classics, 2004.

Gobbi, Tito (b. near Venice, 1913; d. Rome, 1984). Pure, flexible and lovely baritone voice. Outstanding and intelligent actor that helped to compensate for his not so powerful voice. Most famous role was Baron Scarpia in *Tosca*.

The Very Best of Tito Gobbi (2 discs, 36 songs). EMI Classics, 2003.

Horne, Marilyn (b. Bradford, Penn., 1934). Known for her great flexibility and wideranging mezzo-soprano voice. Lively temperament and sound musicianship. A strong stage presence based on her virtuosity and strong concentration, especially known for her Baroque (Handel) and Rossini roles.

Just for the Record: The Golden Voice (2 discs, 32 songs). Decca, 2003.

Hvorostovsky, Dmitri (b. Krasnoyarsk, Siberia, 1962). Russian baritone known for his dark, rich, and lush voice. Conveys a dramatic expressiveness, enchanting lyricism, and sublety. Striking presence with elegant phrasing, distinctive timbre, and brooding intensity. Known for his sumptuously textured and emotion-charged Verdi roles.

Dmitri (15 songs). Philips, 1997.

Netrebko, Anna (b. Krasnodar, Russia, 1971). An outstanding lyric soprano with a very pure, youthful, dynamic, and extensive tonal range. Outstanding coloratura, clear and vibrant in every register. An exceedingly attractive and dramatic actress who projects charisma and passion on stage. Noted for her French and Italian bel canto roles.

Sempre Libera (16 songs). Deutsche Grammophon, 2004.

Nilsson, Birgit (b. West Karups, Sweden, 1918; d. near Kristianstad, Sweden, 2005). Considered the best Wagnerian dramatic soprano of her time. A powerful voice of imposing splendor with great musical stamina. Perfectly in tune and exciting throughout its range. Perfect intonation and purity of tone. Able to reach a climax without a sign of stress. Great dramatic presence on stage.

Ritorna vincitor! The Legendary Birgit Nilsson (2 discs, 32 songs). Decca, London, 2003.

Pavarotti, Luciano (b. Modena, Italy, 1935; d. Modena, 2008). A sweet, bright lyric tenor with a classic legato, and secure upper extension. Known for his purity of tone, smooth delivery and perfect intonation. A charming stage presence and especially known for his lyric roles. Generally regarded as the greatest tenor of his generation.

Pavarotti's Greatest Hits (2 discs, 26 songs). Decca Record Co., London, 1985.

Price, Leontyne (b. Laurel, Mississippi, 1927). A spinto soprano with a rich and sensuous tone, fast vibrato with a distinctive shimmer. Registers and colors well equalized and controlled. Compelling in her intensity and directness of expression, especially known for her dramatic roles in Verdi operas.

Leontyne Price—The Ultimate Collection (2 discs, 28 songs). RCA, BMG Entertainment, 1999.

Schwarzkopf, Elisabeth (b. Jarotchin, Germany, 1915; d. Schruns, Austria, 2006). Known for remarkable musical and dramatic intelligence. Noted for an angelic and carefully controlled voice. Began as a coloratura and later took on lyric roles. Famous for her attention to detail and nuance. Expressive gestures and aristocratic appearance.

    The Very Best of Elisabeth Schwarzkopf (2 discs, 24 songs). EMI Classics, 2003.

Sills, Beverly (b. Brooklyn, N.Y., 1929; d. New York, 2007). Began as a lyric-coloratura before turning to bel canto roles. Noted for her pure, bright, and sweet intonation. Known for her outstanding musicianship, engaging stage presence, breath control, and technical skills, such as fast runs and spiraling cadenzas. Portrayed tragic pathos and lively comedy.

    The Art of Beverly Sills (2 dics, 20 songs). Deutsch Grammophon, 2002.

Sutherland, Joan (b. Sydney, Australia, 1926; d. Les Avants, Switzerland, 2010). Great vocal power, beauty of tone, and flexibility. Known for her flawless intonation, brilliant staccato, firmly defined and rapid trills, and command of cantilena lines. High and wide range with beauty from top to bottom. Great coloratura technician.

    La Stupenda—The Supreme Voice of Joan Sutherland (2 discs, 27 songs). Decca Music Group, London, 2001.

Tebaldi, Renata (b. Pesaro, Italy, 1922; d. San Marino, 2004). A radiant spinto voice with a warm personality. Noted for her creamy smoothness, soft legato, and gentle pianissimo. High standard of musicianship and a sympathetic stage presence. Voice wonderfully designed for the Italian repertory.

    Grand Voci: Renata Tebaldi (15 songs). Decca Record Company, London, 1993.

Te Kanawa, Kiri (b. Auckland, 1944). A lyric soprano noted for her tonal splendor and creamy sound. Very natural singer with a lovely voice throughout her range. Noted for her attractive appearance and sophisticated poise. Excels in mature roles, such as the Marschallin and the Countess Rosina. Not inclined toward highly dramatic roles.

    Kiri Te Kanawa—Verdi & Puccini (10 songs). CBS Masterworks, NY, 1983.

Vickers, Jon (b. Saskatchewan, Canada, 1926). A strong spinto voice well suited for heroic roles, such as Otello, Florestan and Samson. A very imposing physique and powerful voice. Perfectly on pitch and very expressive in lyric parts. Master of diction, tone color, and phrasing.

    Jon Vickers—Italian Opera Arias (12 songs). Video Arts International, 1994.

Warren, Leonard (b. New York, 1911; d. New York, 1960). An exceptional baritone voice. Known for his agility, warmth, strength and sensitivity. Possessed an easy upper extension (even beyond high A). Also acquired a fine control of soft singing. An "Italian baritone voice" especially suited for Verdi roles.

    Leonard Warren—Legendary Voices (15 songs). Preiser Records, 1997.

Appendix C:
Recommended Recordings

CD

Italian Operas

Aida (Verdi). Milanov, Barbieri, Bjöerling, Warren; Perlea, conductor, Rome Opera House, Sony Classics, 2013.

Aida (Verdi). Nilsson, Corelli, Bumbry, Sereni; Mehta, conductor, Teatro dell'Opera di Roma, EMI Classics, 2000.

Aida (Verdi). Millo, Domingo, Zajick, Ramey; Levine, conductor, Metropolitan Opera Orchestra, NY. Sony Classics, 1994.

Il Barbiere di Siviglia (Rossini). Sills, Gedda, Milnes, Raimondi; Levine, conductor, London Symphony Orchestra. EMI Classics, 2000.

Il Barbiere di Siviglia (Rossini). Horne, Nucci, Ramey, Dara; Chailly, conductor, La Scala Theater Orchestra. Sony Classics, 1994.

La Bohème (Puccini). Freni, Pavarotti, Harwood, Panerai; von Karajan, conductor, Berlin Philharmonic Orchestra, Decca, 1990.

La Bohème (Puccini). Björling, de los Angeles, Merrill, Amara; Beecham, conductor, R.C.A. Victor Orchestra, EMI Classics, 1986.

La Bohème (Puccini). Callas, di Stefano, Moffo, Panerai; Votto, conductor, La Scala Theater Orchestra. EMI Classics, 1998.

L'Elisir d'Amore (Donizetti). Freni, Gedda, Sereni, Capecchi; Molinari Pradelli, conductor, Rome Opera Orchestra, Warner Classics, 2011.

L'Elisir d'Amore (Donizetti). Pavarotti, Battle, Dara; Levine, conductor, Metropolitan Opera Orchestra. Deutsche Grammophon, 1990.

Norma (Bellini). Callas, Corelli, Ludwig; Serafin, conductor, La Scala Theater Orchestra, Milan. EMI Classics, 1998.

Norma (Bellini). Caballé, Cossotto, Domingo, Raimondi; Cillario, conductor, London Philharmonic. R.C.A. Victor, 1990.

French Operas

Carmen (Bizet). Price, Corelli, Merrill, Freni; von Karajan, conductor, Vienna Philharmonic Orchestra. RCA, 1990.

Carmen (Bizet). Callas, Gedda, Guiot, Cales; Pretre, conductor, Paris National Opera Theater Orchestra. EMI Classics, 1998.

Carmen (Bizet). Troyanos, Domingo, Te Kanawa, van Dam; Solti, conductor, London Philharmonic Orchestra. Decca, 1998.

Les Contes d'Hoffmann (Offenbach). Araiza, Norman, Studer, Ramey; Tate, conductor, Staatskapelle Dresden. Phillips, 1992.

Les Contes d'Hoffmann (Offenbach). Gedda, d'Angelo, Schwarzkopf, de los Angeles, Blanc; Cluytens, conductor, Orchestre Concerts du Conservatoire. EMI Classics, 2003.

Faust (Gounod). Corelli, Sutherland, Ghiaurov, Massard; Bonynge, conductor, London Symphony Orchestra. Decca Record Company, 1991.

Faust (Gounod). Domingo, Freni, Ghiaurov; Pretre, conductor, Paris National Opera Theater Orchestra. EMI Classics, 1989.

Manon (Massenet). Sills, Gedda, Souzay; Rudel, conductor, New Philharmonia Orchestra. Deutsche Grammophon, 2004.

Manon (Massenet). Freni, Pavarotti, Croft, Taddei; Levine, conductor, Metropolitan Opera Orchestra. Decca, 1993.

German Operas

Fidelio (Beethoven). Vickers, Dernesch, Kelemen, van Dam; von Karajan, conductor, Berlin Philharmonic Orchestra. Classics for Pleasure, 2007.

Fidelio (Beethoven). Ludwig, Vickers, Frick, Berry; Klemperer, conductor, Philharmonia Orchestra. EMI Classics, 2000.

Der Fliegende Holländer (Wagner). Svenden, Heppner, Morris, Groves; Levine, conductor, Metropolitan Opera Orchestra. Sony Classics, 1997.

Der Fliegende Holländer (Wagner). Fisher-Dieskau, Frick, Schech, Wunderlich; Konwitschny, conductor, Berliner Staatskapelle. Berlin Classics, 1995

Der Freischütz (Weber). Mattila, Araiza, Lind, Wlaschiha; Davis, conductor, Dresden Staatskapelle. Polygram Records, 1993.

Die Zauberflöte (Mozart). Wunderlich, Hillebrecht, Wagner, Fischer-Dieskau; Bohm, conductor, Berlin Philharmonic Orchestra. Deutsche Grammophon, 1990.

Die Zauberflöte (Mozart). Janowitz, Gedda, Popp, Schwarzkopf; Klemperer, conductor, Philharmonia Orchestra. EMI Classics, 1995.

DVD

Italian Operas

Aida (Verdi). Millo, Domingo, Zajick, Milnes; Levine, conductor, Metropolitan Opera, NY. Deutsche Grammophon, 2000.

Aida (Verdi). Chiara, Pavarotti, Dimitrova, Ghiaurov, Pons; Maazel, conductor, Orchestra Teatro alla Scala. Image Entertainment, 1986.

Aida (Verdi). Price, Pavarotti, Toczyska, Estes, Rydl; Wanamaker, conductor, San Francisco Opera. Kultur Video, 2004.

Il Barbiere di Siviglia (Rossini). Bartoli, Kuebler, Quilico, Feller; Ferro, conductor, Stuttgart Opera. BMG Classics, 1988.

Il Barbiere di Siviglia (Rossini). Prey, Berganza, Alva, Dara; Abbado, conductor, Teatro alla Scala. Deutsche Grammophon, 1972.

La Bohème (Puccini). Scotto, Pavarotti, Niska, Wixell: Levine, conductor, Metropolitan Opera, NY. Deutsche Grammophon, 2005.

La Bohème (Puccini). Stratas, Carreras, Scotto, Stilwell; Levine, conductor, Metropolitan Opera, NY. Deutsche Grammophon, 2009.

La Bohème (Puccini). Alvarez, Gallardo-Domâs, Hong, Serville; Bartoletti, conductor, Orchestra Teatro alla Scala. TDK Marketing Europe, 2003.

L'Elisir d'Amore (Donizetti). Pavarotti, Battle, Pons, Dara; Levine, conductor, Metropolitan Opera, NY. Deutsche Grammophon. 1995.

L'Elisir d'Amore (Donizetti). Villazon, Netrebko, Nucci, D'Arcangelo; Eschwe, music director, Vienna Staatsoper.Virgin Classics, 2006.

Norma (Bellini). Sutherland, Troyanos, Ortiz; Bonynge, conductor, Canadian Opera, Toronto. Video Artists International, 1981.

Norma (Bellini). Caballè, Vickers, Veasey, Ferrin; Patane, conductor, Theatre Antique d'Orange. Video Artists International, 2003.

I Pagliacci (Leoncavallo). Stratas, Domingo, Pons; Pretre, conductor. Orchestra Teatro alla Scala (Unitel film). Deutsche Grammophon, 1984.

I Pagliacci (Leoncavallo). Kabaivanska, Vickers, Glossop, Panerai; von Karajan, conductor, Orchestra Teatro alla Scala. Deutsche Grammophon, 2008.

French Operas

Carmen (Bizet). Garanca, Alagna, Frittoli, Rhodes; Nezet-Seguin, conductor. Metropolitan Opera, NY. Deutsche Grammophon, 2010.

Carmen (Bizet). Bumbry, Vickers, Freni, Diaz; von Karajan, conductor. Salzburg production filmed in Munich (Unitel film). Deutsche Grammophon, 1967.

Carmen (Bizet). Migenes-Johnson, Domingo, Esham, Raimondi; Maazel, conductor, Orchestre National de France (Rosi film). Columbia/Tristar Studios, 1984.

Les Contes d'Hoffmann (Offenbach). Domingo, Serra, Baltsa, Cotrubas; Pretre, conductor, Royal Opera House. Kultur Video, 2003.

Faust (Gounod). Gheorghiu, Alagna, Terfel; Antonio Pappano, conductor, Royal Opera House. EMI Classics, 2010. Note: Several of the stage settings are not true to Goethe's or Gounod's Faust. For example, the garden scene takes place on a street corner.

Manon (Massenet). Fleming, Alvarez, Chaignaud, Vernhes; Lopez-Cobos, conductor, National Opera of Paris. TDK Marketing Media Europe, 2001.

Manon (Massenet). Te Kanawa, Domingo, Allen; Sinopoli, conductor, Royal Opera House. Kultur, 2003.

German Operas

Fidelio (Beethoven). Jones, King, Neidlinger, Talvela, Greindl; Bohm, conductor, Deutschen Oper Berlin, Deutsche Grammophon, 2008.

Fidelio (Beethoven). Mattila, Heppner, Pape, Lloyd, Struckmann; Levine, conductor, Metropolitan Opera, NY. Deutsche Grammophon, 2003.

Fidelio (Beethoven). Janowitz, Kollo, Popp, Sotin; Bernstein, conductor, Vienna Staatsoper. Deutsche Grammophon, 1978.

Der Fliegende Holländer (Wagner). McIntyre, Ligendza, Rundgren, Winkler; Sawallisch, conductor, Bayerisches Staatsorchester. Deutsche Grammophon, 2008. Note: Vivid and dramatic film version using large sets for ship scenes.

Der Freischütz (Weber). Kozub, Saunders, Mathis, Grunheber; Ludwig, conductor, Hamburg Philharmonic State Orchestra. Arthaus Musik, 2007.

Die Zauberflöte (Mozart). Huang, Gunn, Polenzani, Pape; James Levine, conductor, The Metropolitan Opera, NY. Sony Classical, 2011.

Die Zauberflöte (Mozart). Biel, Dahlberg, Polgar, Frandsen; Ostman, conductor, Drottningholm Court Theater, Sweden. Image Entertainment, 1989.

Die Zauberflöte (Mozart). Popp, Moll, Araiza, Gruberova; Sawallisch, conductor, Bayerische Staatsorchester. Deutsche Grammophon, 2005.

Annotated Bibliography

Batta, András, ed. (1999). *Opera: Composers, Works, Performers*. Cologne: Könemann. A very large volume containing 338 operas with a brief synopsis of each opera. Contains an outstanding collection of over 1,500 illustrations. Text focuses on the origins of each opera with a profile of the composer. A useful appendix containing musical terms, index of works, chronology, and bibliography. Limited information about specific songs from operas.

Beaumarchais, Pierre-Augustin Caron de (1964). *The Barber of Seville* and *The Marriage of Figaro*. London: Penguin Books Ltd. Translated and introduced by John Wood. Includes notes on the characters and their costumes. Both plays are considered outstanding examples of eighteenth century European comedy.

Black Dog Opera Library. Includes eight of the 14 operas discussed in Part I: *Aida* (1996), *Il Barbiere di Siviglia*(1998), *La Bohème* (1996), *Carmen* (1996), *Fidelio* (2002), *Der Fliegende Holländer* (2002), *Die Zauberflöte* (1996), *I Pagliacci* (1998), and other favorites. New York: St. Martin's Press. Each compact edition (size 6" × 7" with about 140 pages each) contains historical commentary, synopsis of the story, illustrations, complete opera CD's (EMI Classics), a complete and annotated libretto, comments on songs and performers. An outstanding value and addition to any opera library.

EMI Classics Librettos. EMI Records Ltd. Manufactured and distributed, New York. Majority of libretto translations in prose rather than rhyme. Includes synopsis of story and photos of the performers, including *La Bohème* (1986), *Norma* (1961), *Les Contes D'Hoffmann* (1989), *Fidelio* (1972), *Der Fliegende Holländer* (2000), and *Die Zauberflöte* (1994).

Fawkes, Richard (1999). *The History of Opera*. New York: Naxos Audiobooks. Traces the history of opera from the 16th century to the present day. Includes four CD's narrated by Robert Powell and interspersed with excerpts from the major operatic composers. Powell's reading is clearly expressed and appropriate for beginners.

Forman, Denis (1998). *A Night at the Opera*. New York: Modern Library, Random House, Inc. This thick volume (over 950 pages without illustrations) contains synopses of 83 famous operas. Each opera includes interesting notes and what to "Look Out For" with a star ranking for each song. An enjoyable text because the author injects his sense of humor throughout as the subtitle suggests: *An Irreverent Guide to the Plots, the Singers, the Composers, the Recordings*. Many readers

273

will be surprised by the omission of Massenet's *Manon* and Offenbach's *Les Contes d'Hoffmann.*

Ganeri, Anita, and Barber, Nicola (2001). *The Young Person's Guide to the Opera.* New York: Harcourt, Inc. Provides an inside perspective on several great opera companies. Young readers learn about the "technical wizardry behind opera's lavish performances." Comes with an introductory CD and charming illustrations. Limited information about individual operas and songs. Contains many interesting and some unexpected anecdotes, such as the 40,000 wigs in storage at the Royal Opera House.

Goethe, Johann Wolfgang von (1990). *Goethe's Faust.* New York: Anchor Books, Division of Random House. Introduced and translated (1961) by Walter Kaufmann. This highly praised translation includes the original German and English translation side-by-side. Kaufmann's translation is in rhyme to match the rhythm of Goethe's rhyming text.

Goulding, Phil (1996). *Ticket to the Opera.* New York: The Ballantine Publishing Group. As the subtitle suggests, this book explores *100 Famous Works, History, Lore, and Singers, with Recommended Recordings* (limited listing). Includes more than 140 operas, opera terms, and black-and-white photographs.

Hamilton, David, ed. (1987). *The Metropolitan Opera Encyclopedia.* New York: Simon and Schuster, Inc. As the subtitle suggests, this book is *A Comprehensive Guide to the World of Opera.* It includes 2,500 alphabetical entries, including biographies, brief opera synopses, operatic terms, geographical sites, guest essays, and hundreds of illustrations.

Hoffmann, E.T.A. (1967). *The Best Tales of Hoffmann.* New York: Dover Publications, Inc. This book is edited and introduced by E.F. Bleiler. It includes ten favorite tales by Hoffmann. In addition to Offenbach's opera, two famous ballets are based on Hoffmann's tales—*Coppélia* and *The Nutcracker.* The book also includes a set of illustrations by Hoffmann.

Mérimée, Prosper (1989). *Carmen and Other Stories.* Oxford, England: Oxford University Press. As part of the Oxford World's Classics series, this book is translated and introduced by Nicholas Jotcham. It contains nine short stories by Mérimée, along with a useful introduction and explanatory notes.

Murger, Henri (2004). *The Bohemians of the Latin Quarter.* Philadelphia: University of Pennsylvania Press. Set in the Latin Quarter of Paris of the nineteenth century, and the source for Puccini's *La Bohème.* It provides a portrait of the difficult life of Bohemians to survive as artists. The four major characters in Puccini's famous opera are present, with Rodolphe (Rodolpho) representing Murger's own experiences.

Newman, Ernest (1996). *Stories of the Great Operas and Their Composers.* New York: Barnes & Noble, Inc. A scholarly treatment of 30 great operas composed by 12 famous composers. The author provides an in-depth account of each opera and background information on each composer. The text is interspersed with lines from vocal scores. No illustrations are included in this authoritative volume.

Prévost, Abbé (1991). *Manon Lescaut.* New York: Penguin Putnam, Inc. The translation from French to English is by Leonard Tancock (1949) with a forward by Jean Sgard. The most popular French novel of the 1800's, and the inspiration for two famous operas: *Manon* by Massenet (1884) and *Manon Lescaut* by Puccini (1893).

Sadie, Stanley, ed. (2004). *The Billboard Illustrated Encyclopedia of Opera.* New York:

Billboard Books. Contains 200 synopses of famous operas and 500 illustrations. Also includes biographies of composers and librettists. Contains six thematic strands: opera houses, stage and scene, the voice, techniques, performances, and popular melodies.

Sadie, Stanley, ed. (2000). *The New Grove Book of Operas*. New York: St. Martins Press. A comprehensive reference to over 250 operas, including black-and-white photographs and color plates. A brief historical background and a full plot synopsis for each opera. Major songs are highlighted. Also contains a useful glossary and a song index.

Schirmer, G. *Schirmer's Collection of Opera Librettos*: *Aida* (1963), *Il Barbiere di Siviglia* (1984), *La Bohème (1954)*, *L'Elisir d'Amore* (1960), *Carmen* (1973), *Les Contes d'Hoffmann* (1973), *Faust* (1966), *Manon* (1963), *Fidelio* (no date listed), *Der Fliegende Holländer* (1964), *Der Freischütz* (1971). New York: G. Schirmer, Inc. All of the librettos above are based on English translations in rhyme. Schirmer librettos serve as the official translations for the Metropolitan Opera.

Simon, Henry. (1989). *100 Great Operas and Their Stories*. New York: Anchor Books, Division of Random House, Inc. Each opera synopsis is preceded by a brief sketch of the composer and background to the opera. The most significant songs are highlighted. Each opera is presented in a compact and easy to read format. No illustrations are included.

Singher, Martial (1997). *An Interpretive Guide to Operatic Arias: A Handbook for Singers, Coaches, Teachers, and Students*. University Park: Pennsylvania State University Press. An in-depth analysis of 151 famous arias by a master teacher and a former opera singer. A technical discussion, including musical notations and phonetic symbols, designed to help singers interpret and master famous arias. Each aria discussion is preceded by the original libretto text and its English translation.

Index

277